Transformative Dialogue

Transformative Dialogue

Co-Creating Conversations
in Communities and Organizations

Edited by
Erik Cleven and Judith A. Saul

ROWMAN & LITTLEFIELD
Lanham • Boulder • New York • London

Rowman & Littlefield
Bloomsbury Publishing Inc, 1385 Broadway, New York, NY 10018, USA
Bloomsbury Publishing Plc, 50 Bedford Square, London, WC1B 3DP, UK
Bloomsbury Publishing Ireland, 29 Earlsfort Terrace, Dublin 2, D02 AY28, Ireland
www.rowman.com

Copyright © 2025 by The Rowman & Littlefield Publishing Group, Inc.

Published in cooperation with the Association for Conflict Resolution

All rights reserved. No part of this publication may be: i) reproduced or transmitted in
any form, electronic or mechanical, including photocopying, recording or by means of
any information storage or retrieval system without prior permission in writing from the
publishers; or ii) used or reproduced in any way for the training, development or operation
of artificial intelligence (AI) technologies, including generative AI technologies. The rights
holders expressly reserve this publication from the text and data mining exception as per
Article 4(3) of the Digital Single Market Directive (EU) 2019/790.

British Library Cataloguing in Publication Information available

Library of Congress Cataloging-in-Publication Data

Names: Cleven, Erik, 1965- editor. | Saul, Judith A., 1946- editor.
Title: Transformative dialogue : co-creating conversations in communities /
  edited by Erik Cleven and Judith A. Saul.
Description: Lanham, Maryland : Rowman & Littlefield, [2024] | Includes bibliographical
  references and index. | Summary: "Dialogue can be an effective response to group and
  community conflict. This book focuses on the many ways of organizing and facilitating
  dialogue in conflict resolution. It delivers a wide range of cutting-edge perspectives from
  experts in the field and shows how transformative dialogue works in a variety of contexts
  to support peace and justice"—Provided by publisher.
Identifiers: LCCN 2024042425 (print) | LCCN 2024042426 (ebook) |
  ISBN 9781538189566 (cloth ; acid-free paper) | ISBN 9781538189573 (paperback ;
  acid-free paper) | ISBN 9781538189580 (epub)
Subjects: LCSH: Conflict management. | Interpersonal relations. | Negotiation.
Classification: LCC HM1126 .T746 2024 (print) | LCC HM1126 (ebook) |
  DDC 303.6/9—dc23/eng/20241113
LC record available at https://lccn.loc.gov/2024042425
LC ebook record available at https://lccn.loc.gov/2024042426

For product safety related questions contact productsafety@bloomsbury.com.

∞™ The paper used in this publication meets the minimum requirements of American
National Standard for Information Sciences—Permanence of Paper for Printed Library
Materials, ANSI/NISO Z39.48-1992.

Contents

1   Transformative Dialogue: An Introduction   1
Judith A. Saul and Erik Cleven

2   Transformative Conversations: The Value of One-on-One
Conversations for Transformative Dialogue   15
Erik Cleven

3   Co-Creation: The Heart of Transformative Dialogue from
the Moment of First Contact   25
Cherise D. Hairston

4   Families in Crisis: A Unique Application of Transformative Dialogue   39
Susan Jordan and Meredith Lemons

5   Working with Transformative Dialogue in Large Healthcare
Organizations   51
Anja Bekink and Angie Gaspar

6   Using Transformative Dialogue to Address Concerns about Racism
in the Workplace   63
Lida M. van den Broek

7   Another Voice in Dayton, Ohio: The Story of a Community Dialogue   73
Thomas Wahlrab

vi   *Contents*

8   Using Transformative Dialogue to Bridge Racial Divides: How Did We Get Here from There?
Vicki Rhoades and Dusty Rhoades   85

9   The Dayton Police Reform Process: Lessons from Transformative Dialogue in Dayton, Ohio   97
Arch Grieve

10   External Constraints versus Party Choice: Transformative Dialogue as a Tool for Planning and Decision Making   109
Judith A. Saul

11   Transforming Conversations: A Journey through Community Dialogue in Somalia   119
Vesna Matović

12   Navigating Dialogue in Complex Conflict Systems: The Transformative Dialogue Experiences of Interpeace Kenya   131
Abiosseh Davis and jared l. ordway
With Lopode Paris, Murshid Dubahir, Kenedy Rotich, Job Mwetich, and Hassan Ismail

13   Asymmetries among Allies: How Working Transformatively Can Contribute to Dialogue in Wartime Ukraine   145
Josh Nadeau

14   Monitoring and Evaluating Relational Outcomes in Transformative Dialogue Processes   155
Erik Cleven

Bibliography   167

Index   171

About the Editors and Contributors   179

1

Transformative Dialogue

An Introduction

Judith A. Saul and Erik Cleven

Conflict is no stranger to groups and communities. Whether it's ten people on a work team, fifteen households in a neighborhood, thirty board and staff members of an organization, one hundred and fifty members of a religious congregation, or five hundred people in a village, groups need to work through disagreements, make plans, or figure out how to live together. Conflict is a normal part of life, but it can be harder to manage when there are deep divisions or when violence exacerbates these divisions.

Dialogue is one response to group and community conflict. Dialogue brings participants together to talk about the situation they share and figure out how to respond in ways that allow them to move forward together or separately. Dialogue is also an important part of group interactions when there is no conflict. We engage in dialogue all the time with family members, neighbors, colleagues, and in our networks and the organizations we belong to. It is through dialogue that we make sense of the world, create meaning, solve problems, and develop relationships. People can engage in dialogue with or without a facilitator. This book will focus on organizing and facilitating dialogue, which can be useful in many different settings.

While there are many different ways to run a multiparty dialogue, this book focuses on *Transformative Dialogue*, a fairly recently defined process that has its roots in Transformative[1] theory (Bush and Pope 2002; Bush and Folger 2005). Transformative Dialogue offers a way to support individual and group interactions and, in so doing, allows participants to shape both the dialogue process and any outcome that results. It is based on a series of premises about people's motivation and capacity to connect meaningfully with others and to make their own decisions, even in situations where they face adversity and constraints. When we have offered training in Transformative Dialogue, people often say that they agree with these basic premises and principles, but then they ask, "But how do you get started, and what does it look like concretely when these principles are applied?" This book is meant as a response to those questions. Transformative Dialogue has been effective in many contexts, as the chapters in this book illustrate, and this book shows how Transformative facilitators co-created dialogue with people in organizations and communities in countries on three continents. We also include a chapter on monitoring and evaluating the relational outcomes of dialogue, a critical component of documenting its effectiveness, something that can be challenging when the outcomes are relational, not material.

WHAT IS TRANSFORMATIVE DIALOGUE?

Transformative Dialogue has been defined as a process where a facilitator works with people in groups and communities to co-create a process that supports participant self-determination as they decide "who needs to talk to whom, about what, and how" (Cleven 2011). In other words, a facilitator helps people as *they* make decisions about participation, content, process, and outcomes of dialogue. A Transformative facilitator also supports changes in the quality of people's interactions, increasing the amount of pro-social interaction. Pro-social interaction means that whether people interact often or rarely, they are able to interact with clarity and strength, being more open and perhaps even responsive to the perspective of others (Cleven and Saul 2021). And this is true whether they agree or disagree about specific issues. People often erroneously think that Transformative work is open and unstructured. This is not the case. What makes a process Transformative is not whether or not it is structured or unstructured but who makes the decision about the structure. In Transformative work that decision maker is always the parties or participants, never the facilitator, mediator, or coach.

All Transformative work is driven by beliefs or premises about people's *motivation* and *capacity* to deal constructively with their own conflicts and to make decisions about what they want to do (Folger 2020). They acknowledge people's inherent desire to connect meaningfully with others and include the belief that people have the capacity to do so. This means that Transformative practitioners support but never supplant people's self-determination and agency as they make decisions about whether and how to interact with others. These premises are taught in basic trainings for Transformative Mediation and dialogue but have not yet been fully presented in any published work. Here we present a full list of expanded premises that are the underpinnings of Transformative Dialogue.

Because the most salient feature of Transformative Dialogue is that practitioners respect people's agency and self-determination, facilitators co-create the dialogue process along with potential participants. Individuals are asked to consider whether or not they are willing to have a dialogue and, if so, to co-create it. The facilitator works with participants to design a process that allows the people involved to make decisions about what they need to talk about, who they want to talk to, and how they want to have the conversation. Second, Transformative theory understands dialogue relationally. This means Transformative Dialogue is understood as a process where perspectives are developed, including people's understanding of themselves and others, and therefore their identities. In a relational world identities and viewpoints are not fixed but can and do change as a result of our interactions and conversations.

Finally, Transformative Dialogue allows people to interact in whatever ways they choose. Transformative Dialogue supports the full range of human interactions: challenge, debate, deliberation, arguing, bargaining, as well as listening, reflection, and so on. That is because Transformative Dialogue facilitators realize that all kinds of interactions can be useful and necessary to people, even those including anger and strong emotion, and that conversations about conflict naturally cycle through all of these forms of communication. This is especially true given that the goal is to transform conflict, as described shortly. In this sense dialogue is as much about people responding to one another as it is about understanding one another. In fact, we would argue that it is only through responding and interacting that one gains true understanding.

Transformative Dialogue's focus on interaction and its unique characteristics flow directly from Transformative theory. Reviewing that theory creates a deeper understanding of this particular approach to dialogue and provides the background to understand the work that is described in the chapters in this book and what motivated the facilitators' decisions at each step of their work.

THE TRANSFORMATIVE THEORY OF CONFLICT

Transformative practitioners define conflict as a crisis in human interaction. Though the issues involved in a conflict or difficult situation may center on disagreements about wants, needs, and values, the conflict is fueled by strong feelings, limited perspective, and difficult interactions between those who disagree. Transformative theory posits that conflict leaves people feeling confused, angry, fearful, and disorganized, in a state of relative weakness. At the same time, they are self-absorbed: defensive, suspicious, and hostile toward those they're in conflict with. This state of relative weakness and self-absorption directly affects a person's ability to communicate effectively, speak clearly, or listen well. So communication deteriorates, becoming negative and destructive. People feel alienated from those they disagree with and, in the most extreme cases, demonize them, no longer thinking of them as worthy of respect and safety. This is crisis in human interaction at its most extreme (see left side of figure 1.1).

But the good news is that people don't have to be stuck in a place of confusion and suspicion. They can and do shift, moving from a place of relative weakness to strength. This shift happens as people are supported where they are, their thoughts and feelings heard without judgment or negative reaction. This support helps people become calmer and clearer, and, once they are able to think more clearly and listen with even a little more openness, they are better able to hear what someone else is saying. They are able to consider both the challenges and the suggestions made by

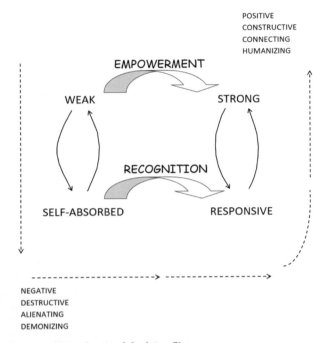

Figure 1.1 The Transformative Model of Conflict.

another person. They shift from being self-absorbed to being responsive. As people make these shifts, their communication becomes more positive and constructive. Their sense of the conflict and of the situation expands as they realize they may not have all the answers. They start to factor in other perspectives. Once participants have shifted to strength and responsiveness, they are better able to figure out if there is a way to work together toward a solution or agreed upon plan. And even if that is not possible, they may be able to disagree without so much anger and hostility and interact in more pro-social ways (see right side of figure 1.1).

Transformative theory is explicit about the premises that are the underpinnings of Transformative practice. We list the first set of these premises here:

- Human beings are inherently both individual or autonomous and social or connected beings. They are motivated primarily by a *moral impulse* to act with both strength of self and compassion for others, with agency and empathy. In all their relations, including conflict, they are motivated to be neither victim nor victimizer but to interact humanely with each other.
- Human beings' social connections are embedded in systems and relations of power and culture. These systems can give rise to human flourishing or oppression.

- Human beings have inherent *capacities* for both self-determined choice and responsiveness to others, which enables them to achieve their desire for morally humane conflict interaction. This is true even when they are confronted with adverse circumstances or embedded in oppressive power relations.
- Because what motivates and matters most to us as human beings is morally humane interaction with others, the most salient meaning of destructive conflict is a *crisis in human interaction* that tends to generate destructive behavior.
- Therefore, the most important *product of conflict intervention* is a change in the quality of the conflict interaction itself, from destructive to constructive, and from negative to positive, regardless of the specific substantive outcome.

That is where Transformative theory starts: with problems in interpersonal interaction. But dialogue often involves people as members of groups and communities, and conflict plays out at that level as well. The way people think of their own identity narrows. They hold tightly to the part of their identity that connects them to their side of the group or community (Maalouf 2000). They become fearful and suspicious of others, think less of those they disagree with, and discount their ideas or suggestions. As the conflict intensifies, it may lead to treating others with disrespect or targeting them. People may even begin to dehumanize others, opening the door to violence (Beck 2000).

But like individuals, groups and communities can change. As interactions improve, people begin to engage with each other. That engagement can help them feel more connected. As they become engaged and connected, they remember that their identities are multifaceted. They reconnect with the ways in which they are similar to those they disagree with, not just how they are different. They begin to trust each other in spite of their differences, first slowly and in small ways. As trust builds, they remember their shared humanity, and relationships become positive. This is not an easy process, and it can take a long time, but dialogue can support these positive shifts at the community level.

TRANSFORMATIVE DIALOGUE AND IDENTITY

Transformative theory understands identity, like interaction, as relational. Identities are a result of social interaction. Though most people see identities as fixed and given, they can and do change. If we see dialogue not just as people coming together to share their identities and the perspectives that go with them but as an opportunity to open up new ways of understanding those identities and how they relate to the identities of others, then dialogue can open possibilities for people that otherwise would be closed. These premises about identity are the basis of how Transformative practitioners work with people in communities:

- The core of human identity is a sense of our own individual agency and our inherent connection to others. Within that core, identities are relational. They are produced and change as we interact with others. People are naturally motivated to connect with others whether they share identities with them or not.

- Human beings have many relational identities simultaneously, including religious, ethnic, political, and social, and have the capacity to choose which identities are important to them. Yet people are more than the sum of their identity categories. People's identity categories label what they are. Who they are can only be known by relating to them directly.
- Each individual's understanding of a given identity is unique to them. This understanding is influenced by collective understandings of that identity. Institutions and cultural systems can constrain people's ability to define their identities for themselves and may try to force particular understandings of identity on people.
- In the face of destructive conflict, people often retreat to a narrow understanding of identity where a single identity takes precedence over the others, limiting a person's understanding of self and their interactions with others.
- Even in these adverse circumstances, people have the capacity to regain a broader sense of self, to choose which of their identities to express and how to do so, and to connect with and fully recognize the humanity of others.

Thus, at both the individual and group level, Transformative theory takes an optimistic view of human nature. Transformative practitioners are grounded in the belief that, fundamentally, people have both the ability and the desire to shift. And as people shift, organizations and/or communities can change. As people remember their shared humanity, they are better able to communicate effectively, restore cooperation, and even find a path to peace.

FACILITATING DIALOGUE

What do people and communities need from a facilitator who understands conflict in this way? The theory described here provides the answer to this important question. A Transformative practitioner is guided by the clear principles of respect for human agency and autonomy, deeply grounded in the framework and its optimistic view of human nature. They believe that people are capable of shifts, even when their words and actions seem to indicate the opposite, and that groups and communities can find ways to reconnect even after the most intense divisions. But that optimistic view is balanced by the awareness that supporting people where they are means a willingness to accept the fact that dialogue may not be right for a particular person or group at a particular time. A successful facilitator is patient, accepting the fact that individual and community shifts will happen in their own time.

Facilitators running a dialogue, individually or as a team, are also in multiple roles. These include educator, coach, mediator, facilitator of group interaction, process resource, process guide, recorder, and manager of content. They are at the hub of the wheel. Because of this, they are often in a position where they could

Transformative Dialogue

manipulate content and/or participants. It is their moral grounding in the values and principles of Transformative theory that precludes this and allows them to manage the tension of both leading and following. Their responsiveness and flexibility allow them to follow the participants where they need to go, accepting and respecting the reality that needs, feelings, self-understanding, and perceptions of others and of the situation itself are constantly in flux. Transformative facilitators are grounded in a humility about their ability to understand another person's situation. As Transformative facilitators we can be with others and support them, but we know that only they can fully understand their situation and what is best for them at any given time.

As the chapters in this book make clear, every Transformative Dialogue is unique. Nonetheless they share a similar set of characteristics. Most Transformative Dialogues begin with a series of one-on-one or small group interactions where a facilitator listens to what people say about their situation and educates them about the potential value of dialogue. This is because a Transformative Dialogue does not consist of a set process or series of steps the facilitator leads people through. Instead, because the decisions about the dialogue are made by participants, the facilitator needs to spend time with people in order to listen deeply to them and to support them in gaining clarity about what would be useful for them. The process of co-creation is rooted in these interactions as participants shape the what, who, and how of Transformative Dialogue. There may be times when a facilitator is invited in to help when large group meetings with different sides have already begun. In these situations, a Transformative facilitator usually talks with individuals and small groups, inviting them to change and modify the existing process in whatever ways make sense to them.

These one-on-one and small group conversations are critical because a Transformative facilitator works from the assumption that participants are the best ones to decide what they want to talk about, the content of a dialogue. A Transformative facilitator believes that those involved in the situation have the best understanding of what the problem really is. This is true in relation to both content and process. Most group and community conflicts are complex and multifaceted. People may not feel ready to talk about some topics. They may disagree about what is going on, about underlying causes, and about the acceptability of various remedies or solutions. That's why participants are the ones who need to decide what to talk about and when.

Participants also decide who they want to talk to. They are in the best position to determine who needs to be part of the conversation to accomplish their goals. Transformative Dialogue does not privilege heterogeneous or intergroup conversations over homogeneous or intragroup or "same side" conversations. Rather than assuming a dialogue begins when people who disagree get together, Transformative facilitators understand that people may need to talk first with others who are part of their own group. While conflict may sharpen differences between sides, it can also obscure differences within sides. It is easy to assume that there is "one conflict-two groups" (Maoz 2000, p. 143), but each "side" has a diversity of viewpoints too, including about how the group should relate to others. There is also often conflict about several issues, and the "sides" are not always the same across different conflicts. Meeting in groups from "one side" allows participants to figure out where they really do agree and to air internal differences.

Meeting in smaller, "homogeneous" groups also gives people an opportunity to think together about who they are as a group and how they want to interact with those on the "other side." That's another important way that participants co-create the Transformative Dialogue process. It's hard to talk to people you disagree with. And many people don't like talking in groups, especially large ones. Asking people to think about how they want to have a conversation allows them to surface any discomfort or concerns and lets them make choices about when to talk with others and how to have those conversations.

It's not uncommon for there to be disagreement between individuals and sub-groups about the what, who, and how of a dialogue. As the facilitator meets with individuals and groups of like-minded participants, that facilitator gathers information and, with permission, shares it with others, going back and forth to shape a process that works for everyone. Sometimes there is no agreement about whether or how to talk. Instead people decide not to meet as a large group with those with whom they disagree. Transformative Dialogue practitioners don't consider that a failure. The individual and small group conversations can lead people to get clearer about their situation and consider ways other than dialogue to react. In this way, one-on-one conversations can be Transformative too (see chapter 2, "Transformative Conversations"). It can also sometimes lead them to consider ways to interact with others more effectively even if they don't have a large group conversation.

But people aren't on their own in Transformative Dialogue. It's a co-created process, which means that the facilitator is also a participant in its creation. The larger the group, the more challenging it can be to figure out how to have a useful conversation. Some things that work for smaller groups, for instance speaking one at a time in a circle or using a talking stick, don't work well when a group is more than ten or twelve. A skilled facilitator can suggest ways to allow many voices to be heard. Also, some dialogues involve managing complex information, regulations, or laws. The facilitator may be useful in helping to organize information and ensuring that technical, legal, or scientific information is accessible to all participants. Finally, while some dialogues may happen over one or several days, others can involve a group or community in months of meetings. A facilitator (or often a facilitation team) can help a group keep track of the larger process and earlier decisions as well as supporting group interactions in the moment.

PEOPLE IN GROUPS

As people interact in groups, they are trying to balance their own needs with the perceived needs of the group. They are interacting interpersonally, with members of their own group and members of other groups. Transformative facilitators work from a third set of premises, these focusing on people in groups:

- People are motivated to participate in groups to experience belonging and connectedness, to give voice to their unique experience, and to consider how the experience of others is similar to and different from their own.
- People are capable of making their own choices on whether and how to engage with groups and can balance their regard for self with regard for others.
- Individuals are capable of learning about and productively deliberating with others on complex and problematic issues that affect their personal and group interests, even when working with people they differ significantly from or strongly disagree with.

It's important to emphasize again that all of the premises presented in this chapter focus on what Transformative practitioners believe about people's *motivation* and *capacity* to deal with their own situation and how they understand it. These premises are what guide Transformative practitioners in all the decisions they need to make as they meet with people to discuss the possibility of dialogue and as they facilitate small or large group conversations.

TRANSFORMATIVE DIALOGUE AND JUSTICE

We have heard people say that dialogue is not appropriate to deal with systemic issues like race unless it contributes to changing the power dynamics between participants, names people's oppressions for them, or challenges systems of oppression. As several chapters in this volume show, Transformative Dialogue has been and is being used in many situations where there are violence, racism, and systemic issues at play. We understand that the urgency of dealing with racism or similar issues of injustice can make it hard to practice Transformatively for some interveners. It is hard to desire change and justice and yet remain nondirective as we facilitate. But there are a number of reasons why we think acting nondirectively does more to support work for justice than directive interventions would.

Because Transformative Dialogue is a co-created process where people themselves decide who needs to participate, participants will not be randomly chosen. Rather, as facilitators meet with potential participants to talk about who else needs to be involved, people will generally mention those from their own group or other groups involved in the situation. In contrast, some facilitators recruit people to "fill seats" and ensure an equal number of individuals from each of the groups involved. This is especially true in in postwar settings or in dialogues about hot topics like abortion. In contrast, the centrality of co-creation has several effects. One is that because those attending a dialogue are connected outside of the dialogue, there is a greater chance of improved future interactions. Also, in Transformative Dialogue the conversation is more likely to reflect the political and social realties of the community, which participants may be satisfied with or may choose to challenge. It will also be about the real constraints—and the risks—people face in making change, as in the case of dialogue in Somalia where neither facilitators nor participants have the ability to change the macro-level political situation in fundamental ways, at least right away.

Transformative facilitators do not try to correct power imbalances or to speak on behalf of parties who they understand to be "weaker" or from marginalized groups. There are several reasons for this. First, it is disempowering for the people we might be speaking on behalf of. In fact, it can be just another instance of oppression if a facilitator from a dominant group decides that he or she can speak on behalf of others. People might question whether the facilitator is speaking because they think that participants' own speaking is not adequate to the situation or not articulate enough. Second, it requires an act of hubris to presume to know what is best for others, especially for those people who have experienced marginalization that we may not have experienced. Third, challenging power structures can be costly, and as Severine Autesserre (2021, p. 163) says, "The people who have to live with the consequences of a decision should be the ones making it." Finally, as Susan Jordan and Meredith Lemons show in their chapter in this volume, sometimes the person who seems to hold the most power, and may be exercising it, is actually acting from the kind of weakness and self-absorption described earlier and needs support to be able to be their best selves.

Directive interventions, even when they have good intentions, as they most often do, miss important opportunities to support people and empower them. If instead of intervening on people's behalf we let them make the decisions about the dialogue and about their situation, then we can support them in finding their own voice and having the courage to speak their own truth. It can also help people figure out what, if any, course of action they want to take outside of the dialogue in their community. Finally, as Bush and Folger (2012, p. 46) remind us, "Support for party-driven dialogue about justice can result in 'weaker' parties claiming justice on their own, and in 'stronger' parties doing justice on their own." If we supplant participants' ability to do this, we also supplant the possibility of transforming conflict.

Press and Deason (2021) have also shown that nondirective approaches are least likely to produce negative effects resulting from facilitator biases. More directive approaches that set ground rules, regulate the form of speech that is allowed, or that discourage the expression of strong emotion can inadvertently contribute to tone policing, racial stereotyping, and color blindness. Transformative practitioners instead follow participants and support them in expressing themselves as they see fit and also respect when they do not want to participate in dialogue. Transformative Dialogue is also entirely consistent with trauma-informed practice.

Finally, it is important to remember that social movements that aim to address injustices also rely on dialogue. In hindsight we think of social movements like the civil rights movement as unified and homogeneous. In fact, it consisted of constant dialogue to understand the situations people were confronting and to figure out and decide what the best strategies were to do so.

For all these reasons, our experience is that rather than being ineffective in confronting power and systemic oppression, Transformative Dialogue is a highly

THE STRUCTURE OF THE BOOK

In the following chapters the authors tell the story of how Transformative Dialogue was applied in a number of different contexts across three continents. This includes Transformative Dialogue in the context of organizations, businesses, and communities of various kinds. These dialogues are about race and racism, police reform, planning and decision making, and family crisis meetings. There are also chapters about the application of Transformative Dialogue in the context of violent conflict. In addition, we include one chapter that details the value of one-on-one conversations, one of the features of Transformative Dialogue that is common to all the stories and essential to the co-creation of dialogue. Finally, we include a chapter on monitoring and evaluation of relational outcomes. This final chapter discusses how to document nonmaterial outcomes such as improvement in conflict interaction and relationships, and how to do this Transformatively.

Cherise D. Hairston's chapter tells the story of a dialogue that involves a faith community. She shows how co-creation of community dialogue happens at a community mediation center. Her story is of a congregation that reached out to her for help and focuses on her work with the pastor in the early phases of the dialogue to co-create a process that would work for them.

In a chapter about Transformative Dialogue in the context of family crisis meetings in Pennsylvania, Susan Jordan and Meredith Lemons explain how their community mediation center works with the child welfare agency and families in crisis to co-create dialogue when there are issues related to a child's safety. Their chapter discusses the ways that the premises of Transformative Dialogue are aligned with trauma-informed practice. They describe how representatives of government agencies are part of the dialogue process and that even though they hold institutional power, even the power to recommend that someone's child be taken from them, they can be weak and self-absorbed and benefit from the support of a facilitator. This chapter provides a very good example of how a Transformative facilitator supports parties rather than trying to "balance" the inequality of power between them.

Anja Bekink and Angie Gaspar's chapter shows us what Transformative Dialogue looks like in the context of large healthcare organizations in the United Kingdom and the Netherlands. In this context dialogue is often held across professional identities as well as ethnic identities in highly diverse and complex settings. Their chapter also discusses how dialogue is co-created when you are a manager working within the organization and what it looks like when you come in from the outside.

Four of the chapters in the book deal with conversations about race and racism. Lida M. van den Broek tells the story of a Transformative Dialogue that took place in a workplace in the Netherlands after a racist incident. In addition to explaining how she co-created the dialogue, her chapter describes the micro-level interactions that took place and how relationships and understandings of the conflict changed through the course of the dialogue.

Vicki Rhoades and Dusty Rhoades write about the Big Conversations about race that have been held over several years in southern Maryland in the United States. Their story shows how Transformative Dialogue helped people confront truths about racism that were invisible to some even though Black and white people had lived in the same community for decades. They show how white defensiveness about racism is an example of weakness and self-absorption and how Black people's stories are examples of strength as they step forward to speak their truths. Their story also explains how they navigated these conversations as white facilitators and shows how a range of activities accompanied and resulted from the dialogues.

Both Thomas Wahlrab and Arch Grieve tell stories about how Transformative Dialogue was used to deal with issues of race in Dayton, Ohio, the home of the Dayton Mediation Center, a community mediation center that practices Transformatively. Thomas Wahlrab's chapter tells the story of a community Transformative Dialogue after the death of a Black man in police custody. Arch Grieve's chapter tells of the police reform dialogue that took place in Dayton after the killing of George Floyd in Minneapolis. Both chapters show how the facilitators created space for people to have hard conversations that confronted painful experiences. They both also give examples of shifts that took place as a result of their facilitation of the conversations and policy changes that resulted from the dialogue process. Arch Grieve's chapter also shows how he and his colleagues dealt with constraints resulting from the dialogue process already having been partially determined by the City of Dayton before he was able to come in and work Transformatively with the community.

Three of the chapters in the book deal with Transformative Dialogue in the context of violent conflict or its aftermath. Vesna Matović tells the story of a Transformative Dialogue she organized over a nearly four-year period in Mogadishu, Somalia. In addition to facing security challenges and the clan divisions that those who are familiar with the Somali situation would expect, her chapter also shows that conflict played out along generational and gender lines too. She explains how she navigated this situation as a European woman. She shows that by respecting people's agency to make their own decisions about the dialogue, there was more, not less, sensitivity to gender issues. But this required first overcoming what she calls a dependency culture where local residents are used to getting something from NGOs in return for participating in "their" activities.

In a chapter about dialogue in northern and northeastern Kenya, Abiosseh Davis and jared l. ordway present a conversation with Kenyans working through the organization Interpeace Kenya. This conversation shows that as in Somalia, organizers of dialogue in Kenya have to overcome expectations of going to dialogue activities for some other incentive, like a stay at a nice hotel or lunch. Their conversation also shows that by respecting participants' agency, local practices come to the forefront. For instance, dialogues were held under the trees rather than in conference rooms at hotels far from local villages. Their chapter talks about the failure of directive peacebuilding and describes how peace agreements and ceasefires in northern Kenya are just a starting point for dialogue, not an end point. Their conversation also reveals that dialogue can take place anywhere, in the marketplace or while doing other things.

Josh Nadeau writes about the possibilities of dialogue in a time of war in his chapter on Ukraine. His chapter shows the challenges that Ukrainian dialogue practitioners were confronted with as a result of the Russian invasion of their country. This caused them to reflect on what dialogue is and should be and led to interesting differences with international interveners. The chapter shows how a Transformative Dialogue approach could help Ukrainian facilitators address the many challenges in Ukraine today as well as address the conflicts and differences between them and international interveners.

Judith A. Saul's chapter shows how Transformative Dialogue can be used as a tool in planning and decision making. As was the case with Arch Grieve's chapter, this is an example of Transformative practice in situations where there are many external constraints and where facilitators need to be extra attentive to the transparency of the process so participants understand the context in which they are making decisions. It describes how, even when processes are designed externally, they can be improved by including elements of co-creation.

In the final chapter of the book, Erik Cleven discusses how Transformative practitioners can document relational changes that result from this dialogue work. Donors and funders often want to know whether projects they are contributing to are achieving the outcomes promised. But how does one document relational changes that are nonmaterial? This chapter shows how to think about developing meaningful relational indicators of change together with participants as part of the co-creation process.

Though these chapters tell stories of Transformative Dialogue in very diverse contexts, there are a number of themes and takeaways that are common to all the chapters. First of all, these stories attest to the Transformative premise that people, when given the right support, have the moral impulse to act with strength and compassion toward others and the capacity for self-determined choice and responsiveness to others. This is true even in complex situations where conflict divides people along identities connected to race, clan, ethnicity, gender, age, and profession.

Second, these stories show that dialogue can have many forms and can happen in many places. It can consist of conversations under the trees or in marketplaces in northern Kenya, as well as in church basements and corporate conference rooms. It can consist of informal conversations over tea or structured meetings to make planning decisions or even tough conversations that are part of county government's child welfare system.

Third, Transformative Dialogue can be applied in any situation. One of the things we have often heard people say is "Transformative practice sounds great and we agree with the premises, but it would never work in a situation where [fill in the blank]." Usually what is filled in is some difficult or complex situation, often involving issues of identity or structural power imbalances. The stories in this book should provide ample evidence that Transformative Dialogue can be applied anywhere, including in the most challenging situations. If Transformative practitioners can organize community dialogue in Mogadishu or police reform dialogue in Ohio, then we cannot think of situations where it would not be relevant. In fact, we would argue that these chapters show how critical it is, especially in these challenging situations, to respect the agency of prospective participants in dialogue if the process is to serve them and their communities.

Fourth, these chapters show how dialogue can help address systemic issues of justice in important ways. This can happen by helping improve the quality of interaction in organizations or communities so that the community has the ability to better tackle policy questions or by helping people figure out together what needs to be done. In these chapters Transformative Dialogue is not an activity that happens rarely in the formal setting of conference rooms because a third party has convinced people it might be helpful. Instead it is at the heart of people's lived experience and what is important to them. It is an essential part of the ongoing conversations that bind communities and organizations together in relationships that create meaning for them.

Finally, the co-creation of dialogue is central to all the processes described in this book. What is central to all the stories is a person who meets people where they are, listens attentively and deeply, and helps them gain clarity and strength to make decisions about what to do and who to talk to. In all these stories facilitators and organizers of dialogue are guided by a fundamental belief in the premises of Transformative practice, namely that people have the motivation and capacity to make decisions for themselves and to connect meaningfully with others when given the right support. We hope that this book will serve as an inspiration for others who want to build stronger relationships and confront tough conversations in their organizations and communities.

NOTE

1. Throughout this book we capitalize Transformative when it refers to Transformative theory or practice.

2

Transformative Conversations

The Value of One-on-One Conversations for Transformative Dialogue

Erik Cleven

Facilitating Transformative Dialogue is about helping people in organizations or communities improve the quality of their interactions and deal with issues of importance to them. This can involve meetings with groups of people that can range in size from smaller groups of five to twenty people to larger town hall meetings with as many as one hundred people. Dialogue, as opposed to mediation, is appropriately thought of as a process involving larger groups. But for a dialogue process to be Transformative, it must leave decisions about a dialogue's participation, content, process, and outcome to the participants involved. Facilitators work with those involved to co-create the dialogue process. For this to be possible, Transformative conversations that happen during meetings with members of a community or organization either individually or in small groups is crucial. The purpose of these meetings is not just to co-create the process or figure out who needs to talk to whom, about what, and how but also to help people decide whether dialogue is right for them at all. These one-on-one or small group meetings are also opportunities for facilitators to get to know people in the community or group and let people get to know them—and to build the trust necessary for a good, facilitated dialogue process. One-on-one conversations are also important for monitoring and evaluation because in a Transformative Dialogue the monitoring and evaluation process is also co-created (see the chapter on monitoring and evaluation in this volume). One-on-one conversations can be useful for people even if they ultimately decide not to participate in larger dialogue meetings. In this chapter I will discuss the value of one-on-one conversations for Transformative Dialogue whatever people decide about participation in group dialogue.

BUILDING TRUST AND GETTING TO KNOW PEOPLE

Trust in the facilitator matters in a dialogue process because without trust people will not be open, dare to be themselves, or talk about difficult or sensitive issues. If people are not being themselves, then the process is less likely to result in increased self-knowledge or changed relationships. If an intervener comes to an organization or community from outside, then people do not initially know this person. When we meet someone for the first time, especially someone who wants us to participate in something, we are likely to be skeptical and suspicious. We are likely to think that this person has some sort of agenda. Interveners do have an agenda—even Transformative interveners do—and being transparent about that agenda is critical to building trust. For Transformative interveners the agenda is to help people get the clarity to make their own decisions about what they need in relation to others.

Being transparent is not enough though. The conversations we have with people are dialogues of a sort too, and we must be ourselves in our conversations. People will feel more comfortable with an intervener if they feel like they know them. That does not mean that we make the conversations about ourselves. The focus of a one-on-one conversation is still the person we are talking to, but we must be authentic in our conversations. Whereas a mediator during a mediation session will say little about themselves and instead focus on reflection and summary, an intervener in a one-on-one conversation needs to connect with people. That means using words and language that are natural to the speaker and that are meaningful to the listener and sharing enough about ourselves to be perceived as authentic. In order to do this, an intervener has to embody the value of respect for personal agency and party choice that are at the heart of Transformative work. If these are things we really value and believe in, if we have truly internalized these values, then it will show in our words and actions naturally. Maintaining and centering these values is therefore critical during one-on-one conversations.

There is a lot of discussion in the mediation literature about intervener neutrality. Some have said it is impossible for mediators to be neutral but that they can be impartial, recognizing that they may sympathize with one side over the other while still acting impartially. I would argue that more important than neutrality and impartiality is gaining and maintaining people's trust. It is possible for people to accept an intervener even if they know they have a particular stance on a specific issue as long as they trust them to fulfill the role of intervener without bias—or at least with an awareness of the possibility of bias and a commitment to the self-determination of the participants. And trust is ultimately grounded in integrity between our words and our actions. If we say we value party choice and agency, and we actually show that in the way that we interact with people, then it builds trust and makes dialogue possible.

EDUCATING PEOPLE ABOUT DIALOGUE

There are things that need to be communicated to people in one-on-one conversations, especially in the beginning of a process when people are considering whether dialogue is right for them or not. People do not necessarily know what Transformative Dialogue is and cannot decide about whether or not to participate unless they know what they are choosing. I have often found that people have their own ideas of what dialogue is. Sometimes they think it means listening very respectfully to others and tolerating everything they hear from them without really responding. Because many communication processes are structured by interveners, people rightfully expect that participation in dialogue means having to participate in some kind of programmed or structured activity that will be controlled not by them but by the intervener.

In a Transformative process, interveners need to inform potential participants about what a Transformative process is, particularly that it is those involved who make the decisions about participation, content, goals, and outcomes. As I have noted elsewhere, I once met a Croat teacher in Bosnia who I was talking to about dialogue who said, "I suppose you want us to be friends with the Bosniaks" (Cleven and Saul 2021, p. 121). Her assumption was that dialogue was about becoming friends and that my agenda was to push interethnic friendship. It wasn't easy to convince her that I was really interested in supporting her in improving relations and communication with others and that becoming friends was not necessarily part of that (though it could be). For her to be convinced of that would require that she trust me. At best that takes time. But it also requires clarity about what Transformative Dialogue is and what it can do for people.

The first thing an intervener needs to explain is why one might engage in dialogue at all and note that the decision to participate or not is their own. If you think that dialogue is about becoming friends with your opponents or enemies, why would you want to participate? Few people seek out contact with those they are in opposition to or who they may even experience as hostile to them. But that is often what interveners are asking people living with conflict to do. Why should they do that? From a Transformative perspective, the answer is that it isn't clear that they should, and getting clarity on that question is one of the main goals of a one-on-one conversation. One reason to consider dialogue is that the person you might talk to is someone you have to have some form of relationship with. It could be that people have to work in the same organization or that people live in the same community and need to interact on some level, whether they like it or not. If that is the case, then it may be that engaging in dialogue is better than the alternative.

Thinking through why dialogue might be beneficial—and why people might not want to engage in dialogue—can be important steps in the process of getting clear about dialogue. As noted, for people to decide whether they want to engage in Transformative Dialogue it is also important that they understand that they are the ones who will make decisions about the dialogue. This includes decisions about who they are going to talk to, who needs to be included in the process, and what the process should look like. Will it be an open conversation or a more structured process? It is the potential participants who need to find the answers to these questions and make the important decisions. It is also important that people understand that in a Transformative process the role of the intervener is to listen and support people in gaining clarity and making those decisions. The facilitator is not trying to push a particular kind of process or outcome.

Transformative one-on-one conversations are also used to discuss practical issues about what an intervener can and cannot promise about confidentiality and what external boundaries or limitations might exist. Anything that is shared with us as Transformative facilitators will be kept confidential and not shared without the permission of those speaking to us. But we cannot promise that other participants in the dialogue process will maintain confidentiality, and we need to make this clear to people. Similarly, as some of the chapters in this book show, external actors can impose restrictions on the process or on aspects of the decision-making process. For example, a city council may seek input into a planning process and then choose to disregard that input. That is something that a Transformative facilitator may want to go over with participants so that they can take this into account when deciding whether to participate or what kind of input to offer.

MY IDENTITIES AS FACILITATOR

Another important topic for discussion with community members who may be interested in dialogue is our identities as facilitators and how our identities might impact those who may participate. When I have worked in places where there has been ethnic violence, I need to talk to people about whether having an American facilitator is the right choice for them. If I am facilitating a dialogue in the United States where people of color will participate, I need to talk to people about whether a white male facilitator is right for them. People may or may not bring this up on their own. If I do it, I acknowledge that it matters and I show that I am sensitive to the fact that this may be important to participants. I also make clear that the decision is theirs, not mine. I can do that in the context of talking about whether dialogue is right for people. I might say, "Another thing you might want to consider is who should be your facilitator. I am happy to work with you, but I am aware of the fact that I am a white male and that you might prefer someone with a different identity."

Sometimes people want a facilitator who looks like them. I have also experienced times when people want a facilitator who is not like them. In some cases, only a facilitator from outside the community can be considered impartial. From a Transformative perspective it is important that people have the opportunity to consider these questions.

My identity can impact people's participation in a variety of ways. When I have worked in Kenya, many people look at me as an authority because I am from the United States, have a university degree, and have a lot of experience working in areas of conflict. Many Kenyans would probably not want to offend me, and they might even accept me as an authority because of my identity. But if I bring the topic up, I give people permission to discuss it without them having to feel like they are being impolite or impertinent in raising the issue. I might also want to give people the space to discuss this without me present so they could speak freely with one another about this topic.

Similarly, because I am a white male who is highly educated, I clearly have experienced privilege. My identity and position may affect how participants experience their agency. It is important to name this for people and to let participants themselves make the decision about whether or not I am the right facilitator for them. If I am not, or even if people are unsure, I need to be able to let go and relinquish the role of facilitator, even if I very much want to help people. My help must not come at the cost of other people's agency.

Sometimes facilitators work in pairs or teams that include people from different groups. In this way a facilitation team can include diversity that allows members of the community to feel that they are "represented" by the facilitators. A few years ago I supported a community dialogue project that began by organizing a steering committee for the dialogue that included representatives from the community where dialogue would be taking place. The members of the steering committee were trusted community members who represented important groups. Whether such a steering committee should be organized and who should be part of it are further topics for one-on-one conversations.

One other thing that can affect a facilitator's ability to have one-on-one conversations is their knowledge of the community and/or the particular issues. I have often been asked how much one needs to know about a community or about people's conflicts to be able to facilitate effectively. Many anthropologists would argue that it takes years to develop real knowledge of other people and cultures. A Transformative facilitator's goal is not to understand people's conflicts or their identities but to support them in making choices for themselves from a position of clarity and strength. So how much do I need to know? I need to know enough that people do not think that I am a dilettante who has no business being there. I must inspire confidence, and some level of local knowledge shows that I care and that I am invested. Similarly, if I have no knowledge of people's culture or their situation I will not be able to effectively reflect what people are saying. I also need to understand local cultural norms. That means I need to develop some knowledge of names of people and places that matter and perhaps cultural practices that come up in conversation. It may also involve understanding local colloquialisms and acronyms, because without a proper understanding of these we can neither understand what people are saying nor reflect them accurately. We can't know everything ahead of time and we also can't know what people find important until we talk to them, but some basic knowledge will help us as we learn through the many conversations we have with people. At the same time, as Vesna Matović shows in her chapter in this book, we must be careful not to assume that cultural norms are fixed and always traditional. As she describes, when people are given the possibility to make their own decisions they might actually go further in challenging their own cultural norms than a facilitator would have thought possible.

HELPING PEOPLE GET CLEAR AND
CO-CREATING THE PROCESS

Aside from informing people about what Transformative Dialogue is and what it can do for them, one of the main purposes of one-on-one conversations is to help people get clear about their situation and to make decisions about what they want to do about it. If they decide that participating in dialogue is right for them, then one-on-one meetings are also important for figuring out who should participate, what the meetings will be for or about, and what kind of process will be most useful to people. Transformative processes are party driven, but people may not know what they want or what would be most useful. Talking through possible options with a facilitator can help people find clarity on this too.

Getting clear will probably not happen in the course of one meeting. After all, as we saw earlier, people need to get to know the intervener first and trust needs to be built. But once people get to know the intervener, then the process of getting clear can begin. In some situations, this is less necessary than others. In a community dialogue process in a city in the eastern United States that I helped support, many people were ready to just show up to a dialogue session. This was because some of the dialogue sessions were general ones to help neighbors get to know one another and were not focused on conflict issues. In places where there has been violent conflict this may not be the case.

A few years ago, a colleague and I spent several months having conversations with people in a community in Northern Ireland who were considering Transformative Dialogue. In the end, the people involved in the conversations decided that meeting with other community members was not right for them at that time. It would be easy to see that process as a failure from the intervener's point of view because a large intergroup dialogue session never happened. Many approaches to dialogue understand success as bringing members of opposing sides together and negotiating some kind of understanding. But it was clear that the conversations we were having with people were helpful to them. The conversations were Transformative in the sense that they helped people figure out and decide whether intergroup dialogue would be helpful at that point in time and helped people understand their situation better. The conversations also revealed a lot of diversity of opinions among people on the "one side." One-on-one conversations can be as Transformative as large group dialogue meetings as long as they are conducted in alignment with Transformative premises.

When people do decide that dialogue is right for them, these one-on-one conversations are important in helping them figure out what the process should look like. This may require repeated meetings with individuals or small groups as well as contact with others to see whether they are also interested in participating. After a Transformative conversation people may need time to think and process what they have discussed and consider the new possibilities that have been raised. In one community dialogue I helped support, some participants wanted to include members of "the Hispanic community." They suggested someone that I could talk to, and when

I spoke to that person they said, "There is no Hispanic community. There is a Mexican community, a Salvadoran community, and a Guatemalan community, and they don't interact with one another." So one-on-one conversations can also be important in clarifying how to think about the individuals and groups in the community.

SUPPORTING TRANSFORMATIVE CONVERSATIONS

So how does one support Transformative conversations? There is no formulaic recipe and, because Transformative processes are party driven, no two conversations will look alike. But there are two things that I have found helpful when having one-on-one conversations with people: maintaining my moral grounding and attending to the person I am speaking with.

Transformative work is based on an ethical relation between the intervener and the parties. By this I do not just mean that we need to think about standards of professionalism or doing no harm—though obviously these are important. Instead in Transformative work the ethical relation to the other is about the way that we meet and encounter the other. Transformative practitioners are always first and foremost motivated by a respect for the ability of others to make decisions about their own issues and relationships, even under conditions of adversity. Because of the deep respect Transformative practitioners have for the human agency of others, they do not supplant that agency with their own categories of thinking or understanding. Instead they try to genuinely meet people as they are and to listen to what concerns and motivates them. Whether meeting with people in groups or one on one, Transformative interveners keep this ethical relation at the center of all that they do. Maintaining this moral grounding is one of the most important things a Transformative practitioner can do. If Transformative practitioners are genuinely grounded in this ethical relation to the other, then it helps us know what to say in different situations as we help people get clear. If people genuinely see that you respect their agency and their understanding of their situation, it will also matter less if you ask a directive question or make a "mistake." Again, trust is a central part of this.

The second thing Transformative practitioners do is attend to the people they are having a conversation with. That means that they give them their full attention and are not thinking about something else or taking phone calls or checking their messages while people are talking. They are fully present for people and ready to give time, attention, and focus to the person they are with. This means that they are listening to people and showing that they are listening by being able to reflect back what they have heard.

As in a Transformative Mediation, reflections, summaries, and check-ins can be useful tools during one-on-one conversations. However, this is a conversation, not a mediation, so it is also important to remember that you need to be yourself. But you need to be yourself with a firm moral grounding in the ethical relation to the other and the nondirectiveness described earlier. Also, community dialogue processes can be very complex. There are many different individuals and organizations that might be involved and there may be many meetings that are part of the process, some large and others small. In addition, there may be serious external constraints that people need to understand and accept. Facilitators may sometimes make process suggestions to people, because people may not be aware of the options they have for how to have community meetings or dialogue sessions. Through all of this, interveners need to be transparent. They need to be open with people about what they are doing at any given time and why they are doing it. And facilitators need to make clear that the people themselves are in control of the process and the outcome, not the intervener. In this way, dialogue can remain Transformative even in the face of the many challenges that exist.

ENDING ONE-ON-ONE CONVERSATIONS

How a Transformative conversation ends depends on what people have decided should be the next steps, if any. Before ending a one-on-one conversation, it can be useful to summarize what has been discussed and any decisions that have been made or actions that need to be taken. If next steps include talking with others, it's important to be clear about what information from the conversation can be shared and what, if anything, is confidential. It may be that a decision has not yet been made and that people need time to consider what they have learned from the conversation. In such cases it can be helpful to note that. A facilitator might also want to check in with people and see if there was anything else they had hoped to discuss that was not covered.

CONCLUSION

One of the most important points in this chapter is that dialogue is not just something that happens in meetings with large groups, for example, with members of different ethnic groups or community groups. Dialogue happens in one-on-one conversations as well as in small and large groups. The process of organizing dialogue is itself dialogical. If facilitators maintain their moral grounding and attend to the person they are speaking with, then any conversation, even an exploratory one or one where you meet someone for coffee just to get to know them, can be Transformative. It is not whether or not someone in the end agrees to meet with others in the community that makes a conversation or a process Transformative. Even if people say no to further dialogue, the conversation with the facilitator can help them get clearer and feel more positive or calm about the situation they are in and help them make the decisions they want to make about their situation.

As discussed in other chapters, there are many different situations where interveners may have one-on-one conversations. In the context of an organizational setting, it may be just one conversation that precedes a large group session; in a country that has experienced civil war, it may be a months-long series of conversations with residents of a particular community. In many cases a Transformative conversation may be one in a series of conversations that really are about building an ongoing relationship with people in a community. Transformative conversations are important in and of themselves whether or not they lead to intergroup dialogue, and they are an important part of the process of co-creating a Transformative dialogue process.

As interveners, what matters is how we meet people. If we meet people without judgment and with a willingness to support them without having a goal of trying to persuade them to participate in something or do something for us, then we are helping empower them to choose the next steps. The premises of Transformative theory include the understanding that people are primarily driven by a motivation to act with both strength and compassion and that they have the capacity for both self-determined choice and responsiveness to others. Supporting people in making their own choices and considering their situation and that of others rather than supporting our own goals and imperatives is what makes a conversation Transformative.

3

Co-Creation

The Heart of Transformative Dialogue from the Moment of First Contact

Cherise D. Hairston

DEEP DIVIDES AND POLARIZATION IN GROUPS AND COMMUNITIES

Most people are unfamiliar with methods of conflict intervention beyond violence, litigation, or avoidance. Even those familiar with dialogue too often think of it as a process designed by a professional who takes responsibility for figuring out what they need. But Transformative Dialogue offers a way that people can figure out what they need themselves, begin to hear each other, and find their own voice. This is true even when they have become discouraged and whether or not they ever reach agreement. From the very first interaction with a Transformative facilitator, people begin to see that other options exist. This is because Transformative facilitators do not solve problems for people or offer a predetermined process they guide people through; instead they work with them as they, the participants, make decisions about their situation. Having to take responsibility for themselves helps people see new possibilities. And in places where there are community mediation centers that work Transformatively, these organizations are well placed to step up and offer support for dialogue to neighborhoods, local groups, faith-based organizations, and businesses.

Like all Transformative processes, Transformative Dialogue puts participants at the center, handing all decisions to them both around content (what's talked about) and structure (how they will talk). The facilitator acts as a catalyst for starting the process. It is the interaction *between* the Transformative Dialogue practitioner and the prospective participant that starts the process. Like a match striking a matchbox to start the flame, the inquiry or initiating contact from an individual or group sparks the start of a journey that leads down a path that is rooted in co-creation.

Co-creation is about partnering with prospective participants to help them answer the central questions: whether a process will occur and the shape and design of that process. As a Transformative practitioner, I do not come in with a predetermined way I will work with a group. I allow the way to emerge in the conversations that happen at the inquiry and initiation stage. Therefore what emerges is truly unique to the people seeking support, their circumstances, and the context in which their situation exists.

This chapter will explore some of the early components of a Transformative Dialogue process from the perspective of someone working at a community mediation center in the United States. In particular, I focus on the practice of Transformative Dialogue in response to a particular conflict within a church congregation. I also provide detailed examples that show how the process of co-creation unfolds to meet the needs of participants as they make decisions about the process. All the elements I discuss lay a critical foundation for prospective participants, grounding them in their own knowledge of the situation and enhancing their ability for perspective taking and decision making. While each step of a dialogue is important, early interactions are particularly important for Transformative Dialogue because only by engaging in conversations with prospective participants can decision making be handed to the participants. These early interactions allow a Transformative practitioner to model the skills and show prospective participants the ways in which they, not the facilitator, are the decision makers. Because of this, a Transformative Dialogue facilitator takes their time working with prospective participants. The time and care spent in the earliest interactions make clear that the Transformative Dialogue process, and the co-creation at the heart of it, is emergent, nonlinear, and ongoing to support people's needs for a different kind of interaction

TRANSFORMATIVE DIALOGUE AT THE DAYTON MEDIATION CENTER

The Dayton Mediation Center[1] is a community mediation center located in Dayton, Ohio, established in 1987 through a partnership between local government and a local university, Wright State University. The center was established before Transformative Mediation was developed, so its decision to practice in this way developed over a period of several years. The two most important influences that led to the transition were the publication of *The Promise of Mediation* by Baruch Bush and Joe Folger and the center's membership in the National Association for Community Mediation (NAFCM), both in 1994. NAFCM's strong ideological focus on self-determination as embodied in the "9 hallmarks of community mediation"[2] aligned with Transformative Mediation's focus on the value of human interaction and bottom-up processes shaped not by "experts" but by participants (Bush and Folger 1994). A third important influence was a commitment to reflective practice, as articulated by Michael Lang, which allowed the center to support both staff and volunteer mediators in a process of continual mediator development by being conscious of what I call the "why" and "what" of practice (Lang and Taylor 2000). Figure 3.1 captures our clearly articulated model of practice.

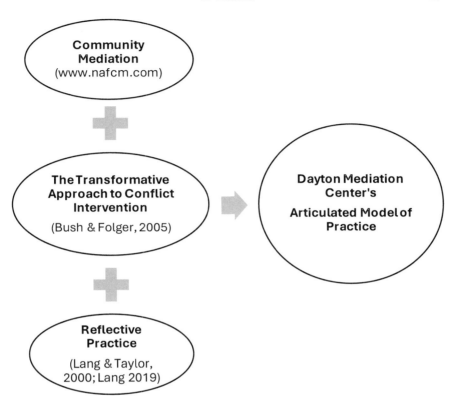

Figure 3.1 Dayton Mediation Center's Articulated Model of Practice

The center has also developed other practice areas beyond mediation to offer a range of conflict intervention processes rooted in Transformative practice. Like many community mediation centers that focus primarily on interpersonal conflicts, the center was sometimes asked to assist organizations, groups, or businesses with conflict situations. When Joe Folger offered a training on working with groups at the center, we adopted Transformative Dialogue as the best way to support groups in dealing with conflict.

"BEGINNING AT THE BEGINNING"; FIRST CONTACT

A "starting point" for the Transformative Dialogue process can be a phone or email inquiry or a one-on-one or group meeting. The typical starting point at the center is an initial contact by a community member, most often by telephone. Those who contact us usually have the same questions, whether or not they ask them in these words: What is Transformative Dialogue and can it be useful for us in our current situation? If so, what would that look like? This *first contact* is when an individual or a group of people locate our service (for example, finding our website or being referred to us) and contact us to explore what, if any, possible conflict intervention support we might offer them. This helps the caller get clearer about their current experience of their conflict situation, helps educate the caller by explaining how the Transformative Dialogue process might be useful, and helps explore "what's next?" after information has been shared and explored. This first contact often leads to one or more additional conversations with the same or other individuals or with small groups. This is because people often need time to process the information they have received and reflect on its relevance to their situation.

Because most people have little experience with formal dialogue processes, this first contact is vitally important. That was the case with Reverend Pat:[3]

> It was a typical day at our community mediation center. A call came in on our main telephone number and I answered it. "Good afternoon, Dayton Mediation Center, this is Cherise, how may I help you?" The caller, Reverend Pat, was interested in finding facilitation services and was seeking general information about our services after a long internet search for local resources. She explained that she was calling the local individuals and organizations that offer facilitation services to find what might be the right one for her situation.

My first important step is to engage in deep and close listening and utilize the core Transformative skills as demonstrated in this next segment. My goal here, at this early stage of the interaction, is to "hold space" for the person to share their experience.

> From the start of the call, I could hear the impact of the conflict. I listened as Reverend Pat explained that there were a host of difficulties at her church that were causing division among members of the congregation. She explained that as the new pastor, her entry into the organization was difficult due to ongoing issues stemming from loss of members, changes in leadership and political issues at the national level becoming an issue in their group at the local level. Most members seemed to be forgetting that their church had clear guiding values and principles.

I was patient and let the story unfold. After listening for a few minutes, rather than suggesting a process for Reverend Pat, I reflected what I was hearing Reverend Pat say. Reflection is a skill used by Transformative facilitators to help participants hear themselves better and to gain clarity about their situation. It also helps them decide whether they want to say more or have covered the main points they felt were important. Reverend Pat responded by elaborating and providing more details about what was going on.

> Members of the congregation were hurting. Their community was no longer a safe space to meet, commune, or do the work of the congregation. There was grief. A long-term, active member had recently died. Their previous pastor had moved on to a different parish, and people were unfamiliar with Pat and not yet ready to trust her. There was

disagreement and anger over a proposal to use the church as a sanctuary, housing an immigrant family who lacked legal standing. This led to heated discussions and debates that went on to strain relationships and further amplify differences. Reverend Pat was seeing destructive interpersonal interactions among members and feared that the congregation could fracture.

As Reverend Pat went into more detail, I heard her own anguish as she described her wounded, divided congregation. I reflected those emotions. Hearing her emotions accurately named allowed Reverend Pat to shift, relax, and be able to express more of what she *and* the congregation had experienced. I believe part of this shift for her was having a space to actually talk about her experience "out loud" and have that reflected back to her. This led to a clear expression of her desire to support healing and change for the congregation.

Once I sense that a speaker is able to listen, I describe Transformative Dialogue in simple terms, for instance: "an opportunity for members to be supported to talk and connect to one another, but where participants are always in the driver's seat, making key decisions about the conversation." I use concrete examples that emphasize how it supports group interactions. I also talk about the benefits and potential risks of dialogue. I keep in mind the central question: "who needs to talk to whom, about what, and how?" (Folger 2010). I begin to ask questions that help the speaker provide more details and discuss what kind of support they are looking for.

As I spoke with Reverend Pat about Transformative Dialogue, she became clearer about what she did and did not want. Some people may be very clear about this from the start, even if they do not fully understand yet how I might help them. Reverend Pat was one of them, and she continued:

Efforts were made by the previous pastor and board to begin addressing the frayed relationships. A facilitator was brought in to work with the congregation and suggested conducting a series of workshops that would focus on helping members begin their healing journey by sharing their experiences of all the difficult events, current and past. This facilitation did occur, but unfortunately the facilitator used what seemed to be a generic process that was highly structured by the facilitator. It did not provide space for group members to express their experiences and share their truth, which left them frustrated. The board promised more facilitated sessions to congregants. Reverend Pat wanted to deliver on that promise and help the community find a way forward, beginning a process of knitting back the relationships and the community.

As Reverend Pat described this earlier effort, I listened, occasionally noting key points. At this point, I didn't need to do as much reflection because Reverend Pat was able to provide a clear picture of the kind of facilitator who could help the congregation:

I feel like as a community, we took several steps backward with the facilitator we had. They did not provide space for us to talk with one another even though I was explicit that having this space was the primary need we had. There was much trauma that had happened to us collectively as a community. Given that experience, I want to make sure that if we bring in another facilitator that they will do what we need. The last facilitator used up all the time we had talking to us rather than allowing us to talk with one another. So my hope is that the next facilitator we find can give us what we need.

Again, listening for key points and themes was important as it also was helpful to hear what did *not* work with the last facilitator. It provided the opportunity for me to offer a thorough explanation of how I work with groups. I did not say negative things about what Reverend Pat described but rather was intentional about clarifying how I work as a facilitator. I stressed my commitment to Transformative premises, namely a belief that the participants know best, and explained that Transformative Dialogue is a participant-driven, nondirective process that allows them to make their own choices about their participation. I explained that I work with participants to co-create a process that serves their needs, not my agenda.

By educating prospective participants about what Transformative Dialogue is, I allow those I speak with to make an informed decision about whether our service can potentially meet their needs. Reverend Pat expressed relief in response to what I shared about both our process and how I work with groups. I believe she was looking for this type of participant-driven process even if she didn't use those words. My patience and clear description of Transformative Dialogue allowed Reverend Pat to provide a detailed description of what the planning group her church had formed was looking for in a facilitator:

> We're looking for a facilitator who could provide multiple "listening sessions" in which people could voluntarily participate and share their experiences, where people would have the space to speak that they didn't have last time. We'd like to have a facilitator present who can help by listening and, when necessary, helping to interpret what was being said by participants in the sessions. Finally, we'd like the experience to help group members feel heard. Together this could create a new foundation for healing and repairing relationships within the community.

The process of careful listening and reflection had now led Reverend Pat to suggest a process, rather than me doing so. I affirmed that the process and skills I offer would be a good fit in terms of this clearly defined request. Though it may seem that there was no need for co-creation because the planning group had defined what they wanted, in fact there was still much to figure out.

Throughout this "first contact" conversation with Reverend Pat, I explored the central questions of the Transformative Dialogue process that help a facilitator begin co-creating a possible process. At the end of the conversation, I worked to get an understanding of the next steps. This typically involves some type of follow-up that allows me to check back in with the caller. I asked before concluding the conversation, "Was there anything helpful to you in our conversation today?" This question allows the person to take a moment to identify what was helpful and perhaps any questions they still have. The first contact call often lasts about one hour.

In the scenario with Reverend Pat, I checked in about next steps and asked if a follow-up call would be helpful to allow time for digesting the information shared. She responded:

> Thank you for listening to me. I'm starting to feel comfortable sharing this with you. You've helped me better understand what went wrong with our last facilitator. I need to take what I've learned back to the planning group.

Hearing this, I asked Reverend Pat if it would be helpful to email her written information about our Transformative Dialogue process. Reverend Pat agreed that would be helpful, and she agreed to get back to me after meeting with the planning group.

In checking in about a next step, I am careful to not be pushy, seeming like a salesperson trying to close a deal. Instead, in line with Transformative premises, my goal is *always* to support self-determination. If a caller responds with a "no thank you," I accept that gracefully, trusting the capacity of the caller to identify what, if anything, follows in terms of next steps. Each first contact is unique, and in this case Reverend Pat seemed to see a strong connection between what I offered and what her congregation needed.

FROM FIRST CONTACT TO NEXT STEPS

In the Transformative Dialogue process, co-creation is present throughout all phases of a dialogue, not just at the start, and is always guided by the central questions of "who needs to talk to whom about what, and how?" There are a variety of ways we engage with participants in this co-creation. I *always* take the lead from the participants and follow them. I may offer suggestions or otherwise act as a guide, because most people have no idea about the options available to them. In other words, I *follow*, not lead. If I make suggestions, these suggestions usually follow from what they have said or asked about. And I am always clear that *they* are the ones who decide whether or not to accept a particular suggestion. Check-ins, a skill commonly used by Transformative practitioners, are particularly useful for asking questions that flow directly from what has been said.

One way that a Transformative conversation evolves from the first contact conversation is that the prospective participant typically identifies others who may want to be involved in the dialogue. That may result in additional one-on-one meetings or a gathering with a small group.

Depending on who is identified, I may do several one-on-one meetings. As in the first contact conversation described earlier, the goal of each is to help the speaker consider their situation, to learn more myself about its complexity and the different perspectives of those involved, and to educate prospective participants about Transformative Dialogue and how I, as a facilitator, might work with the organization.

With Reverend Pat, the next step after our first contact conversation was a small group meeting. Reverend Pat got back to me to say that she had shared the written material I had sent her with members of the church's planning group. They were interested and wanted to talk further about working with the center on their listening sessions. She suggested that we schedule an in-person meeting to do that. I agreed and explained that I would like to bring along a co-facilitator. That was fine with Reverend Pat, so we scheduled a meeting for the next week.

Why use a co-facilitator? One of the luxuries of being at the center is that I am part of a group of people available to facilitate, so, as much as possible, we work together in teams. Having a co-facilitator allows me to balance my strengths and skills with those of another. It also allows the center to use facilitators of different identities. In this particular case, I asked my colleague A. to work with me. Knowing that this congregation included people of diverse backgrounds, I thought that having co-facilitators who were an African American female and European American male would mirror at least some aspects of the congregation's diversity. In addition, A. was new to facilitating Transformatively and I hoped that working with me would allow him to gain valuable experience. I also had mediated with A. and knew his reflection and summary skills and his gentle demeanor. These seemed well suited for this group that had experienced so much trauma and pain. A. had the time in his schedule to work with me, so I filled him in on my initial call with Pat and what I knew about this next step. Together, we agreed that I would take the lead in the conversation with the planning group because I had been on the first call. But I told him I didn't want to dominate the interaction and encouraged him to chime in with questions and comments as that made sense to him.

A week later, A. and I met with Reverend Pat and the planning group. We opened by introducing ourselves to the group and having them introduce themselves to us. The five members all had different roles in the congregation related to supporting the well-being of its members. We stated that our goals were to help them and to make sure they were clear about the next steps:

> We appreciate Reverend Pat reaching out to the Center and giving us the opportunity to meet with all of you to talk about how we might help you accomplish your goals. It's important to us to have a chance to talk with all of you because one of our central questions is always, "who needs to talk to whom, about what, and how?" We've talked with Pat about this and now want to hear your perspective on the situation your congregation faces and what next steps make sense. We also want to answer any questions you may have about who we are and what our facilitation services look like. If we seem to you like a good fit, we'd like to go on to develop a dialogue process with you—one that works for you. As you probably read in the handout Pat provided, our goal is to co-create a dialogue process. And by that we mean we want to talk with you to figure out how to promote conversation within your congregation in the way that makes the most sense to you.

Co-Creation 33

After this brief introduction, we went on to answer questions and talk more about how we support people in having difficult conversations, making them as constructive and useful as possible.

Transparency is central to our work as Transformative facilitators. In response to one question, we described the skill of reflection. We then noted that in addition to answering questions, we had been reflecting what they were saying. We did this rather than ask a lot of questions because what was important was that the participants get clarity, not the facilitators. One member of the planning group responded by saying that he had noticed how well we listened and how good it felt to be listened to. Another noted that after just a few minutes of interaction, he felt comfortable talking with us. A. and I built on that, noting that what people often want is a way to talk to each other even when it seems really scary. We noted that reflection helps people hear not just each other but themselves.

At this point, the group seemed ready to move on. We checked in with them, asking if they would like to begin to talk about how we might support them in designing a process for their congregation. They agreed, so we asked them to share their ideas for a process that might help their congregation talk through some of the difficult things that had happened. A member explained that they already had the elements of a plan. They wanted to use a process called collective story building. Because of all the trauma that had happened to the congregation, they wanted to begin with listening sessions. Those listening sessions would allow people to talk about their experience without others asking questions or challenging what was being said. They also wanted people to see their experience captured. That's where the story building came in. They would create a timeline and have a scribe write down people's experiences in the appropriate place on the timeline. We asked how they saw us, as facilitators, fitting in to this story-building process. They responded by explaining that our ability to listen and reflect would support people in telling their stories. We reminded them that our verbal reflections were open to corrections from the speaker, and they noted how valuable that was to them. This led them to decide that the scribe would also check with the speaker to be sure that what they wrote down accurately reflected what the speaker had said. Thus, these listening sessions would allow a double reflection of each speaker.

Having supported their decision making about how they would have these listening sessions, we checked in with them about who would be attending. They agreed that they would need multiple sessions because they anticipated a high level of participation. They agreed, and together we created a short list of things to cover at the next meeting.

A. and I met with the planning group several more times. Their commitment to maximizing participation led them to create a care team that would be available outside the sanctuary in case a participant got upset. We helped them think about agendas, ground rules, and how best to invite members. A. and I tracked content, offered guidance about process questions when asked, and supported them in making decisions. And in each of the sessions, we reflected what they said to help them gain greater clarity. By the end of these meetings, they had a clear, agreed-upon plan. They were all in concert with each other about how to move forward with the listening sessions. They chose to do all the work to pull together the agenda and let congregants know about this opportunity. It was clear to us that there was great value in how we had allowed them to co-create their process.

It's important to note that in this particular situation, we supported an existing design rather than co-create a process from scratch. Reverend Pat and the planning group had a clear sense of how they wanted to move forward. This highlights another important point about Transformative Dialogue. What defines a dialogue as Transformative is not whether or not it has a structure, or how much structure it has, but who decides what the structure will be. Participants are best situated to make these decisions when they have gained clarity about their situation.

In other first contacts, a caller may want more input from me. When this is the case, I become a process guide, taking a more active role by providing ways forward that may be useful to them. These suggestions come after I have supported them in exploring what might be helpful for their situation. I may ask questions like, "What have you tried in the past to deal with your current situation?" This question often uncovers what wasn't helpful and brings clarity about what might be more useful. Sometimes I follow up their comments with a reflection and then an open-ended question: "Because the last conversation with the group members ended in a shouting match, have you considered what might help the conversation be different?" After the person explores this question, I may explain to them how my facilitation can support a different conversation. I explain how Transformatively facilitated conversations allow people to speak openly about their concerns. I also note that often group conversations end in a negative interaction because people feel shut down or ignored. This can be a helpful piece of information for the caller to consider.

My goal is to customize co-creating so any process suggestions reflect what I'm hearing. Often a caller who is not sure how to move forward may need more time. During a phone call, I may suggest a one-on-one meeting with me to further explore where they are with the situation. Other times I may explain that what can be helpful is to have some preliminary conversations with key people they identify as relevant to the situation. This is particularly important because leaders of groups often act unilaterally, reaching out to the center without speaking to anyone about their decision to seek services. There is a common assumption among these leaders that everyone in the group is "all on the same page" and that there aren't sharp differences. I will often share that it can be helpful to bring people together for initial small group conversations. When this happens, it becomes apparent to everyone where there are common points of understanding and where there are disagreements. In this case, as a Transformative facilitator, I will point out their common areas of understanding and their differences rather than selectively summarizing the conversation. This helps them in two ways. On an individual level, they gain an understanding of what matters to them personally. It also helps them begin to understand that they may differ on this topic and many others.

These one-on-one and small group conversations help participants make decisions about the process. Listening to what they name as concerns, I respond with questions about design and suggestions that take their concerns into account. Listening sessions, like those requested by Reverend Pat, are just one possible outcome of the co-creation process. Each conversation may result in different outcomes as each person and group is different. It's important to not enter this work with an agenda and to stay grounded in supporting groups to make all decisions about what, if anything, to do. Always being guided by Transformative premises helps facilitators stay grounded in this way. Ultimately, some groups may decide not to continue with larger group conversations. I respect that decision, understanding that it is always theirs to make.

LISTENING SESSIONS

I want to return now to Reverend Pat and her church. With planning complete, the congregation went on to have a successful series of listening sessions. They created the safe space that members needed, enabling them to talk openly about their grief, their anger, and their confusion. A. and I weren't facilitators in the traditional sense of supporting interaction between people. Rather, we used our skills to support one person talking at a time, as they themselves had requested.

These sessions reflected the unique expression of the process they envisioned, made possible by our commitment to creating the process *with* them. They achieved their goal, which was to begin a process that could bring healing and restore connection among members of the congregation. As Transformative Dialogue practitioners, we talk about improving the quality of interaction, and this is exactly what happened for members of this congregation. I found that helping to support these listening sessions was not only an amazing experience for me, but I was also deeply moved by seeing the shifts that happened for individual participants. As Transformative practitioners we understand the power of empowerment and recognition shifts. What I witnessed for both individual participants and this entire congregation goes beyond their becoming calmer, clearer, and better able to consider each other's perspectives. It was a powerful, meaningful, and beautiful experience.

I followed up with Reverend Pat a month after the listening sessions were completed. She told me that the process went well. She had heard from many participants who felt heard and who appreciated the opportunity to learn what other people were feeling. Then about a year later I happened to bump into one of the participants who identified himself and told me how much he appreciated participating. He went on to say how much it helped the congregation move forward. He said that some of the specific issues are still there but that it felt different. He described people as being more understanding of each other, even though they still have differences. Transformative Dialogue changes relationships and the nature of conflict interaction so that even when disagreements remain, they can be expressed and handled constructively.

MORAL GROUNDING AND SELF-MANAGEMENT

Working with small and large multiparty groups is challenging work. In fact, it is sometimes downright exhausting because the core skills of Transformative Dialogue require much of us, including being fully present to the ever-changing dynamics of interaction. As these dynamics change and the elements evolve, I do my best to stay clear and on task and maintain my own strength and responsiveness. I can bring my full presence to participants because I am grounded in the Transformative premises that parties know best and that self-determination matters.

Because there is so much to do when attending to multiparty conflict dynamics, having a co-facilitator is so helpful. A. and I worked together with Reverend Pat's congregation, holding multiple listening sessions with more than ten people in each. We primarily used the core Transformative skills of reflections and check-ins. I never realized how demanding it is to "just listen" that closely. A. and I took turns reflecting each participant, and this gave us space to rest. Working together allowed each of us to see and hear interactions and process information through our own unique lenses. Each time we reflected a participant, there was space for confirmation and correction, which supported empowerment shifts for the speaker. We were each better able to pay attention to any biases that arose because we knew there was another facilitator to check in with. We were there for each other, which helped each of us stay grounded in our purpose, our premises, and our practices. Though this work is often challenging and consuming, I'm reminded and enlivened by the simple saying "purpose drives practice."

CO-CREATION MATTERS—FROM THE
START AND THROUGHOUT

As the example of working with Reverend Pat and her congregation illustrates, co-creation means that those of us who practice Transformative Dialogue do our best to be open, flexible, and ready for what emerges from the situation and the participants. We do not resort to predetermined processes or a cookie-cutter, one-size-fits-all approach. Instead we are present with people as they gain clarity about how to best address their situation. This is what I mean by "holding space." This commitment begins with the first contact. And it continues throughout the process because individuals and groups change their minds as a process unfolds. Reverend Pat and her planning group had already crafted a process they wanted to use. A. and I helped them fine tune that process to make it as useful as possible.

But that is not always the case. As I noted earlier, at other times a Transformative facilitator supports individual and small group discussions about how to have conversations and how best to structure them. These early conversations often result in specific plans for a larger group conversation, including how members will participate and what the ground rules will be. However, I often find that as processes begin, participants may decide to change these specifics. What a group agreed to at one point in the process may need to be changed as new information and new perspectives are shared. As a facilitator I help them make decisions throughout the process and support these participant-identified changes. Therefore co-creation is ongoing throughout the process. Because I fundamentally believe that participants in the dialogue process know best, I am comfortable remaining flexible and agile, knowing that the participants may want to design and redesign the process so it works best for them. I delight in seeing participants make these choices for themselves.

The examples shared in this chapter are among many that illustrate the value of co-creation. To me, this is the essential element of Transformative Dialogue. We support people in making *their* own decisions from the first contact through the final session. We are committed to *following rather than leading* because we understand that the participants are the ones who are most familiar with the situation and others who may be involved and also because the participants are the ones who will need to live with the outcomes of whatever interactions occur or decisions that are made. In the process with Reverend Pat, the outcome they wanted was to start healing and improve their interaction as a group. They achieved that. For other groups, there may be different outcomes. Practicing in this way allows for the emergence of clear choices about those outcomes as well as about process.

The power of Transformative Dialogue is deeply rooted in the power of co-creation. In turn, co-creation is rooted in a deeply held belief that people have what it takes to not only speak to what matters but also to consider others' perspectives. And, in my experience, people truly want to find ways to interact and connect with each other despite their differences. Transformative Dialogue holds the promise of helping people do just that, to reduce the destructive heat of their interactions and restore their connection to themselves and those they choose to interact with. From this place of strength and clarity, people in groups often find their way back to their common humanity and are better able to interact with each other, no matter the outcome of their conversations. This is the true heart and soul of Transformative Dialogue.

NOTES

1. https://www.daytonmediationcenter.org.

2. https://www.nafcm.org.

3. For the purpose of this chapter, names and other identifying information have been changed.

4

Families in Crisis

A Unique Application of Transformative Dialogue

Susan Jordan and Meredith Lemons

Susquehanna Valley Mediation (SVM) is a community mediation center in rural Pennsylvania. We were founded in 2010 and serve three rural counties. SVM offers Transformative Mediation and Dialogue. One of the services we offer is family crisis meeting facilitation through the Crisis/Rapid Response Family Meeting Program. These meetings, and the process we go through to co-create them, are an example of a unique application of Transformative Dialogue where we have built in principles of trauma-informed practice. In spite of the extreme power imbalances and the need for a rapid response, and the fact that family crisis meetings take place in the context of government bureaucracy and a strict legal framework, Transformative Dialogue allows a party-driven process that maximizes the agency of all involved including family members and their support networks, child welfare case workers, and occasional additional service providers. It helps case workers do better work and supports families in making the best decisions they can even when they are facing extremely difficult challenges.

In this chapter we will describe the program and how it works and show how Transformative Dialogue is well positioned to respond to the unique challenges we face in the context of family crisis work. Because the premises of Transformative work are so focused on party agency and self-determination, it is a natural fit for trauma-informed practice. This has allowed us to apply Transformative Dialogue to an area that most would think it was not suited due to the legal and institutional constraints present in the child welfare sector.

RAPID/CRISIS RESPONSE FAMILY MEETINGS AS TRANSFORMATIVE DIALOGUE

In 2018, our judicial district's president judge and Children and Youth Services administrator asked us for a meeting. They wanted to start a new partnership between the court, child welfare, and SVM. Pennsylvania's Office of Children and Families in the Courts was in the process of selecting four of the state's sixty-seven counties to pilot a new program called the Family Engagement Initiative (FEI). Our county was applying to be one of the counties chosen for phase one. In order to participate, they needed a partner outside the court system who could coordinate and facilitate crisis/rapid response family meetings (CRRFMs) as an impartial third party. We were already known to our judge because of our Transformative court-referred custody mediation work, so to the judge, this was a natural collaboration. It felt that way to us too, and it offered an opportunity to expand our Transformative work into a new area, much needed in the community. We were also intrigued by the bold aims of the FEI to make meaningful systemic change to the state's child welfare system. We agreed, and our county was chosen to participate.

Historically, when a safety crisis involving a child occurred, the county child welfare agency stepped in to keep that child "safe." This often resulted in the child being removed from their home and being placed in foster or congregate care. With increasing evidence that this family separation caused adverse short- and long-term physical and mental health outcomes for children and families, Pennsylvania's FEI was created. Through the FEI, families would receive enhanced legal representation, and family meetings would be held as soon as possible after the moment of crisis, so that families could be more directly involved in decision making. This provided an excellent fit with our Transformative practice, with its fundamental commitment to involving participants in decision making from the first step forward. The idea was that if there was early intervention, it would increase the likelihood that children would either safely remain in their own home or be able to stay with family. It would also allow resources previously diverted to foster and congregate care to be used to help struggling families directly. And as Transformative practitioners, we believed that the families were in the best position to know what was helpful and possible.

While we had years of experience mediating custody disputes, we had not yet applied principles of Transformative Dialogue to cases referred from child welfare. We felt comfortable stepping into the FEI at phase one because we sensed an openness from our partners to learning together. This fit well with the idea of co-creating, central to Transformative Dialogue. Together we could co-create a program that would help children and families in our community. We knew we had a lot to learn, and since then we have. In 2019, we added a second county to the program, and in 2020, we added a third. We now coordinate and facilitate CRRFMs for three counties and provide training for the program across the state of Pennsylvania. We continue to learn and improve, as each new family presents new challenges and opportunities in our work.

At this point, SVM has coordinated and facilitated hundreds of family meetings. Yet each family is unique and requires our full attention and openness to their individual experience. Transformative values and premises ensure that each situation is addressed uniquely, rather than with a one-size-fits-all approach, and help us stay grounded as we co-create each meeting with the family, their support network, and the child welfare agency. Each process includes many one-on-one conversations and usually at least one family meeting. At times, it may also include mediation.

THE REFERRAL

Referrals occur anytime there is a family crisis that is serious enough that it could result in a child being removed from their home and separated from their parents or caregivers. When the referral comes in from the child welfare agency, and as required by state guidelines, the clock starts and we have twenty-four to seventy-two hours for the entire process. Examples of the kinds of situations that initiate a referral might be a parental overdose, a parent being arrested, domestic violence, child abuse, serious neglect, parental death, a child assaulting their parent, a child sexually acting out against a sibling, a child or parent attempting suicide or self-harm, a family facing immediate homelessness, a serious mental health incident of a parent or child, a child being born in withdrawal from parental heroin use, serious truancy, or a child repeatedly running away or refusing to live with their family.

Often there are multiple, compounding issues a family is dealing with, including generational poverty, generational trauma, violence, addiction, mental and/or behavioral health issues, physical health issues, and more. A family may be referred because a child has truancy issues that are at "crisis" levels. One day in a meeting, one of us asked our judge, "In what percentage of serious truancy cases is truancy the only issue?" The whole room exclaimed, almost unanimously, "Exactly zero!" An example of a referral for truancy may look like this:

A fourteen-year-old boy refuses to go to school and has missed over two months of school in the first half of the year. He has started hitting his mother when she tries to get him to go to school. The child's father died of an overdose when he was a toddler, which his mother witnessed. His mother says she is depressed, overwhelmed, and afraid of her son. She is worried she may relapse and start using methamphetamines again to get through her day. The referral says the family must come up with a plan for the child to start going to school and stop harming his mother. The agency is requesting a family meeting to address the safety concerns.

A referral does not necessarily lead to a case. Instead we begin with a series of one-on-one conversations to explore with prospective participants whether a family meeting can and should take place. These inquiries are rooted in our Transformative understanding that parties know best not only whether or not a family dialogue makes sense but, if it does, who should be there and what the meeting should look like. It may seem strange to some to refer to a family group meeting as dialogue, but it often involves large groups and is co-created like any other Transformative Dialogue process. It can include conversations about a wide range of things that concern participants and their conflicts. And it helps all parties: extended family members, those from the child welfare agency and schools, mental health providers, and others involved with the family make critical decisions about issues that are important to them. Furthermore, using the frame of Transformative Dialogue helps us stay true to our goal of helping each person make the best decisions they can given the situation they face, the perspectives of others, and the legal constraints.

ONE-ON-ONE CONVERSATIONS

We go into every new case rooted in the belief that people have a unique reality based on their life experience and that even in the most difficult circumstances, the people involved are capable of making decisions for themselves and looking beyond themselves. This belief is at the heart of Transformative practice and helps us remain committed to the co-creation process. While participation is voluntary, there is the hope that the process will include a family meeting, with as many natural support people as possible. No two processes are identical because each family is unique and makes different decisions about their situation. While there are some aspects of the process that are set because we are working through the child welfare system, there are a lot of choices people have within existing constraints. Child welfare is an area where parents who are struggling are often told by experts what is best for them. As a result, parents often assume they have no say in the process. Many also doubt their own competence or ability to make decisions. Motivated by Transformative premises about people's motivation and capacity to make decisions, even in adverse circumstances, we will often tell family members during these initial conversations something like, "This meeting is a chance for you to sit down with your support system and do your best work together. We are not going to tell you what best means for you."

We include case workers as participants in the Transformative Dialogue process. Our experience is that they need support as much as parents and family members do to make the best decisions they can in a given situation. Our first one-on-one conversation in most cases is with the child welfare case worker who made the referral. We review the case and get any critical information the case worker wants to share with us. Case workers are often vulnerable to the effects of conflict, which we understand through our Transformative lens as including weakness and self-absorption. Family crises are stressful and complex for everyone involved. Case workers work long hours and may work with families for months or years. Sometimes they have a lot of frustration with the families they are serving. They may feel stressed about making sure children are safe, upset with the behavior of the family, or angry about a confrontation with a parent. Because these are crisis situations, we have received referrals where a parent and a case worker had an angry confrontation minutes before the referral came in. We have had cases where the case worker brought the police to a parent's house to force entry because the parent wasn't answering. We have had cases where the family is threatening the case worker with a lawsuit or worse. Our initial conversations present case workers with an opportunity, if they choose to take it, which allows them to talk through any frustrations and get more clarity about their concerns and what they hope the family will accomplish in the process. This often leads to what Transformative practitioners call empowerment and recognition shifts, and we have seen how these shifts will benefit not just case workers but the families.

Our next one-on-one conversation is with the parent(s) or guardian(s) to help them gain the clarity and strength they need to participate in the family crisis meeting and to make sure they have a chance to ask questions about the process. We also want to make sure that they understand that they have the agency to make decisions within the constraints of the child welfare process. Though there is a sense of urgency with each case, we still see it as critical to conduct this conversation in a way that gives parents a sense of space. While SVM staff have information to share and options to offer, our commitment to Transformative practice leads us to first listen deeply, reflect what we hear, and support their decision making about how to proceed. When they first answer our call, parents may be scared, angry, anxious, fearful, hopeless, and/or suspicious. It is critical to be present with them and support opportunities for them to express themselves, talk through their emotions, and experience empowerment shifts in the form of more calm, clarity, and hope. These empowerment shifts support clearer thinking and better decision making. As a parent becomes calmer, we begin to share information. We are careful not to carry messages from the agency, but we do explain the constraints and that the meeting is a chance for them to have a voice in the decision making about the situation they are in. If there is a risk that their child might be placed somewhere, we talk about that so they are clear about the situation. This is a tension in our work. Our Transformative commitment to party choice means that we do not want people to feel coerced, yet we feel responsible to make sure they have the information they need to make the right decision for themselves about whether or not to participate in the family meeting. We respect their autonomy and do not assume what is right for them or that having "voice and choice" via a family meeting is the best decision for every person.

Transformative Dialogue is defined as a process where participants make decisions about the content, participation, and process of a conversation. If and when it is appropriate, we talk with the parents about who they would like to attend the meeting and what they think would make the meeting most effective for them. In other words, we bring up the basic questions of Transformative Dialogue: who they want to talk with and how they want to have that conversation. There may not be as many choices as in other kinds of Transformative Dialogue, but there are still plenty. Sometimes we may learn that a child would like to attend the meeting. In one situation, a mother states that her son wants to attend. She would also like his maternal grandparents and paternal grandmother to attend along with her best friend, who is the mother of two of her son's friends. She also asks if we could invite the school guidance counselor who has developed a relationship with her son. We discuss any safety considerations and ground rules that might be helpful. The mom explains that whenever her son acts out, everyone tells him he's "just like his father." This sends him into a rage. Because of her son's sensitivity about his dad, she would like a ground rule that no one mentions his father in the meeting. Rather than agree or disagree, we support her agency, a key Transformative principle, and ask her how she would like to bring that up to the rest of the participants. She says she would like to discuss it before her son comes into the room, and she has a plan for how to do that. We also discuss safety considerations for her son. She feels it is important for him to have a voice but thinks he should not be part of the whole meeting. She asks if he can come in for a few minutes toward the end of the meeting to share what is on his mind and so he can see how many people care about him.

From here, we contact each person invited to the meeting and hold as many one-on-one conversations as is necessary to engage each support person from the mom's network. These one-on-one conversations are held to support all the prospective participants in the process and make sure that everyone has a chance to provide input and have their questions about the process answered. These meetings may be quick or more involved. In order to support people through the process and help them gain strength and clarity, these conversations involve the skills of Transformative practice, including reflecting the heat of the conversation, summarizing their concerns, and checking in on how they'd like to participate. Most relationships are not simple. Often a person is invited and there is known conflict with that person and another participant. We listen first, talk through identified barriers to participating, and leave the choice in their hands, putting into practice the Transformative principle of respecting party choice.

FACILITATING LARGE GROUP MEETINGS: THE FAMILY MEETING

The one-on-one conversations usually lead to the development of the family meeting. Even when they don't, the meetings we've held almost always lead to empowerment shifts, helping case workers and family members get clearer about their situation and their choices. As we begin to plan a dialogue session, we are transparent about our purpose, explaining to the family and agency representatives that our job is to support them in creating the best meeting they can. We don't determine what "best" means for them. We clarify any legal responsibilities/boundaries that are nonnegotiable at the same time that we work with the family to help them make the choices that are open to them. The family has options about logistics, including location and whether the meeting is virtual, hybrid, or in person. When meetings are in person, we typically hold them in community spaces. There are often family members who have no-contact orders, are in jail, or who live out of the area. We do our best to accommodate any and all possible circumstances by providing break-out rooms, hybrid options, etc. We keep everyone informed as we consider these logistics, setting up the meeting in a way that is as inclusive as possible. This allows

Families in Crisis

families and case workers to be directly involved in the design of the dialogue session/family meeting.

At the start of the meeting, our opening comments as facilitators explain our role, how confidentiality works, possible outcomes of the meeting, and other important logistical details. We give the group a chance to co-create any ground rules they choose. In line with Transformative practice, we do not impose ground rules but rather invite conversation about them. Sometimes we bring to the meeting ground rules that participants have suggested earlier. Offering the opportunity for a participant to articulate a ground rule at the outset is an opportunity for empowerment. It can also offer an early experience of interparty recognition. Ground rules can also provide some participants with a measure of safety, even if they do not end up following them faithfully. This may sound contradictory, but our experience as Transformative practitioners has shown us that something may seem important at the start of the conversation that later no longer matters. If there are differences about ground rules among participants, we mediate that conversation. For example, if a professional asks for a ground rule such as "Be respectful," that person may understand respect as using appropriate words and calm voices. A different participant might see respect as being heard, not being interrupted or dismissed. This opens up a conversation between participants and gives everyone a chance to shape the process. In one meeting, when a professional suggested "respect" as a ground rule, a family member responded by saying, "I don't want to stay in this meeting because in past meetings I'm always told to 'be respectful.' To me that is just code for telling me to sit down and shut up." When we responded by noting his discomfort and initiating a conversation about what behavior was and was not okay, he decided to continue and participate.

After the opening, the case worker is invited to say what the safety concerns are that started the process. We made the choice to begin this way because it provides transparency and keeps the facilitator's role clear and separate from that of the agency. It also meets the needs of families, who say time and again that they want to know exactly what they're dealing with up front. Meetings often happen in a context of high emotions and conflict. People may be upset, hurt, or embarrassed because of all the things that happened. There may be yelling, blaming, and not listening. As Transformative practitioners, we do not shut this behavior down. Rather, we recognize it as the weakness and self-absorption that we all are susceptible to in conflict. We hear these things as part of the dynamics of conflict and understand them as opportunities for empowerment and recognition shifts. When participants experience empowerment shifts, they are more able to regulate their emotions. They may take responsibility for a mistake they made or state more clearly what they think is best for their child. When participants experience recognition shifts, they may ask a curious question to a person instead of expressing blame and hostility as they may have done earlier. Recognition may come in the form of an expression of gratitude for a family member willing to help out, or a case worker telling a mom who had a relapse that she's a good mom.

Unlike in some Transformative Dialogues, these sessions have a clear goal that everyone is aware of: to develop a plan that will ensure the child's safety. We remind participants of that during one-on-one sessions and at the start of the group dialogue. As we facilitate the conversation about the stated immediate concerns, we may link what's being said to a possible plan. But our commitment as Transformative facilitators means that in spite of this goal, whether or not a plan is developed remains a choice made by those participating. The family is always offered private family time to discuss their situation without any professionals present. While the purpose of the meeting is primarily to discuss immediate safety concerns, participants sometimes disagree about what the safety concerns are or whether other things need to be discussed. There are times the family wants to talk about something from the past that feels important and relevant to them, and the case worker does not want to spend the time on that. As Transformative facilitators we highlight those differences in a summary and let the participants determine how to go forward rather than try to emphasize common ground or avoid conflict. The past often feels very relevant to the family and their current situation. Case workers worry that bringing up the past will distract the group from the task at hand or open up new conflict. As Transformative practitioners, we never make a decision about what to do but understand this as another opportunity for the parties, together, to decide what to do.

The family crisis meeting is focused on an immediate safety plan. That is usually part of a larger, more formal plan that includes other kinds of plans, for example, family service plans that child welfare requires that the family must do. The safety plan that comes from the meeting is written in the family's own words and includes only things they agree to do. It is not imposed on them but rather reflects their best attempt to collaboratively address the issues. Sometimes the plan will include follow-up mediation between certain participants. They may also agree to a follow-up meeting to keep talking or ask for a check-in to see how the plan is going or if something needs to be changed.

We have had people say after a process, "Wow, I thought Children and Youth Services was the enemy, but they really care and were really helpful." We hear that as a recognition shift. We have had people state after a meeting, "I was so scared to do this and thought my family was going to turn on me. If I had known earlier that I had this much support, I might have been honest about my problem sooner." Another recognition shift. Or a case worker who said, "I didn't have a lot of hope coming into this meeting, but I was wrong. You really showed that you want to do this." That is what these meetings make possible. Transformative premises about people's motivation and capacity to make decisions make this possible. Empowerment and recognition shifts increase the family's engagement with one another, with their crisis, and with child welfare and other professionals.

TRAUMA-INFORMED FACILITATION

Very early in our program, when speaking with families one on one and in family meetings, we started hearing about serious trauma, both past and present. Here's one example: when speaking with a mother of a toddler, she tells us that she has relapsed on methamphetamines. She explains that she is a survivor of domestic violence and that she herself went through the system as a child and was sexually abused while in foster care. She is terrified that the same thing will happen to her child. We reflected her fears and concerns at the time, but this and many similar situations made us realize that we needed to know more about handling those who've experienced this kind of trauma.

So as an agency, we began to learn more about trauma and train our mediators in trauma-informed facilitation. We asked ourselves, and then researched, what does trauma look like in conflict? What are the things that we need to know in order to be able to support the participants of Transformative Dialogue, whether or not we know their history of trauma? How do we conduct one-on-one conversations in a trauma-informed manner and support the parties in their decision making about safety and participation? How do we do the same in family meetings, where people might be setting off one another's trauma responses? What we learned is that the Transformative principles and practices align exceptionally well with trauma-informed process. We have incorporated our learnings into our Transformative Dialogue practice, as we explain in detail here.

There are several ways that trauma-informed practice aligns with Transformative premises. First of all, we don't ask people to tell us about their trauma. Probing questions are not in our repertoire as Transformative facilitators. But it usually comes out during one-on-one conversations. It turns out that trauma-informed practice benefits everyone, regardless of their trauma history—even people who may not have experienced trauma or do not think of their personal experiences in terms of trauma. Practitioners do not need to know anything about a participant's trauma history to practice in a trauma-informed fashion. Still, training is critical. It helps us listen more attentively and strengthens our commitment to our Transformative values as practitioners. Because of its focus on self-determination, many elements of Transformative Dialogue are inherently trauma informed, including practices that foster safety, transparency, empowerment, collaboration, voice, and choice, and practices based on cultural humility.

Another trauma-informed aspect of one-on-one conversations that is in line with Transformative practice is the way discussions about *safety* occur. We realize that people define safety differently and do not assume that we know what safety means for them. Instead we provide a chance for them to talk about what they need from the process in order to feel safe enough to participate. We also ask the case worker what they think is needed for safety among participants, including their own safety. The case worker sometimes knows things that a family may not disclose to us, like the presence of a court no-contact order between family members. This allows us to make important process modifications, like having separate rooms available for those who cannot be together. They may also have fears for their own safety with certain family members, in which case we talk with them about their concerns in the same way we talk with anyone else who has a safety concern.

Safety is distinctly different from comfort. The meetings are often inherently uncomfortable and are happening because of a lack of safety. Many clients tell us

they have never felt completely safe in their lives. Yet they may still want to participate in a family meeting. In order to support their ability to make decisions about
the process, we ask them what will help them feel safe enough to participate and
listen closely to what they tell us. If they're not sure, we may offer options. These
generally include reminding them that they have the option of leaving the room
immediately and without explanation, if they need to. We mention the possibility of
breakout rooms so people can be in separate spaces and of staggered entry and exit
times for different participants. Sometimes, if there's violence between participants
or no-contact orders, we may have two parallel meetings going where certain participants have no contact with each other. Our experience has taught us that there
is still value in bringing together the two support systems, to talk about the children
and all the issues, with as much transparency and open conversation as possible. We
have learned of many options that we did not even know about because families will
ask for them.

Another thing we have learned is that when people have had significant childhood
trauma, they may create the worst possible scenarios in their imaginations. Here
Transformative Dialogue's core principle of *transparency* is exactly what's needed.
Our transparency at intake and throughout the process can help them make decisions about their participation in the present process and who they want to include.

A final point is that trauma-informed practice has taught us something important
about Transformative practice. Different people have different levels of tolerance
for conflict and emotion, and that is something we cannot ignore. Transformative
practitioners often pride themselves in saying that they are comfortable with high
levels of conflict. This is because Transformative practice prioritizes "going for the
heat" because that is where transformation of conflict can happen. However, when
we learn that a participant's anxiety or trauma gets triggered by high conflict, we are
not going to say, "but we are okay with high conflict." It doesn't matter what we
are okay with as facilitators. Our job is to support the participants' *voice and choice*
about what they talk about and how. If we notice that someone seems upset by what
is happening, whether we are upset about it or not is not the important thing. This
was an important learning for our mediators, because many had worked to become
more comfortable with high levels of conflict and emotion. But now we understand
that supporting parties means letting them define what they are comfortable with
and that may include saying that they are not okay with high levels of conflict.

POWER IMBALANCES

Another reality of this work is the inherent power imbalance that exists in this kind
of dialogue. The power to take away someone's child is one of the great powers of
the state. While the court, not the child welfare agency, has this power, most families
see case workers as having this power because they work closely with the court and
make recommendations. Thus, families often feel disempowered. Many are used to
the system telling them what to do and being powerless to respond effectively. They

feel that if they stand up for themselves or try to fight back, the system can use its power to come down even harder. While we are unable to change the existing power dynamic in any individual family meeting, we believe, and have witnessed, that when people make shifts to greater empowerment and connection with one another, they are more open and responsive to the needs and perspectives of others in a way that can significantly change outcomes in a positive way.

We have also come to realize that just because you hold institutional power does not mean that you do not experience disempowerment in conflict. Conflict is difficult and can pull all of us into cycles of weakness and self-absorption. Someone who has objective power in a system like the child welfare system and who feels disempowered can use their power in ways that are particularly harmful. This is why we choose to include agency workers as parties in the conversation. The interaction they have with families during a dialogue session often allows them to understand a situation differently. We never use our role to shut down a case worker or to try to "balance" the power of a case worker and a client because of our own judgments about what they are doing. This violates the core principles of Transformative Dialogue as well as trauma-informed practice. We understand it as unethical and working against our purpose to support each person's agency. If we see a case worker making threats to a family member, we understand that as an opportunity for them to experience a shift that may help them feel more connected with the people they are there to help and thus do a better job.

STAYING GROUNDED

As we look back on the learning and growth of the FEI, we realize that our success is closely tied to our ability to embed the skills and the premises of Transformative practice into this work. We stay grounded in the premises of Transformative practice in the way we talk about families and with one another. We conduct regular training with our mediators to keep them grounded also. We come back to fundamental values and premises at every step in the process. This allows us to do the work in a way that has integrity and is ethical, even when we must work quickly.

One of the important values that helps us in this regard is cultural humility. This comes back to the belief in people's unique reality, based on their identities, relationships, and life experience, a premise of Transformative practice. Cultural humility is also an essential component of trauma-informed practice. We train staff and mediators in identity awareness. One training, called "The Urgency of Awareness," encouraged participants to think about themselves and their clients in terms of their normalized/dominant versus nonnormalized/minority identities. Poor and minority families are disproportionately represented in the child welfare system, and our community is no different. This helps us realize the many ways that families involved in the child welfare system are held to cultural norms created by the normalized/dominant groups to which they don't belong. For example, we had a Puerto Rican client tell us that the parenting class they had to attend through the county "teaches us the ways we learned to parent are all wrong. That we have to parent like educated white people." Some of the important aspects of cultural humility are built into Transformative practice. Facilitators don't supplant decision making for parties or make suggestions. They use the language their participants use without making it sound more "presentable" or "professional." This can be a tension with some participants, who sometimes want facilitators to "not allow" certain ways of speaking. If a participant doesn't like a certain way of speaking, they are invited to say that, and that becomes part of the conversation. The group decides what to do about this tension rather than the facilitator imposing something on the group.

One of our mediators said that the most useful tip they ever got in terms of facilitating Transformatively was "name what's happening and give it back to the participants." When things get hard it is easy to get pulled into the need to exert control over things. But we know how to support people when things get hard. We just have to remember that it is not our responsibility, as Transformative facilitators, to figure out the solutions to these incredibly complex situations.

One last anecdote is telling: after our first presentation to Children and Youth Services case workers and leadership back in 2018, the agency administrator caught me in the hallway. He said that when he first imagined SVM's involvement, he thought he was simply getting an organization who could play the role of the neutral third party. He noted that instead what we were offering was aligned with the aspirations of his agency in listening to, and supporting, the voice and choice making of their clients. Most social workers have been trained in "strength-based" approaches, but that training can be hard to operationalize, especially when working with people in a serious crisis.

Transformative Dialogue, in theory and practice, is deeply strength based from start to finish. There are times when we hear the details of an unimaginably difficult situation, and we wonder, "How is this ever going to work?" Then we take a deep breath and start the process anew. Guided by Transformative values and practices, we support families and case workers, one step at a time, for each step we take with them.

5

Working with Transformative Dialogue in Large Healthcare Organizations

Anja Bekink and Angie Gaspar

We write this chapter as facilitators who are called in to help teams composed of staff members in large healthcare organizations. In this chapter we look at the challenges of working Transformatively in this setting and the challenges encountered from the different roles we need to play. We give examples from our practice and the insights gained from this work. We also address the wider benefits of Transformative Dialogue in relation to pro-social interaction. This is imperative for the delivery of safe, research-based, and team-delivered healthcare. Using the Transformative framework as a mediator, trainer of communication skills, and facilitator of group work gives us an ever-growing skill base to work with conflict and teams experiencing difficulties.

Angie has worked in the United Kingdom's health system for over thirty years. For the past twenty years she has been developing support services for a National Health Service Trust (NHS) with fourteen thousand staff members. These services include therapy, responses to traumatic incidents, communication training, stress management, and conflict resolution services. This is an internal service, so Angie is a "staff member" but also "outside" the teams and individuals she works with. In this chapter we look at her role being outside the teams she facilitates.

Anja works as an independent dialogue facilitator, coach, trainer, mediator, and interim manager in healthcare in the Netherlands. She also runs a company together with two colleagues called FeedbackRadar that encourages healthcare organizations to listen to patients' stories and act on them. In this chapter we talk about her role as a manager during which she works as an insider with a team. During the COVID-19 pandemic she worked as an interim manager with various teams in a large hospital, for example, as head of the intensive care unit during the first and second wave of COVID.

The Transformative framework deeply resonates with how we see people and ourselves in the world. We all encounter the struggle to become strong, autonomous individuals who are connected to others—to grow together in our differences and create environments where we can thrive and be creative. Working with the Transformative model has had a major impact on our leadership and facilitation styles. We have learned to really listen and reflect and have a deep confidence that people themselves know what is good for them and that they are able to decide to connect with and understand others' perspectives, even when this is difficult and it may not seem like they have this capacity.

THE CHALLENGES OF WORKING IN HEALTHCARE ORGANIZATIONS

Healthcare is a highly challenging environment. Workplace and system stressors negatively impact the health and well-being of staff and set the stage for conflict. Never has this been as apparent as when we were writing this during the world COVID pandemic. Healthcare is a rapidly changing environment, which means that multidisciplinary teams (MDTs) have to adapt and move forward together as care delivery requires significant interdependence among team members. At the same time, healthcare professionals often work independently (think of the medical specialist in the consultation room, the nurse who cares for a patient), and professional autonomy is a highly valued asset. Teams are very diverse in relation to ethnicity, language, and cultural differences and the organization is hierarchical. The COVID pandemic lasted for a couple of years and increased fatigue and insecurity, further compounding these challenges. After the first wave, healthcare professionals were more likely to face verbal aggression from patients and family members. This was particularly hard because staff were exhausted and aware of the fact that they were unable to deliver the quality of care that they normally do. The lack of capacity was also the cause of difficult conversations. Whereas in the first wave, COVID patients always had priority, in subsequent waves this was not a given. Other patients also needed urgent care. Where in the first wave there was a strong sense of one team, one goal, after that interests were understandably more divided. Different departments saw their own patient groups suffering due to the lack of capacity. The pandemic overburdened the hospitals, and some came close to a situation where difficult choices had to be made about who should be given care and who denied. The long-term situation where staff were working in other departments and in different roles from their usual situation also caused stress. For example, anesthesia assistants were deployed in the ICU; ICU nurse practitioners had to delegate work to others and nurses were deployed in COVID wards.

In the United Kingdom, as the pandemic started, the withdrawal from the European Union had an enormous impact on the workforce: there were divisions and the sense that many people from other countries had that "we aren't welcome anymore." This contributed to a 13 percent vacancy rate across all professions in the NHS, causing considerable stress in the whole system. The shortage of qualified staff was and is a growing problem in healthcare in the Netherlands. Meanwhile, the demand for care is increasing, and this will not change in the coming years. As a result, the quality and accessibility of care are under growing pressure.

Working with Transformative Dialogue in Large Healthcare Organizations 53

Often the groups that we work with have not had the time or the space to have a "different" conversation. Meetings are often formal, or work-process oriented, and there is little time to explore differences, disagreements, and the impact of poor relationships. This happens in spite of the fact that people innately know that "good enough" relationships form the baseline and success of any service, particularly in healthcare where the interdependency among different professionals is critical to delivering care. Strained relationships, challenging communication, and decisions that are not communicated clearly all set the stage for conflict, misunderstandings, and blame. Problems arise and persist due to a lack of clear communication. Hence, Transformative Dialogue provides much-needed support when difficulties arise. Because of this teams are genuinely grateful for the opportunity to talk with one another. They are especially pleased when they realize what characterizes Transformative Dialogue: that all voices are important in the process, that they themselves will shape the process, that they will be supported when the "going gets tough," and that the facilitators believe they, the participants, "have what it takes" to make whatever changes are needed. Our qualities and skills as Transformative Dialogue facilitators or managers are critical and must always be congruent with the relational worldview that we promote.

Transformative Dialogue is paradoxically countercultural in healthcare. Its culture of "diagnose and fix" runs counter to a process where the outcomes, process, and content of dialogue are shaped by the participants, and decisions are in the hands of the participants, even if there is an externally determined mandate. The basic principles of the Transformative model are transferable even to this organizational setting as "people are people" and encounter the same challenges and problems that Transformative practitioners see as opportunities for growth and change. In a healthcare organization a manager may also take on the role as an insider facilitator. Sometimes, however, facilitators are called in from outside. In the following we explore these different roles and what co-creation of dialogue looks like in this context.

Whether as manager or facilitator, when we observe others as they struggle to listen to and understand each other and express their concerns, it is important to remind ourselves that this is their process and that we do not need to "fix" anything. We constantly keep in mind our purpose—to support people as they figure out how to interact and make tough decisions—and the basic premises that form the basis of our work. Reflecting on our own experiences with conflict, we believe that people know best and have what it takes to make personal and collective change in times of difficulty, especially when provided with support as they grapple with difficult issues. We return to this fundamental premise again and again.

THE MANAGER AS FACILITATOR

Does it matter if you are a facilitator working from the outside with teams or a manager working from the inside of teams when you use Transformative Dialogue? There are probably differences and inherent tensions in each of our roles and positions, some of which we explore here; but there is certainly enough in common that supports the value of working this way either within or outside a team.

Managers may think they are not in a position to facilitate interventions because of their existing relationships within the team, which will limit their effectiveness as intervenors in team process or performance. There may be perceptions of favoritism or concerns about their investments in particular outcomes. It's true that when a manager is part of the difficult situation being addressed, it is definitely more helpful to ask an external facilitator to support dialogue. But this does not mean that facilitating dialogue is not a part of a manager's responsibilities. Just as a facilitator of Transformative Dialogue has many roles, such as a coach, mediator, process guide, or communicator of external boundaries, a manager also holds different roles, based on the particulars of a situation. Managers too must often function in the same roles as a facilitator. However, because a manager has final responsibility for a department their role is different from an external Transformative Dialogue facilitator. A manager needs to be aware that their role is distinct and needs to be clear about the boundaries they may set for departmental conversations. When a manager suggests that staff get together to talk about certain issues and possible outcomes they need to be clear at the start about any terms and conditions for possible solutions.

Managers who are also Transformative practitioners have confidence that people have the knowledge and experience to have these kinds of conversations. They trust that those involved are capable of seeing and understanding the different points of view and the impact they have on people. They believe that those directly involved are capable of achieving a satisfying result and want to support them in having these conversations. At the same time, because of a manager's responsibility, it's important to set boundaries for the solutions that are chosen. In this example, it might be the minimum staffing capacity needed or ensuring continuity of certain tasks. In a situation like that it is important to be clear about these boundaries from the start. Then managers can move forward with the co-creation of a dialogue that allows those involved to decide who needs to talk to whom about what and what the best way is to do so. In that way, those involved can come up with the best solutions they can that are consistent with the stated boundaries. Knowledge and training in Transformative Dialogue can enhance a manager's skills and enable them to help groups of people who are struggling or who want to make positive changes to processes in their working lives.

WHERE DIALOGUE CAN HELP

A good example of how a dialogue can help is a situation where a large department with over 150 nurses was unhappy with the way their schedule was organized. Nurses found that they were being scheduled to work in too many different wards. This was because one of the wards, with a different type of care than the other three wards, was short of staff. This shortage was being solved by deploying staff from the other wards. As a result, there was no permanent team working in any of the wards.

Staff felt that this had a negative impact on the quality of care and the team spirit. At their manager's suggestion, nurses started talking with doctors about this, eventually including management in the conversation. The group finally decided to mix the care of the fourth ward with the care of the other three wards so that there were three instead of four teams. In regular times, these wards had sufficient capacity to cope with the requested care. The three teams agreed that if at peak times the fourth ward did need to be open, they would be jointly responsible for staffing it. This had the additional advantage that staff could learn from each other. This solution is one that came about because those directly involved talked with each other about the problem. The solution they came up with was their own, not one that management suggested. And it turned out to not just solve the staffing problem but to increase quality of care and improve team spirit.

A manager or internal facilitator needs to be aware of the many different scenarios where a Transformative Dialogue may be helpful. As in the previous example, there may be a situation where a group, team, or MDT wants to make changes in how they work together or explore concerns they share. Sometimes the "presenting issue" is not clear as it manifests in performance issues such as sickness absence rates, an increase in patient complaints, retention and recruitment problems, poor staff morale, disappointing results of an employee satisfaction survey, or accusations of unfair treatment (for example, racism). At other times groups want to explore poor interpersonal relationships within their own professional group or between the different professions that are part of the MDT. Challenges may also arise during a change process—a merging of services across a geographical area or a need to change working practices (as happened, for example, during the pandemic). In all these situations, the issues threaten the quality of patient care and make it unsafe, so "something" has to happen to change this. In addition, these challenges often represent a loss of the core values in healthcare. This can lead to moral distress in staff members, which in turn can fuel a conflict dynamic of blame, mistrust, and anger. While these interpersonal and interteam conflict situations seem made for Transformative Dialogue, it can have equal value as part of a larger system-wide change process or when people need to discuss a very difficult part of the working environment.

When a manager is able to support Transformative Dialogue themselves rather than call an external facilitator, it is integrated in the way that manager works. It is part of their management style and not a separate process. Because of this, it is important that the staff group know about their manager's style and worldview in order to manage their expectations before the manager starts. If a manager really believes that people have what it takes, it is not up to the manager to be the one who comes up with solutions for the problems that exist. The solutions are already there, they just need the space that Transformative Dialogue offers to become apparent. In difficult situations this space is often not felt, so the group thinks solutions need to come from their manager and might expect a clear plan before a conversation starts. Thus, a manager committed to Transformative practice educates the group about why working Transformatively has value.

THE OUTSIDER AS FACILITATOR

When Transformative Dialogue may be most appropriately run by someone other than the manager, an external facilitator is usually contacted by a senior manager who identifies a concern within a team, often noting a direct link to a decrease in the quality of patient care and staff morale. Clarity comes from the process of co-creation, which often looks something like this. An initial meeting between the facilitator and manager is set up to create a team map: to understand the team, its context, systems and influence, challenges, and the perceived impact of the difficulties. As Transformative facilitators, we understand that at this initial meeting we are hearing the manager's view; it may transpire that this view is very different from the group's view. The facilitator describes their role, and the manager sets expectations of change and/or success. The facilitator often provides an "overview" of possible process designs and explores which might be most appropriate, who needs to talk with whom about what, and the operational constraints (for example, shift patterns, twenty-four-hour service). The questions discussed will depend on the situation but often include things like: If all staff cannot be involved in the conversation(s), how can we engage with them in different ways or keep them aware as the process evolves? How do we organize as many initial conversations as possible so that staff can shape the process at an early stage and have a notion of the value and hoped for outcomes of the dialogue? The final design is determined by how many people are in a team, whether different professional groups are involved, and of course what will ensure that staff have "buy in" to the process. Our experience is that teams are not used to talking about their relationships and the impact they have on the services they deliver.

THE PROCESS OF TRANSFORMATIVE DIALOGUE—HOW CO-CREATION HAPPENS

Making connections and building relationships is intrinsic to our work. Each conversation, telephone call, and email is important. Trust grows when people experience that you have a sincere interest in them. Listening, reflecting, being curious, and recognizing the strengths of each person or group creates a sense of openness. This is because people feel you "with" them, being alongside them in each interaction. Whether as manager or external intervenor for the team, informal contact builds trust: drinking cups of coffee, attending meetings, visiting people, and listening to their stories: How long have they been working there, what do they do, why did they choose this profession, what was it like in the past, and what is it like now? These interactions also allow the team or department members to co-create the process. By speaking to different people, you get an idea about who wants to speak to whom about what, and you can facilitate that. By organizing meetings around certain subjects and asking who would like to participate in them, people get to choose how to be involved. By sending out a questionnaire that people can fill out anonymously, by finding out how things really are instead of the story that is going

Working with Transformative Dialogue in Large Healthcare Organizations   57

around, and then sharing what you learn with those involved, people feel heard and are more likely to be open to changes in their perspective.

Including as many people as possible in these initial conversations supports people in shaping the process from an early stage. Defining your roles as facilitator or manager and listening to the different perceptions of the "problem" and what change might look like really engages the participants from the onset. If you are in the role of interim manager, part of building trust is being clear why you are there, how long you will stay, and what your assignment is—and then to keep to it. For an external facilitator, being honest about time or money constraints often elicits creative suggestions from the group as to how to connect their conversations to other groups involved in the process or to make decisions about how a whole group might "come together" if there are large numbers of staff involved.

Several examples demonstrate how participants develop processes that work for them. One dialogue involved three different professional groups and provides a good example of starting with small group sessions. Each professional group had a separate meeting to begin with, and all three had difficulties within their own teams as well as between the teams. Each wanted to spend time on their own functionality before meeting with the other groups so that they could have a clear idea about how they could work better together. This demonstrates the importance of intragroup dialogue rather than expecting to begin with intergroup dialogue. When they were ready, they decided that the best way to meet would be with representatives from each group. This was critical because there were too many people for a whole group meeting and the service had to keep running, precluding the possibility of everyone being at one meeting. The representatives would then carry key ideas from the large group back to their teams for further discussion. As the groups met, they became clearer and clearer about a way forward, how perceptions of the "problem" were often not shared, and what they might need from each other to improve the patient pathway and talk more honestly in the MDT meetings as problems arose and the dialogue groups had come to an end.

In another group it was not possible for all members to meet, so they decided to start with a questionnaire that was sent out to every member of the team, to be completed anonymously. The external facilitator then analyzed the information in relation to the perspective of each professional group and discussed the findings in a smaller meeting with representatives from each group, which illuminated "who needed to talk with whom about what." They decided to proceed by having representatives from each group for a series of meetings, which enabled the participants to design the process from the beginning. We saw this as an empowerment shift, a movement from blaming the other teams for the dysfunction to a curiosity to talk with others about what is going on in the MDT.

DIVERSITY IN COMMUNICATION FORMS

Transformative Dialogue is flexible enough to allow many different forms of communication. Our experience is that working with images enables deeper transcultural communication. With a trust that has over one hundred different nationalities and where many staff have English as a second language, expressing emotions and impact through images deepens the group's experiences of the challenges they face together. So as a manager or facilitator you can increase creativity, choice, and "voice" with simple resources such as colored pens, Post-its, or postcards. It is critical to offer this tentatively to groups, explaining why you sense it might be useful, but then allow them to make the decision about whether to adopt it. They will soon tell you if it is not useful! One group seemed to express themselves best through images. Offering a collection of postcards for them to depict "where the team is now" and "where you would like to be" seemed to "unlock their voices" as they collaboratively created the pictures and were then united in shock as to how bad the team had become and how they shared the resulting distress. The picture of "where we want to be" enabled an empowerment shift toward "we really need to talk about this" and "we can do this." After several hours of talking about how this might have happened (increased workload, crammed team meetings with little time to reflect, decrease in social gatherings, "lunch at our desks," etc.), the group became very emotional, almost mourning the sense of each other that they had lost. After a much-needed break, they returned with a resolve to improve the situation with an immediate plan that involved changing team meetings and having more opportunities to talk together and a longer-term plan to create a business plan to increase staffing in line with the increase in referrals and workload. Often people who work in the healthcare sector take on more and more work out of a sense of necessity. This propensity to "overwork" ends up being detrimental to the individual worker and of course to team functioning. Sometimes, as illustrated in this example, this can build up unnoticed and unprocessed. Giving workers opportunities to explore and talk is of immense value to the team and ultimately to the larger service.

Sometimes, regardless of how well designed a process is, a group may have become so weak and self-absorbed that they find it hard to talk productively, instead expressing themselves mainly through blame, criticism, and interpersonal hostility. In a group Angie facilitated, interpersonal relationships had broken down to such an extent that participants had difficulty talking to each other during the dialogue. Angie reflected this and then asked if this mirrored their working environment. One member spoke up and said that relationships hadn't always been like this, that there was a time when they always greeted each other, talked, shared breaks and food, and helped each other out. She said that the normal "glue" that held them together and helped them to function as a team had "solidified" and that nothing flowed easily between them. She felt communication was "stuck" and that members didn't reach out to each other in the way they did before. She was at a loss as to what to do, of how to mend this, how to start. Silent nods indicated agreement, and another member said, "we don't even say hello to each other in the mornings—that's how bad it has become—and we are all guilty of this." More nods from the group indicated that the experience was shared and that they were all responsible. Angie wondered out loud if an exercise might be helpful, allowing them to say to each other individually what they might need from each member of the team. The exercise was

Stop-Start-Continue (also affectionately known as "speed dating"). Angie explained that every team member had time alone to really think about their relationship with each member of the team and write on a Post-it what they wanted from the other: for example, to stop (ignoring me in the morning), to start (saying hello again), and to continue (bringing in those cakes you always used to). Chairs were put in two parallel rows, with only one row moving at two-minute intervals. Each person had one minute each to voice their needs. In this way, each individual had the opportunity to speak with and listen to everyone on the team. The group liked the idea and discussed several concerns. They then came to a group agreement that the requests were not to be seen as demands and that they should be simple, direct, respectful, kind, and confidential. The Post-its would be given to their partner after voicing what they requested only if their partner wanted to receive it. The facilitator's job, in this instance, was to ensure that people kept moving within the agreed two minutes. Angie observed laughter, tears, discomfort, and people talking and listening. The group agreed to evaluate any outcomes at next week's meeting. There were many, including an increase in positive communication with each other.

There is always a risk for facilitators and managers offering such an exercise. A Transformative facilitator needs to ask herself what her purpose is: "Am I trying to 'fix' this group? Am I taking them down a path they are not on? What benefit might this bring to their process?" It is also critical to be transparent and explain why a particular suggestion is made. In this instance it was tentatively offered and received with some concerns. Because participants defined how the exercise would run before they started, there was ownership and a willingness to try something that might help them start talking to each other in a different way. The physical action (putting out the chairs, moving to another person every two minutes) seemed to alleviate some of their fear. It also encouraged thoughtfulness (having time to really think about what would make a difference with each of their colleagues) and allowed them to express loss, need, and appreciation.

In the previous examples all of the processes were very different, but what they shared was that it was the participants who were making the decisions about what the process should look like. The facilitator's role was to support people as they became clearer about the choices they needed to make about how to interact in the dialogue and in the wider workplace.

CO-FACILITATION

As either a facilitator or manager, it is really important to have the confidence that comes from understanding the changing dynamics that arise in dialogue groups and knowing that through these dynamics Transformative premises ground us by constantly reminding us of our purpose. An awareness of group dynamics also increases the ability to reflect, not only individual voices, themes, and agendas but also group/organizational dynamics and norms.

For this reason, external facilitators work as a team to co-facilitate groups when this is possible. This enables a co-reflection about the process and the facilitation between and across groups. What did we see, what did we miss, what are we intuiting, and what choice points have we offered during a dialogue session? How are we working together and what shifts have we seen in the group—what is emerging? This also enables us to have input into the evaluative phase of the intervention as this can be done in each dialogue session. Check in with open questions like "how have you done today in your conversations," "how is the process working/not working for you," "how do you see your ideas going into the wider group," and "what might be useful now?"

As a manager co-facilitation is rarely an option. But there are other ways to respond to group dynamics. One example is to have everyone submit agenda items and, if there are too many of them, jointly determine what needs to be discussed and which items can be moved on to the next meeting. It is important that meetings have the character of a dialogue and not be a monologue by the manager. A manager who practices Transformatively needs to make sure that there is a lot of space for voices other than the manager's and that there is space for disagreement.

INCREASING PRO-SOCIAL INTERACTION

Both as a manager and facilitator, one goal is to support pro-social interaction, meaning that people make choices that are not only good for themselves but that are also valuable for others. Pro-social interaction is growing when a team starts thinking about the effect of their actions on other departments or teams—when there is greater awareness of the importance of connection.

One example of supporting pro-social interaction came about in responding to a conflict about the patient visiting scheme in a hospital during COVID. In the first wave, the hospital had drawn up a very limited and uniform visiting arrangement for all departments and was not willing to make any exceptions. The aim was to keep traffic in the hospital as low as possible in order to prevent infection. In one department, different professionals had widely varied opinions about these rules, and emotions were running high. The differences were mainly based on personal standards of good and bad care in these circumstances. One group felt strongly that it was indeed better to admit as few people as possible to the department and to let communication with the family take place, as much as possible, over the telephone or iPad. They were very concerned about their own health and the health of their loved ones at home. The other group experienced moral stress because, in their view, they were unable to provide quality of care due to the lack of visitation arrangements. In their eyes the arrangement was inhuman; they found it unacceptable that family members were only allowed to be present to a very limited extent, even when their loved ones were dying. In their view, digital communication was no solution at all. The first group adhered strictly to the rules and regularly had difficult conversations with the families about this. If a colleague from the other group then allowed the family more visits, it was felt as betrayal. The other group felt that in certain situations you had to be flexible with the rules and therefore became angry when they were told that they were not collegial. Both groups agreed that the conflict would lead to sick leave due to the staffs' moral distress and that something had to change. However, they came no further than repeating their opinions to each other and demanding that management come up with a solution.

As a manager grounded in Transformative practice, Anja initiated a meeting with representatives from both groups, so that they had the opportunity to listen to each other. Anja supported their conversation with reflections and summaries, so that it became increasingly clear to everyone what was important to them but also what mattered to others. Ideas arose on how to find a balance between limiting the presence of visitors in the department and ensuring the quality of care. For example, they agreed that it was more important to allow two visitors to visit the patient instead of one, so that people could share experiences at home, rather than to increase the duration of the visit or to allow them to come more often. They also agreed that it was more important to extend the visit in the event of admission or imminent death than when the patient was stable, even if he or she had been on the ward for a long time. This group then took part in the hospital-wide conversation (chaired by another manager) about the visiting rules, so that they could explain for themselves what was important for their ward and also listen to the views of other departments. From this conversation it became clear that it was not desirable to make a uniform visiting arrangement for the entire hospital. By listening to each other, they understood the different situations (pediatric ward, ICU, maternity ward, wards with multipatient rooms versus wards with single rooms), and it turned out to be possible to make a visiting arrangement with exceptions for certain wards. While it was not be an ideal situation, it was a more acceptable one.

CONCLUSION

In this chapter we described how Transformative Dialogue can be useful in a healthcare setting, whether practiced internally, as a manager, or as an external facilitator, and what co-creation of dialogue looks like in this context. In our experience, whatever role you have, the key to success is that you see people and yourself in the context of a relational worldview. This worldview posits that we need each other to function well in the teams that we work in; that in times of difficulty, we need to share our differing and collective thoughts and co-create ideas that can enable communities of work to thrive and function well. Conflict separates and divides us, and the Transformative framework is a valuable guide for facilitating conversations that lead to change and better understanding.

Our commitment to Transformative interventions reflects our belief that staff are our greatest resource. If staff are given opportunities to talk (individually and in groups), they can improve their working lives and the care they collectively deliver. They best understand the complexity of healthcare. They have what it takes to use the opportunities that Transformative Dialogue provides to grapple with their situation and challenges. Working with Transformative Dialogue makes a person humble about their own role. It is impressive to see that teams often come to insights or solutions that you would never have thought of yourself.

From the examples we provide, it is clear that no two dialogues are the same. But when we as facilitators make connections and build relationships with individuals, it enables team members to move into conversations with each other to address what is important to them. We are not afraid to suggest creative processes, if the group finds this helpful, but our offerings are tentative and in service to the groups' process.

One outcome of Transformative Dialogue is the likelihood of increased pro-social interaction during and after the dialogue. This is vital in healthcare as care is delivered in MDTs that rely on each other. If the whole system is able to interact, understand their differing roles and relationships, and listen and talk together, they will be able to light a way forward for good practice in a rapidly changing and complex environment.

6

Using Transformative Dialogue to Address Concerns about Racism in the Workplace

Lida M. van den Broek

An employee of a large insurance company in the Netherlands comes to the office early and finds a drawing on a whiteboard in the office garden. A drawing of a hung slave, as we know it from the history books, with the text: Sylvana, a good start. The drawing is based on a picture that appeared on social media, in which a picture of Sylvana Simons (a woman with a Surinamese[1] background and founder of the political party Bij1[2]) is pasted onto an old Ku Klux Klan picture of a hanged slave.

How to discuss a racist incident? White people already find it difficult and often uncomfortable to raise the subject of racism in one-on-one conversations. In a larger group it may be even more difficult. Yet it is very important. In the Netherlands employees of color often talk to each other about incidents and unpleasant experiences, but never or hardly ever with their white colleagues. Or rather, they "no longer" talk about it with their white colleagues because they are so often disappointed when they raise the subject of racism that they are getting tired of trying. Too often white colleagues react with denial, with amazement, or attempt to justify what has happened. Because these uncomfortable conversations are not being held, white colleagues have no idea that racism is occurring on the work floor and what impact it has on cooperation with their colleagues of color. It would be in the best interest of all to find a way to have these uncomfortable conversations effectively.

As an organizational anthropologist, I have been working for over forty years in both profit and nonprofit organizations in the Netherlands, and now and then in Belgium and Germany. Kantharos, the consultancy and training firm I founded together with my colleague Ida Sabelis[3] in 1983, specializes in managing ethnic diversity and unlearning racism. In the first years we concentrated mainly on training in unlearning racism and advising on diversity and affirmative action policies. Now that the workplace in the Netherlands is more ethnically diverse, I am increasingly asked to address ethnic conflicts in the workplace. With Transformative Dialogue, I found a method not to fix conflicts but to give colleagues the opportunity to engage in "uncomfortable conversations" with each other in order to gain more insight and awareness of what underlies the conflict and to clarify and possibly improve the relationships between them. Thanks to the experience in fighting racism that I have built up over all these years, people of color accept that I, a white woman, can facilitate discussions about racism between white people and people of color.

This chapter analyzes the organizational dialogue that resulted from the previous event. The case has been anonymized and the type of organization in which it took place has been changed. As part of monitoring the process, I recorded all conversations. I asked permission for the recording, explaining that my goal was to use it to help me guide the entire process. At that time there was no intention of using it for an article. Later I realized the recordings were valuable resource material to use in my writing, as long as I changed the context and ensured the absence of any identifying information. The recording made it possible to more accurately describe a dialogue process, including initial conversations and the first group session.

CO-CREATION BEGINS

The diversity officer of a large insurance company calls me for help. There has been a racist incident in the organization and the diversity support group has complained. Because this was not the first racist incident, the diversity officer wants to approach it structurally. She briefly describes the case over the phone, as presented at the beginning of this chapter. The employee who found the drawing is first stunned and then very angry. She feels hurt, shocked, and indignant, and all kinds of thoughts run through her head. She takes a photo of the drawing. Being very upset, she goes to find a colleague who is also a member of the ethnic diversity support group. When they return together, the drawing has been erased. Who drew it and who erased it is not clear. What is clear is that the whiteboard belongs to the financial administration. Incidents have occurred in that department before. The members of the ethnic diversity support group do not want to address the financial staff directly and certainly not publicly. They decide instead to contact the diversity officer and visit her immediately.

The co-creation of the dialogue process starts during my first meeting with the diversity manager and her assistant. They indicate that it is not just about this incident, because it is not the first time. Apparently, there is an environment in which this kind of thing can happen and where people accept it silently. For this reason, the ethnic diversity support group was formed by some employees of color not long ago. The diversity officer wants to initiate a discussion about the incident in the organization. They decide that the goal for the process is not only to fix the incident but also to start a discussion about "desired and undesired behaviors, with a focus on ethnicity and the incident."

I describe the Transformative model to them and suggest initiating a Transformative Dialogue process. I emphasize the co-creation process, explaining that

Using Transformative Dialogue to Address Concerns about Racism in the Workplace   65

participants are involved in co-creating the dialogue. I also describe my role as facilitator and how they might be involved. They invited me because I work from the Transformative perspective and because of my extensive experience dealing with racism, so they are pleased to hear all this.

The next important question I ask them to consider is "who should talk to whom, about what, how, and when?" As initiators and my initial conversation partners, the diversity officer and her assistant will work with me to develop a plan of action that will later be presented to the CEO and management team. We talk about the different parts of the organization that should be involved. They explain that the person who made the disputed drawing does not work in the financial administration, nor even on the same floor. And what makes it more complicated is that this person himself has an immigrant background. So the financial department, the owners of the whiteboard, have been falsely accused. This accusation has spread throughout the organization. The financial employees and their manager are annoyed that the ones who found the drawing did not come to them. Now they feel wrongly discredited, which affects the good name of their department, and they are not happy about that.

As I talk to the diversity officer and her assistant, I understand much of what they are concerned about. As a process guide, I suggest possible ways to move forward. explaining that the decisions are theirs and those of the participants in the dialogue process. We talk about a dialogue process that involves several steps. The first step would focus on the employees who are directly involved: members of the ethnic diversity support group, employees of the financial department who own the whiteboard and feel wrongly accused, and the employee who made the drawing on the board. Because the management of the financial department feels wrongly accused, and the incident is much discussed by the departments working on the same floor, we decide to invite them for a second round of discussions.

Finally, because the initiators want to go beyond merely fixing the incident and involve the CEO, the management team, and the managers of other departments, they decide that the process needs to be evaluated. The evaluation will include specific results of this dialogue and highlight potential management action and policy changes that may be needed to address incidents in the future.

This three-step proposal is presented to the CEO and the management team. The diversity manager has her own budget and therefore does not need financial approval for this process. But because she wants the results of the dialogue to be discussed at the highest level, it is important that the CEO and management agree. Moreover, there is room to accommodate their wishes if they have additional suggestions or specific requirements. At this stage, management makes no changes. In fact, they insist on starting the first phase quickly to see what it brings.

INTRAGROUP MEETINGS

As a start to the dialogue process, separate meetings are organized with the different groups involved. Meetings between people on the so-called same side are often not given much attention in dialogue processes, but they can be very important. So first there is a meeting with the members of the ethnic support group, a meeting with the employees of the financial administration, and a meeting with the so-called perpetrator. This is followed by an additional meeting with the managers of the financial administration and a meeting with other managers working on the same floor. A similar meeting with the CEO and the management team is not organized because we already talked to them about the proposal and about the methodology of Transformative Dialogue.

In these conversations, I explain what Transformative Dialogue is and the process as it has been co-created thus far. I talk about the roles of the participants and the facilitator. Participants talk about what is important for them to discuss during the dialogue session and which members of their group will participate in the dialogue. Because a conversation about a racist incident in an ethnically mixed group can make people feel vulnerable, we ask participants about special needs or conditions they might suggest for having a fruitful conversation, making clear that this is their decision. The ethnic support group indicates no special needs. Above all, they want to make clear that this incident is racist and not acceptable. The employees of the financial administration especially hope that there is room to make clear that as a department they are not involved in this incident and are very annoyed that the ethnic employees jumped to their conclusions too quickly. The so-called perpetrator hopes above all that it will become clear that it was all based on a clumsiness and that there was no intentionality. So no one identified any special needs. All feel assertive enough and are not afraid to engage in the conversation and hope above all to say what they have to say.

When we meet with the managers, they suggest that participants of the first round and those involved in the incident attend the session with them because they were directly involved. As managers, they only have secondhand information. Moreover, participants from the first session can bring in ideas for follow-up steps from management. We agree to share this request with the participants of the first round at the end of the first session. This back and forth is an important part of what it means to co-create the process.

INTERGROUP CONVERSATIONS— INITIAL INTERACTIONS

The first intergroup session takes place between five employees of the financial department, all ethnically Dutch; three members of the ethnic diversity support group who come from different backgrounds; and the so-called perpetrator, who I will call Fatou, who also migrated to the Netherlands. The diversity officer and her assistant are also present and part of the conversation.

When the first joint dialogue session starts, I open the conversation by summarizing what has already been discussed in the earlier conversations about roles and about the process. Then I ask, "who wants to start?" The conversation starts quietly.

Using Transformative Dialogue to Address Concerns about Racism in the Workplace 67

In the first three turns employees of the financial department explain that they want an open conversation, to hear each other's stories, but especially want to discuss how cooperation can be continued. I reflect briefly after each speaker by saying out loud what has been said and stay as close as possible to the words and emotions of the speakers themselves. Then one of the participants proposes that a representative of each group shares what they think has happened. I reflect this in such a way that it remains a proposal of the speaker and not mine: "You propose that a representative of each group tells what they think has happened." This is an important part of my Transformative practice. If I had adopted the proposal immediately, then I would have become part of the conversation, and the participants could feel less ownership of the conversation. A proposal from the facilitator might also be experienced differently by the participants. They could feel pressured, and this could evoke more resistance than a proposal from one of them. This is an example of how, during the dialogue, I ensure that the participants retain ownership of both the content and the process so co-creation continues. Co-creation happens throughout the dialogue!

A member of the diversity support group then turns to Fatou, the person who made the drawing: "It seems to me that you should tell your side of the story first, that you explain why you did this, because we have a lot of questions and would like to hear your side first." Fatou responds that there was no special reason to use that particular whiteboard except that he just happened to be standing before it. He was explaining to a new non-Dutch colleague the kinds of discussions about racism going on in the Netherlands at the moment. As an illustration he had put the drawing and the text on the board, saying, "It was stupid that I didn't erase it afterward and that because of that it was misunderstood, but this was the context." The employees of the diversity working group ask him more questions. The conversation is going on now, and parties respond to each other quickly. I do not intervene and let the interaction take its course because participants are having a good conversation with each other. They are taking responsibility for the conversation: letting each other speak, listening, and responding to each other. An intervention could disrupt that process and take the attention and the ownership away from the participants and focus it on me, negating my party-centered commitment as a Transformative facilitator.

A member of the support group asks the colleagues of the financial department what their reaction was when they saw the drawing and the text on the board. "I immediately erased it," says the person who found the text. One responds: "I didn't know if someone from the department had done it, but something like that doesn't belong on the whiteboard, so I erased it."

MISUNDERSTANDINGS AND DISAGREEMENTS

So far, the group has been exploring the different perceptions of what happened. Then there is a turn in the conversation. When a member of the diversity support group tells how it has affected him and that everyone will understand what it means to them, he is interrupted by an employee of the financial administration, who responds: "No I don't understand it at all." He continues: "Why didn't you come directly to us? Why do you connect it with previous incidents? You immediately discredited us as the perpetrators." This is followed by a fierce discussion in which the support group is blamed for their reaction to the drawing and for involving the diversity officer. A member of the support group responds: "Apparently, you understand that this drawing should not be there and have therefore erased it, but you do not understand what the effect is on us." Then the conversation falls silent for a moment. I use the pause as an opportunity to summarize their comments about how the incident was handled and what the different points of view are. My summary is inclusive and detailed enough to help participants get a sense of where the conversation has gone and allows them to decide where to go next.

Then the conversation takes a more strategic turn, focusing on how to react to such an event. Fatou indicates that as far as he is concerned, there are two ways in which you can react: "You can defend yourself, but then you end up in a victim role. Or you can think: 'Okay, that's what they think, I don't agree at all, but I won't react.'" The support group states that it's not about defending: "What we want is for people to understand that this is racism. Racism is not an issue that only affects people of color, just as sexism does not only affect women. It's a problem for all of us, including you." And then a discussion arises about victimization versus active action against discrimination, about freedom of expression versus the limits of what is acceptable, whether this is an isolated incident or a structural problem, whether actively raising the issue of discrimination actually provokes a counter-reaction, and who decides what is racism and what is not. The conversation now grows more heated, and it is difficult for people to get a word in.

A Transformative facilitator often experiences a tension between guiding and following. I follow the conversation, reflecting what is said from time to time, including the accompanying emotions, and occasionally summarizing the different points of view. Because parties have chosen to raise their hand to get into this jumble, I also point out the order of speakers. At times I even ask whether new speakers are responding to what has just been said or want to bring up something new, so they can decide if this is the moment to make their point. Calling on speakers and asking whether they are bringing up a new point or responding to the previous speaker can seem directive and not aligned with the Transformative model. But because speakers raise hands to take turns, this intervention seems to be in line with the wishes of the participants. In a large group and during a fierce discussion, sometimes more direction is needed than just reflecting and summarizing. As a facilitator, it is important to consider whether the intended intervention remains in line with the Transformative model, that is, whether the decisions remain in the hands of the participants. One way to do this is to ask yourself as facilitator why you are doing what you are doing. If the answer is that you want to calm things down, then your actions are probably not in line with Transformative practice. If the purpose is to support parties where they seem to be, it might be. As a facilitator it is important to check in with participants from time to time to ensure that your actions are aligned with their wishes. Staying morally grounded requires always remembering what one's purpose

Using Transformative Dialogue to Address Concerns about Racism in the Workplace 69

is: to support but never supplant the decision making of participants. Transformative Dialogue is not about whether a process is open or structured but about who makes the decisions about the structure.

SHIFTS TOWARD UNDERSTANDING AND RECOGNITION

When I summarize the fierce discussion, I also note that some of the participants have not said much so far. Then, because I have made the group's pattern of interaction visible, the discussion takes a different turn. An employee of the administration, who has said little, expresses that she would like to share what is happening for her: "I acknowledge that as a white person life is easier for me, and I realize very well that this incident is racist, and I want you to know that." This is an explicit acknowledgment of what another participant has said and an attempt to make a connection, what I understand as a recognition shift. This then evokes recognition and appreciation from a member of the support group: "That is good to hear." I summarize this piece of dialogue in order to make explicit the connection that occurs here for the first time in the conversation. I repeat what each of them has said using words as close as possible to theirs: "You, M., acknowledge that as a white person life is easier and you realize that the incident is racism, and you want them to know that. And K., it's good for you to hear that." This then evokes a reaction from Fatou: "I can understand very well why it can be racist, insulting, and discriminating. I myself have been insulted often enough in the past because of my origins." Here we see how recognition leads to recognition and resonates when this speaker shares the experiences of the support group. This does not mean that the parties agree with each other, because Fatou continues: "What I have learned from personal experience is that you don't have to experience a situation like that as an insult. You can also look at it in a different way. Why does a person think like that? Often someone has no intention of offending." At this point, for the first time, a member of the ethnic support group asks Fatou a direct question: "How do you react when you find yourself in a setting where you are discriminated against?" Here, in the conversation, a cycle has started in which the recognition of one evokes recognition and appreciation from the other, which then evokes recognition and connection from the third party, followed by an interested question from someone else. In Transformative terms, this is a series of recognition and empowerment shifts, which allows the conversation to change direction. And then someone picks up again on the differences in their approach: "Do you let these insults pass by, or do you bring them up for discussion?" But it becomes clear that the content has changed when a member of the support group says: "Okay, you (Fatou) think of it one way, but can you respect that we see it differently?" Fatou responds to this and indicates that he respects that the support group takes a different approach, but that he is not happy with the changes they want to achieve "because that stands in the way of freedom of expression." So although they do not agree, there is improvement in the conflict interaction.

70   *Lida M. van den Broek*

At this point I offer a summary of the conversation and focus on the main difference of opinion regarding whether this is an isolated incident or a structural problem. I also note that part of the group is silent. Attending to the conversation is a basic skill of Transformative practice, and noticing is something that I frequently do as a Transformative facilitator. It allows the group to consider its own interaction and often creates space. This allows one of the silent participants to take this opportunity to speak. She, an employee of the administration, says, "I am really on your side in this and I dare say that I do not agree with the other perspective, but I do not know what to do differently were this to happen again. Do you have a suggestion?" Again, a hand is reached out with an invitation to express needs. That gesture is accepted: "We (the support group) are not only looking for understanding but also solidarity. In order to be able to show solidarity, you must first understand what these kinds of situations mean to us." At this point the two people who found the drawing talk about what they could have done instead of erasing it.

The administrative staff members indicate that they prefer to talk about how they can deal with each other better in the future than about the differences of opinion that seem to exist between Fatou and the support group. They are now convinced that this was an incidence of racism. One member of the administrative team, however, dissociates himself from what appears to be a common point of view and indicates that he still thinks it is only an isolated incident: "There are always people who think they can do something *'cool'* under group pressure, and for me this is still an incident and not structural racism." Someone else argues, "But because it is *'cool'* does it mean it is not racist? And do you have to accept things just because it's *'cool'*?" After this a discussion arises about intention and impact. Should you judge a situation on the intention—it's not meant to be racist—or on the impact—it is experienced as racist and so it is racist. This raises the question of what the relationship is between freedom of expression and impact, particularly for Fatou. He indicates that, as far as he is concerned, "freedom of speech is paramount, but that should not lead to people being excluded." In this phase of the discussion, we see alternating expressions of rapprochement—wanting to talk about the common future—and differences of opinion—"it is an incident" versus "it is racism."

After a short break at the request of the participants, the discussion resumes, with one of the speakers requesting that we focus on the future. Before we start, the administrative employee who previously distanced himself from the group position takes the floor: "I want to say that even though I just supported Fatou in the discussion, I did so because of the discussion. But if you (diversity support group) experience it as something that keeps coming back, yes of course I think it is also important that things like these are addressed. I think there is a consensus that everyone should feel safe and respected in the organization." This comment builds a new bridge among participants.

The group also talks about how they want to deal with each other in their daily work: when do you greet each other, speak to each other, the contact at the coffee machine, and other kinds of everyday interactions. In between, they talk again about their different experiences with the situation, considering briefly why it went this

Using Transformative Dialogue to Address Concerns about Racism in the Workplace 71

way and how they can respond differently and in solidarity in the future. They say to each other that if such an incident happens again, they know where to find each other and will be open for discussion, hopefully directly and immediately, when an incident occurs.

WRAPPING UP THE INTERACTION

As facilitator, I conclude the conversation by summarizing the agreements made and indicating that the next meeting will be with the managers of the financial administration and managers of the other departments working on the same floor. The managers invite the participants of this initial dialogue to attend the next session as well, so that the initial conversation can be built upon and agreements can be made for future collaboration, and they agree to come. This is another example of how co-creation happens throughout the dialogue process, because participants in this first session have decided to change who will attend the next session. This was possible because as a facilitator my commitment to following the participants—rather than a predetermined process—allowed it to happen.

With this rather extensive report of the first dialogue I wanted to show how a dialogue can go and how the specific interventions of a Transformative facilitator can support a group's interactions. As is often the case, the conversation develops slowly and moves from being initially negative, offensive, and defensive toward a more constructive conversation. That development is not linear, but it is erratic, with forward and backward movements. In this case the result is a significant agreement about the way participants view the particular incident they discussed as well as a willingness to take more joint responsibility for similar situations in the future. There is a great deal of agreement, but not a total agreement on everything. Fatou and the support group continue to have fundamental differences of opinion about the definition of the situation (isolated incident or structural problem) and the strategy you should follow (let it pass or tackle it). However, they also expressed their respect for the differences and their willingness to keep talking to each other. Even with the disagreement the interaction has become more constructive and positive.

A lot has happened for all the participants. Initially, the different groups of employees stood diametrically opposed to each other. None of them talked directly and openly to the others. When entering the first dialogue session, no hands were shaken. People more or less entered and sat down together in their own groups. This was also reflected at the start of the conversation in the way that the diversity support group was attacked for the way they reacted to the incident. Slowly the atmosphere of the conversation changed. Offensive questions changed into interested questions. A sincere discussion arose about the differences of opinion. Someone supported the point of view of what at first seemed to be the opponent. Then others joined in. In the end they left the room expressing respect for the difference of opinion that was still there, with agreements to deal better with each other next time. As they left, they shook hands and said, "see you at the next meeting."

The dialogue continued, with several additional sessions that are not described here. The second meeting was with the same group, together with the managers and a delegation of employees from other departments on the same floor and more representatives from the diversity support group. Subsequently, a conversation took place between the management and the board of directors in which the results of the conversations were discussed. They discussed the steps that management and the board of directors should take to make the organization safer and more reliable for everyone.

Finally, at the request of the diversity support group, a second meeting was held with Fatou. As employees with an ethnically diverse background, they wanted to speak to him separately, without their white colleagues, but with guidance of a Transformative facilitator. In this conversation the differences in points of view were discussed again. Although the support group had hoped to convince Fatou of their point of view, this did not happen. However, Fatou did indicate at the end of the conversation that though he held on to his point of view in this interaction, his opinion actually corresponded with theirs more than the conversation indicated. The support group invited him for one of their regular meetings and he agreed.

SUPPORTING INTERACTIONS INCREASES CLARITY

Transformative Dialogue, as I have shown with this case study, is a method that can provide space to engage in controversial and uncomfortable conversations. It is a model that gives participants space to listen to each other and to be heard. It does not force anyone to change their mind or agree with each other. It provides room for a personal process of reconsidering points of view and searching for connection. In the discussion described here, all this has taken place. Participants in Transformative Dialogue do not always reach agreements or find solutions. But its focus on supporting interaction usually allows people to understand different points of view and make connections across differences even when they do not agree. In this way, it increases clarity. And, according to the model of Transformative Dialogue, this is a positive result.

NOTES

1. Suriname is a former colony of the Netherlands. Because of our shared history, many people with a Surinamese background live in the Netherlands.

2. Bij1, a shorthand for the Dutch word "bijeen" meaning "together" in Dutch, describes itself as an intersectional party that stands up for equality between people. Combating discrimination is one of the party's main priorities.

3. Associate professor of organization studies/CMS at Vrije Universiteit Amsterdam; Professor at EduRight Unit; faculty of education, NWU, Potchefstroom, South Africa.

7

Another Voice in Dayton, Ohio

The Story of a Community Dialogue

Thomas Wahlrab

On July 16, 2011, in Dayton, Ohio, Kylen English, a Black man, had been arrested as a burglary suspect. His girlfriend's aunt reported that he had been kicking in her door to reach his girlfriend. Following his arrest, Mr. English was transported to a hospital to be evaluated for his mental and physical health. While en route to the county jail after being released from the hospital, and while passing over a bridge, he broke the police vehicle's window and exited from it. He then jumped over the guardrail of the bridge to his death below.

The questions, accusations, and judgments about the circumstances of how Mr. English died were immediate. While no official conclusions will likely bring ease to anyone who continues to question these circumstances, internal and FBI investigations all exonerated police actions. A Facebook post by a pedestrian who witnessed the event also corroborated what had happened.

This chapter is about both the reaction to how a man died in police custody and the response to this reaction by community members, including the role that Transformative Dialogue played in helping the community. Before "Black Lives Matter" and even before "Black Power" were inspiring memes and slogans, Dayton, like many cities, experienced protests by Black people who were angry about the way they were treated and their lack of acceptance by the community. I write this chapter aware of my responsibility for Dayton's history, as a life-long member of this community, as well as to share the opportunity I had to make a difference. That opportunity came when I was the executive director of the City of Dayton's Human Relations Council (HRC), the city's civil rights monitoring and enforcement agency. I was also an experienced Transformative practitioner.

At the heart of this story are the community dialogues that came to be known as Another Voice, which were a response to a reactive trajectory, the end of which appeared likely to be destructive and violent.

CO-CREATING THE PROCESS

Officials in city government, including the police department, held press conferences and private meetings with Mr. English's family. Community leaders gathered angry, mostly young community members and rallied and marched in protest of what they saw as evidence of police brutality. They also spoke at city commission meetings and wrote articles in the press. The city's attempts to explain were contested or doubted and their spokespersons were vilified.

As I watched these divided and ineffective responses continue, I reached out to the HRC board chairperson, Robert Walker. We talked about what possible actions the HRC might take. Walker and I knew that what the city officials were doing was not providing clarity for the people who were speaking at city commission meetings—where no dialogue could take place because speakers were permitted to speak for only three minutes, and responses by council members were prohibited. City officials were not involving community members in their actions, and those community members appeared to be more and more confident in their use of threatening behaviors. While Walker and I knew that historically the HRC did not intervene in high-profile situations, we decided to act. We agreed that an important first step for HRC was to provide a space for dialogue, an opportunity for city officials and angry community members to talk with each other.

As a committed Transformative practitioner, I believed the most effective dialogue would be one co-created by those who chose to participate. Consistent with this understanding, with each personal invitation, I emphasized their role in co-creating the dialogue, assuring those I spoke with that their thoughts on both the content and the process of the dialogue would be factored into the design of the dialogue process. This open invitation was based on my understanding that formalized and controlled actions by city officials were counter to a belief in the capability of people to act responsibly. Per protocol and law, city officials were acting effectively, that is, investigating police actions, reporting to proper authorities, and so on. But these actions were not seen as effective by community members. The invitation to not only attend a dialogue but also to decide how it would unfold was a direct result of my belief in the capability of community members to engage with each other constructively, that is, to make decisions about who to talk with, how to talk with them, and with support make decisions and act on those decisions. With agreement about this approach, Walker and community member Darryl Fairchild began inviting people to engage in a dialogue of their own creation. The design of our invitation process was intentionally informed by the premises and practices of a Transformative practitioner, that is, that people are capable of making decisions that serve their own needs as well as the needs of others and that open and honest communication among those involved would improve decisions made about how to deal with the situation.

While these community conversations were developing, other actions were simultaneously taking place, including a civil rights investigation by the FBI and community engagement sessions with the Community Relations Service of the

Another Voice in Dayton, Ohio

Department of Justice. The community conversations provided a space for many people to express themselves about the situation but also led to multiple mediation sessions between city officials and community organizations and their leaders and other initiatives, including a community statement, youth forums, a prayer vigil, and conversations between youth, city and county officials, and a community-police committee that evolved into a formalized council.

FIRST GROUP MEETING

The invitation to this first meeting was accepted by a wide range of people. They were both Black and white. Their roles and identities in the community included ministers, community organizers, community violence interrupters, unaffiliated community members, and HRC board members. I intentionally left time for people to mingle and interact with each other before any formal interaction began. This decision avoided a hard announcement to begin and gave people a chance to interact the way they wanted to and to get comfortable with each other at their own pace. As facilitator, I did not call for attention but waited long enough for people to chat and reintroduce themselves to each other, as many of them knew or knew of each other.

Guided by a commitment to participant self-determination, the first thing I did was check that the group was comfortable with me as their facilitator. They accepted my offer by responding with words of assent and with no one objecting. I asked if they might want to talk about process issues, for example, ground rules or confidentiality. Hearing none, I said that I would be sensitive to how they were talking and would check in with them periodically to see if anything about the dialogue needed to change. I also noted that while they may not have concerns about confidentiality, I would not be communicating to anyone what I heard in the meeting without explicit permission from them.

Holding up another decision point to participants, I then asked how the people would like to proceed. Transformative practitioners often say, "Purpose drives practice." My goal was not to gain agreement from people but rather reflected my purpose, which was to begin the conversation as facilitator, not as a decision maker, making room in the process for the participants to be the decision makers, including any decisions about how they would talk with each other. This way of beginning is critical to a Transformative Dialogue as my actions supported my words: the dialogue was theirs to create and use in the ways that made sense to them.

One person began talking about what was happening in the city following Mr. English's death. She ended by saying, "We need to try to ratchet down the noise, so we can address the heart of the situation." This statement set a starting point, that is, sharing events she had noticed and a possible process for the dialogue while creating an opening for others to also share what they had noticed. I reflected some of her story and ended by repeating her statement that ended with, "addressing the heart of the situation." I waited for less than a minute during which everyone was silent. Then one person said, "We should all be responsible to speak our minds."

Following this statement, one person after another spoke, speaking about the events following Mr. English's death and their understanding of what was happening in the community.

For the most part the participants spoke one at a time. There was less conversation between people at this time and more of a sharing of each person's understanding of events and comments about what the group was or would be embarking on. As one person said, "There are questions on everyone's mind about what happened concerning the circumstances of Mr. English's death." Someone said she wanted to hear from others about who was fueling the escalation of the community's reaction as it had "fractured a trusting relationship in the community between multiple individuals and groups and shocked many." I noticed the emotion in this statement and heard her suggestion that the group speak to their personal awareness of events since the death of Mr. English. While the participants in this dialogue had been individually invited, I saw the request to "hear from others" as an opportunity to support their intention to determine who else was needed in the room. Wanting to support this act of self-determination but not highlight it above other previous talk, I provided a summary by reviewing this round of dialogue that included mostly a reporting of recent events and personal experiences and included in my summary the suggestion to hear from others about their firsthand knowledge.

I also checked in, asking, "Do you want to continue sharing what you were noticing or talk about hearing from others who may not be present or maybe something else?" Again, it was my intention to include everyone in the process of decision making and to provide the opportunity to notice and use their agency in the moment to create the flow of the conversation.

Several people quickly spoke up generally agreeing about wanting to move from talking about events to being specific about those who were influencing events and talking about how they were connected to those people and what kind of influence they might have with them. Then multiple conversations began at once, and it became difficult to follow them. I heard snippets of conversations where people were saying what they knew or heard, including identifying names or organizations and, for some, identifying how they themselves were or were not connected with these individuals and organizations.

With multiple small group conversations going on, I saw that it was difficult for everyone to hear each other. When the room quieted for a moment, and wanting to both support what was happening and suggest a different option, I asked if they wanted to come together and share any information with the whole group. Again, as a Transformative facilitator, I didn't assume that I knew what was best. Rather, by attending to the conversation, I noticed what was happening and suggested an option, checking in to see how people wanted to proceed, making sure to be clear that the decision about how to proceed was the group's decision. Most of the people remained quiet as several of them shared their conclusions about who they knew and who they felt comfortable talking with. Because of the webs of interrelatedness within the community, there were people in the room who had a good rapport with some of the youth who were protesting and with the leadership of the local civil

Another Voice in Dayton, Ohio 77

rights organizations like the National Association for the Advancement of Colored People (NAACP) and the Southern Christian Leadership Council (SCLC), including the board members of these organizations. I summarized that many in the group had offered information to each other about their connections in the community and concluded with a check-in by asking them, "How do you want to use this information or how would you like to proceed?"

A seemingly self-organizing process happened then as the participants proceeded to self-appoint who would talk with whom in the community. When their talk subsided, I summarized what the group had done by confirming who would be speaking to whom and then waited for anything I may have missed.

Another round of dialogue began when someone asked who else should be in this conversation. He then said, "This is something to be addressed urgently and I feel everyone needs to have the opportunity to be heard." Someone named a person who was leading many of the youth in their demonstrations. The naming of this person increased the level of emotion and expressions of strong opinions. And after some time, one voice got everyone's attention by saying, "There is grieving, and the rhetoric voiced is responding for the voiceless." At this the group fell quiet. Up to this point I had chosen not to intervene. As a Transformative practitioner, I intentionally supported rather than suppressed this elevated emotional level of talk. The group's process had evolved from individuals speaking and listening, to several people speaking in elevated voices that may have been difficult to accept or understand, and then to a moment of quiet. When people talked again, there were several statements about inviting the youth leader and affirmations that anyone could be invited.

I offered a short summary of the entirety of the meeting, including decisions made, and suggested setting a next meeting date. After a short discussion a date was determined and the participants ended the session.

SECOND GROUP MEETING

Once everyone was present and settled in, I suggested that everyone introduce themselves as there were several new people there. With more than twenty people present, to save time, everyone simply offered their names. I then asked for their permission to provide a summary of the first dialogue session. Both of these moves informed the group that my role as facilitator included being a content recorder and a process guide. Everyone may have known each other, even if they were new to the dialogue, but by introducing themselves again, they were all being welcomed and accepted in the room together. By offering a summary, I was providing a way for them to remember content of the previous session and to know that everyone had the same information. Because my first commitment was to be responsive to the group, if anyone had responded negatively, I would have reflected that objection and the session would have had a different beginning.

Several rounds of talk followed that centered on current events in the community, what had been seen or heard, and what had been reported in news outlets. I supported this conversation by offering periodic summaries and check-ins. I did not provide reflections as there was an easy flow to their talk. Eventually a suggestion was made that one action this dialogue group could take was to offer another voice by writing a statement to the community about what was going on and what this dialogue group would promise to do about it. One person reasoned that more trust building was needed. He said, "We have to stop the wound" and that "whatever we do would be just the beginning." In addition to a promise of trust-building actions between multiple sectors in the community, including the police and the community, they talked about a need to specifically provide forums for youth to speak and be heard. As this conversation progressed, I intervened only a couple of times with summaries that included their discussions about these topics and check-ins to support any decisions they needed to make about which of the lines of conversation to continue or not.

At this point, the tone of the session changed. The person who was leading the youth in their demonstrations spoke for the first time. He simply yet forcefully, and in an accusatory tone, asked, "Why didn't I get invited to the first meeting?" Another person followed quickly and in a similar tone said, "You weren't invited because you're part of the problem." Several people then spoke spontaneously and over each other while the person who had asked the accusatory question was silent.

This heated moment in the conversation had changed the content and the atmosphere of the conversation from proposing concrete actions to an eruption of accusations of blame, as well as some attempts to acknowledge and understand actions taken. As the interactions became more challenging for the group, I became more active as a facilitator, intervening with more frequent summaries and check-ins as well as several reflections of various points of view and of impassioned statements about the person who had asked the question. I included the strong emotions in my reflections because my goal here was not to calm people down but to help them hear themselves and each other. In a lull after one such check-in, the person responded by saying he wanted to help. Because no one immediately responded to this offer, I reflected what he had said, "You want to help." This reflection allowed the group to hear again what had been offered and to hear it in my voice rather than that of the person with whom many were angry. After my reflection, another person repeated the offer and added, "Then you should be a part of what we're doing." Other participants murmured sounds and words of assent.

I provided a summary at this point that included the recent heated exchange, the acceptance of the youth leader, and even the previous round of talk about actions the group had started with. A check-in followed as it was my intention to make room in the conversation to say more about what seemed like an agreement to accept the youth leader or to possibly change the topic of conversation. When one participant expressed the desire to continue talking about the proposed statement to the community, I again asked the group if this was okay with everyone. These interventions allowed the group to continue to co-create the dialogue by making decisions about the content of their conversation as it unfolded.

Another Voice in Dayton, Ohio

Rather than anyone explicitly responding to my question, participants began to make suggestions about specific commitments that would begin to build trust, including writing a statement. Two people offered to draft the statement. I repeated their offer and checked in to be sure that the group's silence was an acceptance of this offer.

Someone then raised the question as to what they would do with the statement. Several people offered suggestions, and following a summary and check-in the suggestions were accepted as reasonable. Then someone questioned how they should document who was offering the statement to the community, including who would sign it. This portion of the conversation generated immediate and forceful statements. Some thought the chief of police should sign it, while others thought that would send a confusing message.

I entered the conversation with an overview of the various opinions and followed with a check-in by saying, "Was this summary complete? Did I miss anything? And how would you like to proceed now?" It was my intention to provide a pause to decide if they wanted to talk further about who should sign the statement. When one of the participants suggested that they think about this and discuss it further at the next meeting, many members of the group assented to this. This ended the second meeting.

THIRD GROUP MEETING

By the third community dialogue meeting, thirty days had passed since Kylen English had died. In the interim, city officials had met with me and the director of the Dayton Mediation Center and committed to participating in any mediations requested by the participants. The possibility of mediation was raised in response to several things, including a rift in a longstanding collaborative relationship between the police and the youth leader, who continued to accuse the police of causing Mr. English's death, and accusations and demands for the firing of city officials that were made by executive directors of two civil rights organizations.

The people attending the third session included those from the second session and a few new people. I again suggested they introduce themselves and summarized the content of the first two sessions, which included the outstanding question of who was to sign the statement. A participant then mentioned that the draft of the statement to the community was ready to be reviewed.

The group then engaged in an editing session of the statement. I didn't intervene much because the interactions of those who were engaging in the editing of the document were serious, purposeful, and, while intense at times, appeared respectful. When I noticed that someone had made a suggestion that was not heard, I offered to act as a co-recorder for the group by writing on a white board. The offer was accepted and I facilitated and recorded until the edits were accepted.

Once the draft was completed, with everyone having either witnessed or contributed to the writing, I asked for any final thoughts. The room was quiet. Then one of the participants stepped up to the whiteboard and wrote at the top of the statement, "Another Voice." I checked in, saying, "So the statement as named and written is accepted?" The continued silence confirmed the agreement. (See appendix for the full text of the statement.)

Again, in my role as process guide, I was aware of at least two outstanding content topics the group had raised earlier and that therefore needed further attention. I reminded them of their intention to think about who was to sign the statement and how they were going to share it in the community. This is part of my job—tracking content and checking in to see if there was still interest in issues that had been raised at earlier sessions. When one person suggested that anyone in the dialogue group and anyone in the community who agreed with the statement were welcome to sign, everyone agreed. They also agreed with the suggestion made by two people that no city management officials, including members of the police department, should sign the statement.

The group then listed several suggestions about what to do with the statement, for example, post it on various websites, read it at church services, read it at a city commission meeting, etc. Different participants committed to reading the statement and others, who had access to websites, promised to post the statement. I offered to summarize the previous discussion topic about these decisions and, with their agreement, did so. I then checked in to ask them what else they needed to talk about or whether there was something else they wanted to do.

This third and final dialogue session authorized me, along with the city's Dayton Mediation Center, to manage mediation sessions between those who still needed to talk with each other, including city officials, police officers, and community members. The group agreed that these mediations were critical if the community was to understand or accept how Kylen English died and for the community to heal.

PARTICIPANT REFLECTIONS

So far I have focused on my own experience of organizing and facilitating this dialogue. But what was it like for those who participated? And what difference did these conversations make? I learned about that when I interviewed some of the participants years later. One participant said, "The dialogue evolved into something that changed what was happening in the community." One of the mediation session participants said, "We stayed in the room. We kept talking. We were able to push each other. Gain respect for one another."

Another person, who later participated in one of the mediation sessions with someone who had attacked him, said, "Because of the mediations, the truth begins to come out." Another mediation participant said, "Both sides went into a holding pattern, so all could put a process in place. It was an open and respectful process. I felt all had an opportunity to be heard."

One of the concrete actions that resulted from the conversations was a police-community committee whose purpose was to build trust between the police and the

Another Voice in Dayton, Ohio

community. The organizing sessions were facilitated by an elected official and there were always two mediators present. During one of the sessions, several of the participants expressed a belief that someone was saying one thing in the meetings and another to their followers and that, "If this duplicity wasn't addressed, some of the group participants probably would leave the effort." The city official was hesitant to respond as he seemed to be concerned about opening a conflict. Another participant pointed out that two mediators were present, and he could hardly see a better time to address the situation. I summarized what was being said, including the tension in the room. A mediation took place then and there during this organizing session.

SHORT- AND LONG-TERM IMPACTS

This chapter describes a dialogue facilitated by a Transformative practitioner. An incident, the death of a Black man while in police custody, precipitated nearly an immediate reaction on the part of some individuals and organizations. Some of these reactions were spontaneous, some were organized, and day by day there was an increase in the number of people participating and an increase in their seemingly threatening behaviors.

Both then and now in this description, I have refrained from offering my feelings and opinions about the actions of city officials and community members. Instead I offered my services as a known mediator and as the director of the HRC. This Transformative Dialogue provided an opportunity to change a negative community reaction to a positive community response.

The "Another Voice" statement that the dialogue participants wrote to the community included recognition of the tragedy of the death of a person, belief in the sincerity of everyone's authentic concern about this tragedy, hope for a moment of reflection, and specific commitments the authors hoped would benefit the welfare of the whole community.

Nearly three years after this dialogue, John Crawford was shot by police while casually walking in a Walmart store in a Dayton suburb. Four days later, Michael Brown was shot by police in Ferguson, Missouri. A mediation participant later told me that the work we did made a difference in Dayton: "Mediation allowed the people to address the situation." She continued, "Because of this, we've not had 'Ferguson.'"

Transformative Dialogue and mediation, both undergirded by a belief in people's capability to speak for themselves, changed how Dayton was responding to tragedy. The claim, that because of what Dayton did another "Ferguson" was averted, must be left to others to prove. But a statement similar to that claim was reiterated by another dialogue participant when he said, "I believe that because of our response to the death of Kylen English, our community responded to the death of John Crawford in a different way than Ferguson and how other cities have responded to similar crises."

Some years later, in a private conversation, one of the dialogue participants said, "I was free to talk, and I had a voice." How often do we leave meetings knowing we didn't speak or weren't heard, where the process did not support our ability, our need, to be heard? In a Transformative Dialogue people are supported to hear each other, to make choices about how they want to talk and what they want to do about their situation.

A long-term community activist and dialogue participant said, "After the death of Mr. English, the news media messed with everyone's perceptions. The news media provoked the people to have the distrust they had." In the beginning, when Robert Walker and Darryl Fairchild made their invitations to dialogue, one participant said, "There was little hope that anything could change minds and feelings." Afterward she said, "The effort evolved into something that changed what was happening in the community." Transformative interventions had an immediate and long-term impact on Dayton.

FINAL NOTE

I want it to be clear that I understand that Mr. English's death elicited pain and suffering for his family and friends and many community members. Even today this suffering continues for some. I do not assume that any of the interventions we brought to bear on the community's reactions to Mr. English's death eased their hurt or lessened their concerns or doubts about who was at fault for his death.

This chapter is not in any way a statement on anyone's feelings or thoughts then or even today about Mr. English, the Dayton police, or the Dayton municipal government. Mr. English left behind a son, his family, and a community of friends. My heart goes out to all of those who knew and loved him, and I take full responsibility for this aspect of the community's response to the reaction to his death.

APPENDIX—ANOTHER VOICE STATEMENT

The recent death of Kylen English is a tragedy for the greater Dayton Community. We are saddened by his unfortunate and untimely death which has elicited a wide range of reactions and emotions throughout the community, all of which have not been voiced and/or acknowledged. We recognize that many families in our community have felt the sting, pain, and grief from the loss of loved ones though their stories have not received the same degree of public attention.

It is our belief that while there are different understandings regarding the events concerning this tragedy, we all care for our community. We know that Dayton has not always lived up to our highest ideals. Past events, many of them polluted with racism, have left issues unresolved that have fostered mistrust. The tension provoked by this recent incident reveals a deeper malaise in our community that must be addressed. We know that many individuals and organizations have worked over

Another Voice in Dayton, Ohio

many years to build healthy relationships that help move us beyond brokenness and mistrust.

- It is our hope that in the midst of our current tensions the positive work of the past will continue with renewed fervor.
- It is our hope that everyone will take a moment for reflection or prayer for our community.
- It is our hope that all withhold judgment until investigations are completed.

The issues of poverty and violence in our community compel us to seek the following:

- We commit to working for the well-being of our community including those persons most directly affected by this tragedy.
- We commit to inviting all members of our community to participate in this work.
- We commit to providing opportunities for all voices to be heard, particularly the voices of our young people.
- We commit to working for a fair and transparent resolution of the tensions in our community.
- We commit to creating a public space for the community to grieve and pray.
- We commit to continue working for justice, peace and vitality throughout our Dayton community.

Michelle Zaremba, Sherry Gale, Darryl Fairchild, Patricia Rickman, Dormetria Robinson, Marlon Shackelford, Earl Thompson Jr., Daryl Ward, Rodney Kennedy, Cathy Shanklin, Tom Wahlrab, Allen Elijah, Robert Lyons, Tommy Owens Jr., Judy Zimmerman, Jerry Bowling III, Alex Freeman, John Gantt, Marsha Greer, David Larson, Francisco Pelaez, Robert Walker.

8

Using Transformative Dialogue to Bridge Racial Divides

How Did We Get Here from There?

Vicki Rhoades and Dusty Rhoades

It was a long slow process. One that took patience and persistence . . . and a lot of profound listening. We first trained as mediators in 2001, learning Transformative practice from Irv Foster and Tom Wahlrab from Dayton, Ohio. Vicki, with her background of liberal arts education and human services employment, fell into the model fairly comfortably. Dusty, having completed a career as a senior Naval officer, carrier pilot, and engineering test pilot, took a bit more time to acclimate. Still we both soon found our bearings and greatly appreciated the concepts of conflict as a normal human condition and shifts of empowerment and recognition as the principle features of interaction. And having mastered the skills of profound listening, reflection, and summary, it seemed a natural step to apply those same skills to facilitating multiparty conversations.

Looking through the rearview mirror over the span of time and space of over a decade, we could not have imagined holding facilitated conversations on racial issues with over two hundred community members in attendance. Not to mention the depth of rich conversation with people from different races, religions, genders, ages, and economic status. It would have been hard to believe that we would be instrumental in gathering twenty-eight partnering organizations to support conversations on race and privilege in southern Maryland.

Living in southern Maryland, composed of Calvert, Charles, and St. Mary's counties, makes this accomplishment even more impressive. Calvert County, where we live, is nine miles wide and thirty miles long, surrounded by the water of the Patuxent River and the Chesapeake Bay. It is largely a wealthy white bedroom community for Washington, DC, and northern Virginia. But it wasn't always that way.

As late as the 1960s, the local economy was largely based upon fishing, oystering, and tobacco farming. The population was over 50 percent African American. That changed as a nuclear power plant was built; a bridge was constructed over the Patux-ent River, connecting Calvert to St. Mary's County; and white people moved out of Prince George's County to escape middle-class Black people moving in from DC. Housing prices increased and drove many locals out of the market. Today, only 12 percent of the population of Calvert County is African American.

While no longer legally segregated, we are largely separated by race, custom, and economics. People like us, in their seventies, grew up experiencing segregated schools. African Americans have memories of having to sit in the balcony of the local theater, not being allowed to go to certain beaches, and being treated in a separate Black ward in the local hospital. That didn't begin to change until the mid-1960s. As a result, the generational trauma of the past survives and affects relationships in the present. Racial tension is alive and well in southern Maryland, but no one wanted to acknowledge it and talk about it. No one "wanted to pick that scab."

SO HOW DID TRANSFORMATIVE DIALOGUE BEGIN?

Gently. We didn't start out talking about racial issues . . . they evolved on their own. Our intention was always to support community conversations. Fifteen years ago the Community Mediation Center of Calvert joined with the local library and others to support public conversation about issues important to southern Maryland. They had nothing to do with race. At least we didn't think they did. These conversations evolved through the years, growing from ten or fifteen participants at first to twenty, fifty, and even one hundred community members who came together to discuss everything from affordable housing to aquafers and oystering. As we began these community conversations, the committee recognized the need to have facilitators to support the group interactions. Most members were reluctant, feeling that they didn't have the skills to lead such conversations. We, on the other hand, saw that our Transformative skills were perfectly suited to support such potentially difficult interactions among people of different identities and backgrounds. We didn't plan these early conversations to focus on race or privilege. But we discovered that no matter the topic, the conversation somehow touched on racial concerns.

As we continued and broadened the scope of our planned conversations, we real-ized race needed to be an issue we talked about, but how we introduced it would determine whether anyone showed up to participate. People shied away from the topic of race, even though it was always the elephant in the room. Then, nine years ago, we were invited by a local church to facilitate a workshop on race. The organiz-ers realized that no one would come if they called it an antiracism training or even had the word "race" in the title. So they called it "Seeing the Face of God in Oth-ers." In the workshop, rather that talking about "white privilege" and "internalized oppression" of African Americans, the topics became "What it's like to be white in Calvert" and "What it's like to be Black in Calvert." The organizers felt it was important to be sensitive to language so people would feel willing to participate. We were not part of the organizing group, but we agreed to facilitate, believing that,

Using Transformative Dialogue to Bridge Racial Divides

eventually, participants would start feeling more comfortable with the terms and the definitions, and more honest conversations could occur.

An example of the kind of honest conversation that took place is when one white male participant, a community leader, said, "Well, I don't see the problem. We all just got along. I was raised side by side with Black kids all my life here in Calvert County. I had plenty of Black friends growing up. We played ball together." We recognized that he was defending his upbringing, feeling somewhat uncertain and anxious. We listened carefully and reflected his words so that he could hear what he had just said. Another participant, a male African American and also a community leader, replied, "Well, Jack, my experience was different. Sure we played ball together, but I couldn't go to the same beaches as you or swim in the community pool. When I went to movies, I had to sit in the balcony." We saw that this man was annoyed by the other's comments and anxious to correct the record with regard to how the community actually interacted. Again, we reflected his comments, using his own words and tone of voice, to allow the speaker and those listening to hear these comments spoken by a different voice.

As facilitators, this type of communication is a gift. We supported both participants equally by reflecting what they each said when they said it and then summarizing that "although you were both brought up in the same community, you had very different experiences growing up in Calvert." And from there the conversations continued, each person seeing the other's perspective a little more clearly because of the reflections and summary. The two men had known each other for decades, but this was undoubtedly the first time they had ever had such a frank and honest exchange. Others began feeling more empowered to express their own life experience. Seeds were planted to continue and grow the conversations.

BUT WHAT CREDIBILITY DO TWO OLD WHITE PEOPLE HAVE TO FACILITATE RACIAL ISSUES?

Fair question! It's tricky because there is mistrust on both fronts. Many in the white community just don't see a problem. We hear things like, "I worked hard for everything I have. I grew up poor. Don't tell me about 'white privilege.' I'm not going to feel guilty for slavery that happened a hundred years ago. I had nothing to do with that. Why can't we just get past it!"

Many in the Black community have lived their whole lives in systems that have worked against them. We hear things like, "I've had to work harder, faster, and be smarter to get ahead, and even then I was passed by. I'm sick and tired of living in fear for my kids. It's exhausting to have this conversation over and over and over again. I live with racism every single day!"

Versions of these comments showed up in every conversation. They were indications of weakness and self-absorption in the first examples and feeling stronger to voice their experiences in the second. All were excellent opportunities for us to reflect their words and tone so that they could hear themselves and others. Heat is where the opportunities lie. Although the feelings were strong, there was still an underlying desire to understand one another—they all made the choice to participate. They made their own choices to share their understanding and life experience. As Transformative facilitators, we believe that when people are given the opportunity to sit down together, person to person, and talk with one another, there is a desire to connect and discover new ways of being together. It is human nature to want to connect with others. We supported them by carefully listening to them, reflecting their comments when we recognized opportunities for empowerment and recognition shifts, and offering to summarize portions of their conversation when it appeared to be a good opportunity for them to review elements of their interaction.

The first step for two old white people was to recognize our whiteness. Facilitator know thyself. As in every conversation, we come with our own experiences, biases, and baggage. To be effective as a Transformative facilitator, we needed to understand ourselves in a way that included an awareness of our bias so that we didn't let those biases make decisions for us. While we also reacted negatively to terms like "white privilege" fifty years ago, in retrospect we can clearly see that we benefited from the color of our skin. This was especially true of Dusty as a white man in America. Skin color never made it more difficult for him to move ahead. Although having this information about oneself and sharing it in community conversations isn't the job of the facilitator, it gave us understanding of that perspective. There are many white Americans who do not have an awareness of white privilege, and as facilitators we support the conversation wherever it goes, realizing that people find their way if given the opportunity to talk freely and openly.

Earning the trust of Black community members was a different challenge. It was pretty clear that we were not experts on being Black. We had a lot to learn. We recognized early on the importance of inviting people of color to the table to help plan dialogue events. The leaders that joined us for the planning sessions were key to bringing others into the conversation. Their input was essential in co-creation of a program that would be meaningful to participants, provide good information, and encourage open and meaningful sharing of participants' lived experience in the community. Our involvement with facilitating previous community conversations hosted by the library helped to build a reputation for being trustworthy. They recognized that our commitment, as Transformative facilitators, was to support the conversation so participants could have a better understanding of themselves and each other.

We were facilitators of this process, but we were also community members. That holds both challenges and potential. Being part of any initial planning for these community conversations was important. Not because we needed to insert our influence and opinions but because we needed to find a way to create a safe space where everyone would feel comfortable. Listening was much more important than speaking at these planning sessions. Our experience as members of several different service organizations and activities in the community was helpful. But we realized we needed more diversity. So we brainstormed names and invited a variety of other community members to meet with us. They were able to share information from

WHEN DID THE BREAKTHROUGH COME?

A group from Middleham and Saint Peters Episcopal Parish had been hosting what they called "Big Conversations" on immigration, healthcare, gun violence, and veterans for several years. This group had formed a more organized steering committee for these community conversations. Around 2015, they also saw the need to focus on race, but being a mostly white congregation they felt uncomfortable about broaching the subject head on. They were apprehensive and didn't feel qualified to take on such a huge topic, even though they knew the need was there. Additionally, their annual events had taken the format of a panel presentation followed by questions from the audience. That format had created some uncomfortable moments as audience members presented politically charged comments.

Committee members were aware that we had been engaged in this work as volunteers for the Community Mediation Center of Calvert (CMCC), dating back to the earlier civil discourse conversations with the Calvert Library beginning in 2007. We were invited to join the committee in hopes that we would be able to assist in structuring the events in a way that would support constructive dialogue. We assured them that we felt confident we could support people as they ventured into challenging conversations. We were not afraid to take on the topic or afraid of conflict. We were not experts on the issues but we were experts on conflict and on facilitating difficult conversations. We were invited to join the steering committee with a focus upon facilitation of small group conversations.

At our urging, they also invited representation from the NAACP and Concerned Black Women of Calvert to make the committee more racially diverse. The steering committee's approach was that we were all learning together. Mistakes would be made, and they would be seen as "learning opportunities." Again, the diversity of our members provided contacts in multiple parts of our community that we could meet with to shape the content of our offerings. We were literally partnering with our prospective participants to co-create conversations that would be engaging and valuable to them. The trust that was built over time on the steering committee would eventually spill over into the room with over two hundred participants.

The Big Conversation planning committee's preparations had included reading the curriculum *White Privilege: Let's Talk* (Blackmon et al. n.d.). In the introduction, the authors say:

> It is important to have facilitators for these conversations. The most successful facilitators are persons who do not function as the group's expert on race but rather are passionate about having conversation, open to new ideas, careful listeners, attentive to nonverbal communication, and comfortable with the complexity and tensions that

surface when discussing race. While having one facilitator is adequate, having two group facilitators is ideal. Co-facilitators often feel more confident and are able to accent one another's leadership.

As transformative facilitators, we were a perfect fit. We could offer process options that would allow many voices to be heard and were willing to follow the participants' conversation wherever they chose to take it. We were in the right place at the time to make a difference in how community conversations were seen and valued. As one example, we introduced the planning committee to the format of breaking into facilitated small group conversations after the panel presentation and then return to the large group format so the facilitators could report the highlights of small group conversations.

HOW MUCH PREPARATION WAS REQUIRED BEFORE LAUNCHING SUCH AN AMBITIOUS PROJECT?

We had no idea what we had gotten ourselves into. The steering committee, of which we were now a part, needed to do a great deal of homework to prepare itself and the audience for the topic of dismantling racism and privilege. It was a multistage planning process that lasted more than a year, with members suggesting resources and activities they thought would be helpful, including:

- A book study on *Living into God's Dream: Dismantling Racism in America* edited by Catherine Meeks (2016). More than sixty people, including all of the steering committee members and a diverse crowd of local residents, participated during six Sunday sessions. Two different steering committee members facilitated each session. Catherine Meeks, the editor of the book, participated in one of the discussions via Skype.
- Interviews were conducted over the course of many months as the steering committee prepared for the event. Committee members listened to the experiences and concerns of a diverse group of community members who expressed a wide range of awareness and understanding of the interaction among races in our community. As members of the committee, we were able to use our listening, reflection, and summarizing skills to support enlightening exchanges that would inform our upcoming programs, making them interesting and valuable to a wide range of participants and relevant to their lived experiences.
- A white privilege workshop: Because this term was both foreign and off-putting to many white Americans, this workshop gave participants the opportunity to explore its meaning in a safe place. The twenty-five people who took part, both white and Black, found it to be a profound experience.
- Public viewing and discussion of the film *13th*, titled after the Thirteenth Amendment (DuVernay and Moran 2016). In this documentary, filmmaker Ava DuVernay explores the history of racial inequality in the United States,

Using Transformative Dialogue to Bridge Racial Divides 91

focusing on the fact that the nation's prisons are disproportionately filled with African Americans. Over one hundred people attended the program at Middleham and St. Peter's. A large group facilitated conversation after the film was rich and moving. Here are just a few of the statements from the exit cards:

- "I did not realize how systemic the problem of racism is."
- "Today was my third viewing and for the first time I cried. My tears would not stop. It made me sick. Why—because things have not changed in view of the words and actions of the current government administration. But in God all things are possible."
- "How did you not know as white people what Blacks went through and are still going through? Is it that you didn't want to know? Or because your rights were not affected?"
- "This film has opened my eyes to the progression of institutional racism and to the fact that it is still in full practice. Change is imperative and I hope we can start that right here in Calvert County."

SO WHAT DID ALL THAT PREPARATION LEAD UP TO? HOW DID IT GO?

The steering committee arrived at the title "I Didn't Know . . . Exploring Racism and Privilege in Our Community" after the Catherine Meeks book study and the viewing of the film *13th*. Many of the participants voiced concern and surprise that they were unaware of so many things regarding the unequal treatment of Black people in America. Many white participants had no idea of the history and the role that white privilege continues to play today in the United States. They had never examined the myths, misconceptions, and stereotypes surrounding race.

Partners of Big Conversation on Dismantling Racism and Privilege (BC-DRaP) at this time included Middleham and St. Peter's Episcopal Church, the Calvert Library Prince Frederick, the NAACP of Calvert and St. Mary's Counties, Concerned Black Women of Calvert, Community Mediation Centers of Calvert and St. Mary's Counties, and the College of Southern Maryland.

The Big Conversation took place in January 2018 in the Great Hall of Middleham and St. Peter's. Six local presenters (Mike Shisler, a public high school principle; Dr. Carmen Phelps, the director of the Institutional Equity and Diversity Office at the College of Southern Maryland; Michael Kent and Joyce Freeland, past and present NAACP presidents; Kirsti Uunila, the county's historic preservation specialist; and Sandy Walker, the supervisor of equity and school Improvement for Calvert Public Schools) shared their personal experiences of race.

After the presentations, we broke up into thirteen small groups of ten to twenty-five people. With the help of our database of participants and local library staff, we successfully endeavored to ensure racially diverse participants for each small group. Conversations focused upon white privilege and racism and what is being done or not being done to address it from the perspective of community members. Dialogue was supported by seventeen white and Black co-facilitators, male and female and representing different age groups, mostly from CMC Calvert and St. Mary's. Each facilitator was provided with a guide containing detailed information on the program and carefully crafted questions to invite group discussion.

After the small group conversations, we regathered in the large group and a facilitator from each group shared highlights of their group's discussion. Here are a few of the comments regarding establishing common ground toward dismantling racism in southern Maryland:

- "The power of our stories and hearing each other's stories make us aware of what we didn't know. We don't know what we don't know."
- "We need to build relationships to overcome."
- "We need to understand and correct history, elevate African American leaders in history. Be proud of African American history."
- "We have to be proactive in changing the systemic and personal racism."
- "We need more diversity in the police and local schools. Role models are important."
- "Interpersonal, intentional engagement toward building better, more equitable community."

WHAT WERE THE KEYS TO SUPPORTING HONEST, RICH, AND POWERFUL CONVERSATIONS ABOUT SUCH CHALLENGING LIFE EXPERIENCE?

We exercised our Transformative Dialogue skills. We welcomed participants into the conversation, introducing it as an opportunity to share from one's own life experience. Setting the tone, we assured participants that they had the power to say how they wanted to have the conversation. We listened carefully and supported them in their dialogue with reflection and occasional brief summaries, remaining aware of sensitivities and loaded language. It was important to create a climate that enabled people to speak about what was important to them in a language that was comfortable for them. We met people where they were so they had the ability to meet others where they were. As one white male participant said, "I never had a conversation with a Black person before."

As Transformative facilitators, we were mindful of treading gently—getting dialogue started is often fragile and tentative. It was important for us not to force, direct, or lead the discussion. Truth has to come before reconciliation. You can't have an honest conversation without sharing each other's truth—the stories, the history, the experience of being in this world. People will not discuss openly and honestly until and unless they feel safe. Until they are ready. That was the case throughout the process, from initial meetings with stakeholders, to planning build-up events, to supporting deep and meaningful exchanges of experience and understandings on the day of the Big Conversation. Other committee members had lingering concerns about opening conversations to potential racist comments from some community members. We knew that as we stayed with the individuals, reflecting their words and their tone of speech so that they could hear themselves and others, the conversation would be self-correcting.

An executive summary, based upon notes from small group discussions and participant surveys, was created after each Big Conversation. This executive summary served as a report back to all stakeholders and participants and formed the basis for planning future events and programs.

HOW DO YOU KNOW IT'S WORKING?

The participants tell us. They keep coming back for more. The contact list for the Big Conversation grew to over one thousand names and email addresses of participants. Two subsequent Big Conversations on race and privilege focused on areas steering committee members felt were important: "Progress and Challenges in Our Schools" and "Many Wounds to Heal: Health Care (In)Equity." More than 220 people participated in each, held virtually due to the COVID-19 pandemic. Participants continue to be diverse in race, age, gender, and religion. They bring their friends and family members. There is a desire and a need to connect, even when we don't share the same life experience. Knowing that people can experience shifts with our support and observing participants as they shift gradually from being weak and self-absorbed toward becoming stronger and more responsive is gratifying as the effects of these shifts are seen over and over again.

Coalitions continue to grow, both in terms of who's involved and their outcomes. The team has now grown to include twenty-eight partner organizations. Each of the partners support the Big Conversations and also work in many other areas of our communities. Talk results in action, and these Big Conversations moved participants to do many different things. They organize follow-up events that continue to build upon the concerns that were expressed in the Big Conversations:

- The need for advocacy was a key aspect of the summary of the September 13, 2020, Big Conversation on health inequities, so the Calvert Library sponsored an Advocacy Program, where people could learn how to advocate for themselves and others.
- Participants of Big Conversations stated the need for representation of people of color in the healthcare arena, so St. Mary's Library sponsored a program called Black Men in White Coats, which talked about the lack of Black doctors and how to address it. There was a follow-up session with four local Black doctors addressing the issue.
- Participants of the conversations expressed a need for Black history. As a result, the NAACP, the Historical Society, the libraries, and others are exploring ways to document oral histories from the African American community. The

compilation and consolidation of resources will be shared with schools and the general public. This initiative has since grown to partner with numerus agencies, schools, libraries, and nonprofit organizations that have been formalized in a Southern Maryland History Coalition. They are identifying and cataloging historical references that will be available at numerous sites and virtually to the schools and citizens of our southern Maryland area. This capability will support the understanding and teaching of the true history of southern Maryland.

- The Mediation Centers have helped address specific issues of racial tension in the schools, facilitating discussions and talking circles.
- The board of education approved an antiracism policy for the public schools, which met much resistance from some community groups. The Big Conversation partners came together to support the BOE antiracism policy by writing an open letter to the local newspapers.
- The Health Department coordinated an effort with partners to provide COVID vaccinations to the homebound and the underserved areas of the county and those with lack of transportation. The Health Department created a "home visit vaccination program."

Support by our network of Transformative facilitators has grown. Originally, we were able to support the Big Conversation with facilitators from our local Community Mediation Centers in Calvert and St. Mary's Counties. We have since reached out to Transformative mediator friends and colleagues across the state, including members of the Maryland District Court, state Mediation and Conflict Resolution Office (MACRO), and Louise Phipps Senft's Baltimore Mediation team to gather additional support. With their help, we have been able to field up to fifteen teams of Transformative co-facilitators—each diverse in gender and race. Our colleagues across the state have given generously of their time and energy in support of these efforts.

GOOD GRIEF, CHARLIE BROWN, WHAT NOW?

Stay the course. Our communities are rife with polarization and conflict. Transformative skills enable us to support productive, honest conversations so community members can gain a better understanding of each other. Honest and meaningful dialogue helps us to dispel myths, misconceptions, and long-held stereotypes about each other. Such productive dialogue is essential in our world today and, indeed, has the potential to transform our world. It has the ability to open our eyes to the pain that is felt by others as well as within ourselves. It has the power to begin healing old and painful wounds. There is no topic that offers more opportunity and challenge than conversations on race and privilege.

HOW WILL YOU KNOW WHEN YOU'RE DONE?

We don't overcome centuries of social constructs in a couple of conversations. Even today, the very mention of phrases like white supremacy, white privilege, critical race theory, racial disparities, and "true history" often send people to opposite sides of the ring and ready them for conflict. These terms are often misunderstood and mischaracterized. It's not the Transformative facilitator's job to define the terms, set the rules of engagement, or even referee the dialogue. The gift of the Transformative facilitator is to work with participants as they find their own way. This work is a lifelong commitment—it's never "one and done." Progress will continue to be slow and will require an ongoing commitment. We are in it for the long term.

Note: Vicki Rhoades passed away on June 10, 2023, after weathering a long series of health challenges. She and Dusty met in high school and were friends and soulmates for sixty years. They were co-mediators for the past twenty-two years and authored the first draft of this article together. At the Celebration of Her Life, several mediation colleagues from around the state noted her significant contributions to the advancement of mediation and Transformative practice in Maryland. She is missed by many.

9

The Dayton Police Reform Process

Lessons from Transformative Dialogue in Dayton, Ohio

Arch Grieve

STARTING—NOT AT THE BEGINNING

Can Transformative Dialogue play a productive role in a high-stakes, bureaucratic-ridden situation like police reform? And to what extent can Transformative practitioners make a difference when they are called in midway after a process is underway? In this chapter I will tell the story of my role in the police reform dialogue process in Dayton, Ohio, which may provide at least a partial answer to the two questions posed here. In 2020 the Dayton Mediation Center (DMC) was asked to assist in a series of dialogues on police reform and, as a staff member and mediator at the time, I became involved.

After the May 25, 2020, murder of George Floyd in Minneapolis, protests occurred in many parts of the United States, including in Dayton. The protests in Dayton were met with tear gas, pepper balls, rubber bullets, and other "nonlethal" methods of crowd control by the Dayton Police Department. A curfew was announced after many arrests, and the local police response to these protests resulted in a great deal of outrage on the part of local activists and residents. One City of Dayton employee who oversaw community-police relations for the city resigned in protest.

In response to the frustration in the community and growing mistrust of the police, Mayor Nan Whaley decided to start a working group for police reform that she hoped would bring all sides together. The mayor's office organized the process, stipulating that there would be five areas of police reform for community members and city employees to focus their efforts on: recruitment, use of force, community engagement, training, and oversight. The mayor set goals for each of the working groups. She determined that one member of the Dayton city commission would co-chair each of the five working groups and sought out elected officials and community members, many of whom were well known and respected. The groups were made up of community members volunteering their time to serve on these committees, officers from the Dayton Police Department, members of the volunteer Community Police Council, and individuals with a background in the criminal justice system. City staff and University of Dayton law students provided administrative support and assistance with research. Finally, Dayton Mediation Center staff were asked to facilitate each group. I was assigned to the use of force committee, one of the most controversial topics of the five, and one that saw some of the most heated exchanges.

Had the DMC been tasked with designing the process from the beginning, we would have been guided by Transformative principles centering people's agency in the process, beginning by meeting with many different stakeholders and members of the community to co-create the process. Instead we were brought in at a point where many decisions had already been made by the mayor's office about the structure and process of the dialogue. The mayor and the commission member co-chairs were also the employers of all the city staff members who worked on the efforts, including the police, the city's law staff, the commissioners' personal aides, and us, the facilitators themselves. This did pose a challenge for some of the group's participants who felt that working for the city would jeopardize our impartiality, a legitimate concern that made it difficult for some of the citizen volunteer participants to truly buy into the validity of the process as a whole. Nonetheless, my colleagues and I were committed to working Transformatively from the moment we became involved. We worked within the structure to find as many places as possible to hand decisions about the content and process of the dialogue to the participants themselves, while recognizing the constraints put in place by the city. This is therefore a story about how we dealt with the external constraints that ran counter to how we would have organized the dialogue had we been free to create the process from scratch. In addition, as in any dialogue about a hot topic, we also had to deal with challenges including strong emotions about the topic, issues of race and authority, and juggling the multiple roles we occupied during the process.

HAVING CHALLENGING CONVERSATIONS

This process presented many challenges to the facilitators. Perhaps the greatest challenge, however, was the conversation topic itself: police reform. There are many aspects that make this topic challenging, including systemic racism and the highly polarized debates around police reform. Dayton is a city that has many historical challenges in dealing with race, and the city itself is still largely divided by it, with the western side of the city being predominantly Black, and the east side of the city being populated with more white residents. As with most cities, Dayton's police force does not adequately represent the minority population it polices. Dealing with the problem in 2020 presented its own challenges, as reform efforts in general tend to put police departments on edge and leave many community members feeling disempowered. There were also many different goals, with some community members wanting reform while others wanted to defund or even abolish the police. The latter two options were not ones that the city commissioners were willing to consider, and so, as a result, the group was constrained from the start to "reform." This imposition did, by necessity, limit the scope of the conversation in a way that was decidedly not Transformative. Still, given these constraints, we did our best to ensure that the conversations themselves were supported as Transformatively as possible.

Even speaking about reform, however, did not sit well with many in the police department. From their perspective, they were already following best practices and had no systemic issues to speak of. Many working group members saw things differently, however, and wanted to see real changes within the department. Many saw very real and damning differences in the ways in which the police treated Black residents of the city compared to white residents. Needless to say, race would remain a central theme in the conversations as the process progressed.

There was also a tension built into the process for all working groups between trying to balance open and honest dialogue with the need to have some formal way in which the groups could put forth recommendations to the city commission, which was previously defined as the process's ultimate goal. A greater concern, however, had to do with the process' "chain of command," to borrow a policing term. It was sometimes difficult to know who was in charge of the effort. Was it the city commission as a whole? The mayor herself? The co-chairs of each of the groups? Or was it in fact the bureaucrats behind the scenes who were really in charge? At times it felt like it could be any of those people or groups. Complicating the matter further, the co-chairs insisted that the community members were in charge of the effort when, in reality, all of the commissioners were in charge (from a legal/governmental standpoint) and none of them were in charge (from a leadership one) at the same time. The confusion and resulting challenges stemming from this issue were obvious in each of the groups from time to time but especially whenever there was a major issue within a group that pitted community volunteers against city employees, and even more so when those topics involved police officers or legal department staff members, as both groups often held the most rigid views surrounding policing reform.

So how did we respond when asked to participate? DMC staff talked together about what was possible, given the way the process was already structured, the volatility of the topic, and the confusion about authority. We agreed that in spite of these limitations, what we could do, as Transformative facilitators, was to help each working group communicate more effectively, supporting each participant in the dialogue as they struggled with these difficult topics, the many differences they each had, and the different goals held by each of the groups' members. In addition, one of the key things that helped us facilitate the dialogue and support the participants was transparency. At every step of the process, we reminded participants of our role, our relationship to the city of Dayton, and what possible outcomes actually existed within the process as it was designed. Though at times the struggle felt like trying to kick a ball through a goal in the dark, as Transformative practitioners, we acknowledged and held up those areas of confusion in order to better support participants as they struggled to identify a viable path forward. Our commitment to respecting each person, regardless of their perspectives or opinions, allowed us to use our Transformative skills to support participants in the conversation. One way we did this was through the skill of reflection. Rather than trying to control the conflict or high emotions, we reflected them back to the participants, allowing them to hear themselves better and to hear each other better. This led to real empowerment shifts, allowing each person to feel heard and understood. This in turn opened up the possibility of recognition shifts, maximizing the opportunities for people to begin to hear and perhaps understand each other, even across their significant differences.

HOW THE DIALOGUE STARTED

When the Dayton Mediation Center got involved in the process, groups were already formed. Nonetheless, the mayor agreed that we could begin by talking with each of the group members individually to do some conflict coaching before organizing the first meeting. Our goal in requesting this was to support each participant in getting clear about their own personal goals for the effort and consider how they wanted to "show up" for each meeting. This intervention was designed to help them in their own efforts at strength and responsiveness before the group discussions even began. These initial one-on-one conversations were crucial for participants as we helped individual group members, including city employees and community members, as they began to articulate what they wanted to come out of this process. From a Transformative perspective, this was helpful, as many of the group members were coming into the conversation individually from a relatively weak and self-absorbed standpoint. For example, many police department members expressed concern about being considered as the "bad guys" by the public and felt that label was undeserved. Similarly, members of the community felt like a true reform effort was not possible given how powerful the police and city were. Helping each of the participants become clearer about their own goals and desires for participating, therefore, helped increase the chances for pro-social interaction once the discussions began. This is, of course, one of the main goals of any Transformative process, to improve the quality of conflict interaction from negative to positive and to support people as they get clear about what they want to do about their situation.

One of the roles of a Transformative facilitator is as process guide. Participants are the ones making decisions about the process, but this requires that they are aware of the options that are open to them. After meeting with each group member, DMC facilitators therefore suggested listening sessions for each of the working groups, and this was accepted as a good next step by participants. The sessions allowed people to introduce themselves to one another, learn more about each other, and gain insight into why each person wanted to participate. Individual participants chose what they shared. Many talked about their upbringings, about their interactions with and exposure to policing, or about their individual identities and how those identities (as someone who is Black, queer, or disabled, for example) shaped their views of policing. Some of these experiences were powerful and elicited strong emotions. This was a sign to us, as Transformative facilitators, that we were on the right path with regard to "following the heat" and getting to the heart of what was important to people.

These listening sessions helped participants better understand where other members of the committee were coming from. The result was an increase in pro-social interaction throughout the whole process as participants began to see each other as individuals rather than as members of the "police" or "clergy" or through their role as a "public defender" or "law department director," for example. This didn't eliminate conflict. It was still in the room much of the time. Community members and police exchanged occasional heated remarks with one another, and at times emotions were high. For the most part, however, there was a greater understanding of where everyone was coming from. The result was fewer personal attacks than perhaps would have been the case had we not started with listening sessions. And even when conflict was heightened in the conversation, people now knew where they stood and had in mind what they wanted to see happen as a result of their participation, and members slowly became more comfortable with uncomfortable conversations. We consider this a very positive return on the time we spent meeting one on one and having those listening sessions.

One of the tenets of Transformative Dialogue is to value intragroup conversations equally with intergroup conversations. This is based on Transformative premises about people in groups. It is also based on the reality that no group is homogeneous nor are group identities and views fixed. They are shaped by interaction. There was perhaps a missed opportunity in not having groups of more similarly minded individuals participate in some intragroup discussions in advance of the larger meetings, as described in this book's introduction. For the most part it seemed that the desire to get the conversations going outweighed the desire to spend more time preparing participants. Had those discussions taken place, however, they likely would have provided participants with an opportunity to discuss their goals and objectives with others who shared similar, but not identical, ways of thinking and to figure out what they truly wanted to get out of the process both individually and collectively. The large group conversations also often revealed rifts between participants who were thought of as being on the "same side." I believe that having intragroup dialogue beforehand could potentially have made the larger group discussions more productive, as ingroup fighting and bickering frequently took up a great deal of time. As facilitators, we could have offered these types of smaller "separate sessions" more often for participants when those conflicts arose, as long as we made sure to be clear that the decisions about process were up to the participants themselves, which is critical to us as Transformative facilitators. Though this was not done, there were instances where mediation was offered to group members who were spending a great deal of large group time with interpersonal conflict, and this was a valuable intervention that my colleagues and I did well. On occasion small group sessions were used when there was a topic that some group members wanted to discuss further that they didn't have time to do during the normal sessions, and this was also very useful. At times like this, I would note that some participants seemed interested in continuing the conversation and suggest that a small group session might allow them to do that. But I made it clear that the decision about whether or not to do that was up to the participants, not me.

As expected, we were dealing with high emotions during much of this police reform process. We felt ready to tackle this because, as Transformative facilitators, we understand the importance of high emotions and believe "there are facts in those feelings." When conversations got heated, my colleagues and I supported people in expressing these strong emotions by using the core Transformative interventions of reflections, summaries, and check-ins. So sometimes we intervened frequently when emotions were high. Other times, however, we backed out of the discussion and allowed participants the space to express their frustrations and concerns. This choice was made when people were communicating in spite of the high emotion. Transformative Dialogue makes space for people to freely express what is on their minds, even when this involves strong emotions. Again and again, we see that allowing this expression helps a speaker get calmer and clearer and provides listeners with important information about what matters and why.

GROUND RULES

At the beginning of the process each group also talked about potential ground rules for the conversation. As Transformative practitioners, we leave the question of creating ground rules to the participants, including the question of whether or not participants want ground rules. Working in a governmental setting posed a unique challenge in this area, however. There was a clear expectation that the working groups would be developing recommendations to be sent to local government, so the commissioners wanted each group to have an agreed upon way to make decisions. And the default mode for meetings connected to local government is Robert's Rules of Order. When facilitators from DMC began to work with the groups, they helped participants co-create ground rules that worked for them, building from the default of Robert's Rules. This co-creation of ground rules happened within each group and was in line with Transformative best practices. Including everyone in this process did help in enhancing the degree to which individual participants felt some ownership over the process. However, as the process unfolded, group members felt more constrained by the rules they had agreed to. Some of this was due to the different communication styles of the various participants, while some of it was due to the fact that the rules were very formal, which was often at odds with the fact that participants were trying to have open and frank conversations. Many group members struggled because they didn't know how to suggest changes in the context of the ground rules they were working with. Still others had difficulty feeling like they had the ability to even weigh in at all when louder voices dominated the discussion. Both of these challenges proved frustrating for many members.

Throughout the conversations, we dealt with the awkwardness of trying to balance open and honest dialogue with the need to have some formal way in which the group could put forth and advance recommendations to the city commission. Eventually the groups came up with a compromise that helped strike a balance between these opposing styles of communication. Participants agreed to the use of a motion, second, and roll-call vote whenever a formal proposal would emerge or an amendment was suggested. But outside of this, a much more relaxed environment emerged that allowed open discussions without formal motions so individuals could share their thoughts, ideas, and perspectives. This satisfied the city's need for formal recommendations that had resulted from a democratic process while also accommodating the need for a more relaxed atmosphere that allowed those unfamiliar with Robert's Rules to fully participate. As facilitators, we helped this compromise to emerge by being vigilant in ensuring that everyone felt heard. We made frequent use of the core Transformative skill of checking in to see if the discussion was "working" for all participants. We also reminded the groups that Robert's Rules were developed to allow everyone to be heard, so modifying the rules to be sure that was happening made sense.

At times, many group members felt constrained by the ground rules that they themselves had agreed upon. One guideline in particular that caused many problems was the rule that group members should avoid making generalizations. It came about because of a fear that generalizations would cause the police representatives, in particular, to shut down or become frustrated. However, it ended up frustrating the group members more, as they felt they could not truly say what they were thinking about the police. In the end, the group decided to relax this guideline so that they could have a more authentic conversation. This is consistent with the Transformative principle that co-creation of the dialogue is ongoing throughout the process and made possible by facilitators following, not leading the parties.

THE CHALLENGE OF ZOOM

The police reform dialogue was taking place at the height of the COVID-19 pandemic, which presented an additional challenge. The process stipulated that biweekly meetings be held of each working group, with meetings taking place over Zoom. Facilitating conversations on such a controversial topic involving so many stakeholders both within government and from the community at large is a difficult endeavor to begin with, but having interactions on Zoom rather than in person definitely had an impact, although not an entirely negative one. Another challenge to the process was the size of the groups, which was set at about twenty-five people per group. This made it difficult for everyone to be able to participate fully. Meetings, on average, lasted for ninety minutes, so theoretically each speaker would have less than four minutes per meeting to speak if everyone participated equally. This inevitably led to some individuals having less time than others, something that was a structural challenge that had an impact on the way discussions unfolded.

In addressing these concerns, my fellow facilitators and I did our best to utilize the tools that are available to an online facilitated discussion that do not necessarily exist for an in-person one. For example, using the chat feature on Zoom helped individuals to weigh in by writing a message whenever they couldn't get into the discussion as quickly as they wanted to verbally. This had the advantage that the entire group could see the message at once, which was an unexpected benefit of holding the discussion electronically that is hard to replicate in an in-person setting. As facilitators we also did our best to help reflect nonverbal communication cues, such as expressions of frustration communicated by shaking of the head, to ensure that those who felt frustrated by the conversation felt heard, even when they weren't saying anything. This is important to do as a Transformative practitioner regardless of the setting, but doing it was arguably more important while hosting the discussion virtually given that it was hard to see other forms of body behavior that participants might exhibit in an in-person format, such as fidgeting or balling of the fist, to name just a couple of examples. By paying even closer attention to the (albeit fewer) visual body language cues that *were* on screen, we were able to overcome some of the technical challenges posed by meeting virtually as opposed to being in person, something that much of the world was also becoming more comfortable with at the time.

CHALLENGES OF RACE AND IDENTITY

Once the process began (and throughout the entire police reform effort), there were many challenges to our goal of supporting this effort Transformatively. One exchange, in particular, seemed to distill much of the conflict down to its essence. It was near the end of one of the use of force committee meetings, when a simple question from one of the community members in our police reform working group threatened to derail the entire effort when he asked an officer in the group, "do you believe that this reform effort is necessary?" The officer took a minute to explain his reasoning before giving his conclusion, "so no, I don't really think that it is needed." The meeting did not end well that night. The fact that the community member who asked was Black and the officer who responded was white laid the crux of the challenges faced bare.

As I've alluded to, race was a recurring issue throughout the process, and eventually a pattern emerged whereby community members would bring up police biases, not only along racial lines but also against those with mental health issues or individuals facing homelessness, and police would present themselves as being unbiased in their work. This didn't sit well with a lot of the participants, however. As a result, some of the participants committed more to the process and trying to work to correct what they perceived as institutional bias, while others became more disillusioned with the effort and drifted more toward other ways they wanted to advocate for police reform (or abolishment). As facilitators, my colleagues and I understood that we needed to address this issue head on.

Being a straight white man, and the only straight white man to serve in a facilitator role during the process, I was acutely aware of the fact that my experiences were very different from those of the majority of the process's community participants, who were African American. Acknowledging this, then, became a very important part of my own personal involvement in the process. I most often acknowledged my privilege during the one-on-one discussions I had beforehand with participants. I was transparent, wanting them to know that I was aware of the fact that I lacked the unique perspective that comes with experience. This was a critical part of establishing their trust in me. It also helped to support the legitimacy of the effort as a whole. When a Transformative facilitator recognizes and acknowledges their own potential areas of bias, they establish legitimacy and create an environment of greater trust and transparency for all participants.

MANAGING MULTIPLE ROLES

As I noted earlier, one of the roles of a Transformative facilitator is as a process guide. There are other roles as well. The fact that we had to deal with multiple roles during the dialogue process was another challenge, common to Transformative facilitators but complicated by the way the groups were set up. We were not just facilitators but also process consultants, coaches, and even trainers. We ended up wearing each of these hats at some point in the process, and it was important to be explicit with each stakeholder about which hat we were wearing at which time. Transparency at all times is a key characteristic of Transformative practice, and this also requires self-awareness and attention to both the process and each individual participant. At some times this was easier, such as when we were simply facilitating in the meetings and helping the group become more productive in their conversations with one another.

Since this process was happening in the height of COVID, all of the events were virtual and we were all getting used to this new virtual world. This raised our awareness of the importance of one-on-one conversations in between meetings because there were no informal one-on-one conversations happening before or after meetings. These one-on-one meetings were often coaching sessions. In one coaching session, the facilitator helped a group member think through how they might raise a challenging issue. With this help, the group member was able to raise the issue in a way that invited conversation rather than shut people down.

In addition to being process consultants, helping the city manager or commissioners better understand the dynamics of the process itself, we often worked as coaches, helping individuals consider what was going on with the larger group and what they wanted their role to be in that process. When working with the co-chairs to develop an agenda, one group facilitator supported the co-chairs as they wrestled with strong differences about the direction for the next meeting. This group was the only group that hadn't made any recommendations yet. One of the co-chairs felt it was essential to get a recommendation made by the end of the next meeting. The other chair wanted to take things more slowly, seeing the value in the dialogue and deliberation and the potential to create meaningful recommendations. The facilitator reflected each of their points of view to help them get clear for themselves and better understand each other. After summarizing the struggles between the external pressures to get moving and the time needed to create meaningful recommendations, the chairs decided to create an agenda that gave people time for the conversation and deliberations and had clear steps to keep the group moving toward a decision. After a few more meetings, the group was able to put forward one of the most significant recommendations of the whole process: the recommendation for alternative responders.

Legislative aides played a significant role in many of the groups, including reviewing agendas, managing time, and drafting recommendations. This could lead to blurry roles. With co-chairs, facilitators, and legislative aides, there were a lot of leaders in the group. For one of the facilitators, having a one on one with the legislative aide helped create some clarity around roles and expectations. Talking directly about the various ways both the aide and the facilitator could support the process produced less confusion for the group members.

Finally, we were also trainers at times, helping individuals acquire the skills needed in order to be more effective group participants. Figuring out what was needed from us in our conversations with each of the different stakeholder groups, and even within those groups at other times, was an important part of the process. At times this could feel like groping in the dark, but as Transformative facilitators we had some experience being in all of these roles.

INTERACTIONAL SHIFTS AND POLICY OUTCOMES

As I look back on DMC's role with these working groups, I realize there were positive outcomes because of the Transformative facilitation that we provided. Everyone involved experienced shifts as a result of these conversations, even though we were not able to be involved in the process design from the beginning. As facilitators, we noticed empowerment shifts, with individuals becoming clearer about their own concerns and better able to express them to others. Some participants also experienced recognition shifts, becoming more open to what others were saying, whether or not they agreed with them. Some, hearing challenges faced by police, became more receptive to the unique concerns described by the officers. Others, upon hearing the police insist that they were simply "doing their duty" in such a way that held no racial (or other type of) individual or institutional bias, gained new clarity about the limits of what was possible in this process with regard to police reform. Thus, whether the conclusions were heartening or discouraging, the individuals who came to these realizations were shifting and gaining clarity, which is a major goal for a Transformative practitioner. Thus, Transformative Dialogue's support of interactional shifts allowed participants to feel heard and to increase their understanding of the situation. This is not to say that this was true all the time, or even for every participant, but as a whole it did seem that individuals tended to make shifts toward strength and responsiveness after such interventions were made.

But more happened than interactional shifts. In fact, the working groups recommended significant policy outcomes that resulted in real changes to public safety in Dayton. The one-on-one meetings, listening sessions, coaching, occasional mediations, and Transformative facilitation resulted in concrete policy changes. These include:

- The introduction of body cams for police officers
- The creation of a mediation response unit to handle nonviolent conflicts/disputes
- Deescalation training for Dayton Police Department officers
- Policy changes to how use of force can be implemented

Most significantly for the DMC, a city-funded mediation response unit (MRU), which many in the community view as a success story, came about, in part, from the police reform process. The DMC describes the MRU as "an alternative response team that responds to low emergent 911 calls within the City of Dayton . . . [and whose] program was formulated after the police reform talks began in 2020 and the working groups identified recommendations for the community of Dayton."[1]

POSITIVE CHANGES AND MUCH LEFT TO DO

While the positive outcomes of this police reform process were real and are making a difference in Dayton, it must be acknowledged that significant cultural change is hard and does not happen overnight. There is still much more work to do to create the kinds of changes some would like to see. Unfortunately, less than six months after completing this police reform process, there was an incident of police mistreatment of a Black man that led to national headlines and a civil rights lawsuit, the exact types of actions and consequences that commissioners wanted to avoid through these reform efforts. Changing deeply embedded cultural realities of racism and police overreach require much more than a single attempt at reform.

But as noted earlier, the police reform effort did make a difference, not just in greater understanding but also in effecting some positive changes to public safety policy in Dayton. The working groups improved the quality of their conflict interaction among participants and resulted in new initiatives. Whether individuals came to the end of the process with greater or lesser faith in their local institutions or a desire to protest further, the effort can be labeled a "success" because a majority of individuals got clearer on their goals and objectives as a result of the process. In that sense, I do think we succeeded from a Transformative standpoint in spite of the many constraints.

In conclusion, any city that decides to embark on such an effort is likely to face similar challenges given the nature of policing throughout the United States. My experience from Dayton suggests that even when the process is less than perfect from a Transformative perspective, Transformative facilitators can still effectively support people in having difficult conversations as long as they are transparent about their identities and roles and engage in co-creation from the start of their involvement. Part of that critical component of transparency is acknowledging to participants that while they are unlikely to get everything they want, they may at least get clarity on the possibilities and limitations of what they hope to change. They may not accomplish all that they hope, but they are likely to experience more positive conflict interaction even when particular issues remain unresolved.

NOTE

1. https://www.daytonmediationcenter.org/blank-1.

10

External Constraints versus Party Choice

Transformative Dialogue as a Tool for Planning and Decision Making

Judith A. Saul

One of the hallmarks of Transformative Dialogue is its commitment to a bottom-up process that involves participants in decision making at every step. As noted frequently in this volume, Transformative Dialogue is often described as a process co-created by the facilitator and participants. But when a government or organization wants help with planning or decision making, the outcome is often defined: a recommendation or plan with specified parameters. And in these situations, a facilitator is often asked to submit a proposal that defines what the process will be, who will participate, and how the process will result in the predefined product. Does that mean a Transformative facilitator is precluded from submitting bids? The good news is that the answer is not necessarily "no." But in a case like this, a particular set of questions arise: How can a predefined process be Transformative? What must a facilitator be thinking and doing to ensure that participants are driving the process to the greatest extent possible? When does the balance tip, requiring an ethical Transformative practitioner to turn down an opportunity?

There are other times when a plan or decision is announced by decision makers only to be met with angry protests by those affected. If the decision maker asks a facilitator for help, how does a Transformative practitioner respond to a situation with sides defined, tempers high, and issues of power and authority front and center?

These are the questions I will explore in this chapter, based on my experiences facilitating a wide range of dialogues, primarily in the United States. A fully co-created dialogue may be the ideal, but it is best not to let the perfect be the enemy of the good.

GOALS AND VALUES

A facilitator's decision about submitting a proposal and accepting a job is a question of ethics. Because of this it is worth taking a moment to be reminded of the core values of Transformative Dialogue. These goals and the values that underlie them are the same regardless of the way in which a dialogue begins.

The goal of a Transformative Dialogue is to support change in the quality of people's interactions, increasing their ability to interact from a position of clarity and strength and to consider the perspectives of others, whether or not they agree. This is what we mean when we say that Transformative Dialogue increases pro-social interaction among those involved.

In the case of a client-driven process, the outcome, most often a recommendation or plan, is often a given. Though the goal of increasing pro-social interaction is explicitly separate from the idea of reaching an agreement, improved interaction usually increases the quality of any agreement that is reached. Thus, a Transformative facilitator maintains the goal of supporting pro-social interaction, realizing that as trust and respect among participants increases, decision making improves. Said differently, the increase in pro-social interaction allows participants to hear and be heard in ways that have not been possible before. In addition to allowing clearer thinking, a Transformative Dialogue has the potential to build relationships that allow members of an organization or a community to work together more effectively in the future whether or not an agreement is reached on a specific issue.

THE CLIENT-FACILITATOR RELATIONSHIP

An important and often overlooked part of designing and running any dialogue process is the relationship of the facilitator to the person recruiting the facilitator, most often referred to as the client. This client generally selects the facilitator, sets the terms for the process, and finds or supplies the resources available to complete it. Thus, before there is any interaction with participants, the facilitator has a relationship with the client. Perhaps the most important element of this client-facilitator relationship is transparency: between the facilitator and the client as well as between the facilitator and the process participants. The facilitator becomes an "honest broker" working between the two.

First and foremost, the client defines what they hope the process will accomplish. This goal may be to make a recommendation, develop a plan, or come up with a set of acceptable options. It is important to note that in many of these situations, dialogue participants are not decision makers. Rather, they are making recommendations to an entity tasked with making a decision. For example, a local town's legislature wants public involvement, but the legislature cannot give away its decision making power. The client also sets a time by which an outcome needs to be reached, based on legal or financial constraints or their own best guess about the time required.

Often a client seeks facilitation for what's referred to as a proactive process—one that is planned before there is a crisis. This happens when organizations or governments decide that they would like to involve many voices in a planning or decision-making process and invite facilitators to submit proposals. There are many kinds of proactive processes. Examples I have been involved in include drafting a regional transportation plan, recommending best land use practices for a national forest, and helping two related organizations consider whether or not to merge.

There are other times when a facilitator is contacted by a client who is dealing with an unexpected situation. These reactive facilitation processes are a result of dissatisfaction expressed by people affected by a proposed decision. A neighborhood or other subset of a community or an organization's members or employees express their anger and concern about decisions made or actions taken by those in control. Suddenly leaders realize that continuing as previously planned may not be a good idea. In an effort to regain control, minimize damage, or correct their mistake, they decide to involve people in modifying or reimagining the existing plan or decision. At this point, leaders may turn to a facilitator for help in figuring out how to deal with the situation. While more open ended than proactive situations, these reactive situations often require a quick response to the pressure of angry and sometimes public protests. These situations are often more amenable to a co-created process, generally with the client as one (often weightier) voice in that creation. Situations like this that I have been involved in include dealing with the disposal of specialized waste and working with a religious congregation upset by plans for new leadership.

Both proactive and reactive processes involve a combination of negotiable and nonnegotiable issues. Boundaries may be set by regulation, law, or resources. Opportunities for participant input may be limited by time or resources. While some of these boundaries are in fact fixed, it is common for things seen by one side as nonnegotiable to in fact be much more flexible than participants are initially willing to admit.

While these proactive versus reactive scenarios can be very different, they are best thought of on a continuum with characteristics varying based on a range of internal and external factors.

TO ACCEPT OR NOT?

A Transformative facilitator's first decision is whether or not to respond to a request for assistance. In many proactive processes, the request is made when a government or organization issues a request for proposal (RFP), inviting facilitators to apply through a competitive process. Other times a person may be contacted directly and asked if they can assist in a particular situation. This is most apt to happen in a reactive situation, when those in control are caught off guard by a reaction they were not anticipating. In either case, the critical first step is to engage with the client in conversation, in a one-on-one meeting when possible or through a series of questions and answers when direct interaction is not possible. As in other one-on-one meetings, the facilitator is listening and learning about the situation from the perspective of the client. And the facilitator is educating the client about the value of using Transformative Dialogue, explaining why they choose to work this way, how it would be useful in this particular situation and what the process might look like.

This conversation also allows the facilitator to determine what leeway exists to move a predefined process in a Transformative direction. The less formal the process, the more likely it is that this is possible. Sometimes an entity that has issued an RFP is unwilling to engage with a facilitator before a proposal is submitted. In this situation, a facilitator finds out as much as possible about the situation through formal and informal channels and then includes information about the value of Transformative processes in the proposal, including links to additional information to clarify ways of working that may be less familiar to the client.

My experience has demonstrated that in both proactive and reactive situations, there are many opportunities to move a dialogue in a Transformative direction. I will use examples from the work I have done to demonstrate how a Transformative facilitator can do this.

RESPONDING TO AN RFP THAT PREDEFINES A PROCESS

As mentioned earlier, more formal processes that begin with an RFP can create the biggest challenges to working Transformatively. One example of this is a transportation planning initiative I co-facilitated. The RFP was issued by a local transportation council, a joint agency representing county municipalities and allowing access to federal transportation planning funding. The goal was to create a multimodal plan that would address the needs of drivers of cars, buses, and trucks as well as bike riders and walkers. The RFP required that any recommended plan include input from all of these groups. Representatives from the transportation council would provide oversight but not be directly involved. A timeframe of fifteen months was defined and the main task was to facilitate a working group composed of representatives of the various interest groups and municipalities that the transportation council would appoint. While the agency head was willing to answer questions, the proposal was not open to negotiation.

The single most important question that I asked was what the transportation council would do with the recommendations that resulted from this process. In the past I had been involved in facilitating public input processes where the hard work put in by members of the public was essentially ignored by those who were the decision makers. For me to be an honest broker, I needed to be assured that the recommendations would be used by those who sought this input. I was reassured about this by three things included in the proposal. The first was that the staff of municipal transportation departments would function as technical experts, ensuring that recommendations were legally feasible. The second was that the funding available for improvements was part of the proposal, and recommendations needed to be financially feasible. The third was that while council members would not participate in working group meetings, they would receive regular updates about the working group's activities so they could intervene if the group was moving in ways that the legislators could not support.

Given these assurances, I then considered my ability to work within the imposed structure. The proposal I submitted involved opening the process up to involve the public at several crucial points. It didn't change the structure that the RFP imposed but allowed for a more co-created process by giving more voice to the public.

The RFP specified that members of the working group, responsible for formulating recommendations, would be selected by the transportation council. To allow for public input from the start and democratize the selection process, I proposed that the first open meeting be held before the working group was selected. At this meeting, members of the public would have a chance to learn about the process and its goals and to brainstorm the interest groups that needed to be represented in the working group. Then interested individuals from those groups could apply or be recruited.

I proposed three other public meetings. One would happen two months after the working group was formed to allow the public to have input into defining the problems. Too often the public is asked to review solutions but not to weigh in on the definition of the problem. This limits the value of public input. At this second public meeting, people would be invited to share specific problems they encountered as they walked, biked, or drove through the defined area. The third and final open meeting would happen at month twelve or thirteen of the process and allow public input on solutions that the working group was recommending.

RESPONDING TO AN RFP THAT HAS FEWER CONSTRAINTS

A very different example of a proactive process involved working with a not-for-profit organization that was considering a merger. Two organizations with similar missions were located in adjoining counties. Both were well respected but under financial pressure from declining funding. The board of one of the organizations decided to approach the other about the possibility of merging. The second organization had some serious concerns but agreed it was worth exploring. So they issued an RFP, requesting a process that would bring the two organizations together to consider whether or not to merge. Funding was limited, and the organizations hoped to do as much work as possible on their own, using the facilitator in targeted ways. They also hoped to reach a conclusion in no more than six months. Beyond this, it was up to the facilitator to propose the specifics of the work.

Because the RFP was skeletal, especially compared to the one described earlier, it was easier to proceed in a way that followed the precepts of Transformative Dialogue. My first step was to request a meeting with one or two representatives of each organization. I left it up to them to determine if they preferred to meet with me separately or together. They suggested a joint meeting that included each organization's executive director and board chair. During this meeting, I used the basic skills of a Transformative practitioner. I did a lot of listening, asked a few questions to check in on what I was hearing, and also educated them about how a Transformative approach could work well in their situation.

After listening to their goals and their initial concerns, I described Transformative Dialogue as a co-created process where they would consider "who needs to talk to whom about what and how." I noted that even this initial conversation was shaped by their decisions, which is how I would continue to work with them if I were chosen. As we began to talk about the "who," they told me that so far the idea of merging was known only to the executive directors and the boards of directors. Because they wanted to move fairly quickly, their current thinking was that no one else needed to be involved. I reflected that and checked in with them about who else would be impacted by the decision. The list was long and included staff, clients, funders, and local partners.

I invited them to think about the pros and cons of making a decision like this without broader input. They agreed that broader input was important but expressed concern about creating an "uproar" only to have it come to naught. My suggestion was that they consider a staged process, where input and involvement would increase gradually if deliberations indicated support for a merger. This met their need for control and enabled a slow widening of the circle in a way that made sense to them.

This "one-on-one" meeting resulted in a proposal that had a series of decision points allowing those involved to end the process or continue with the next level of involvement. Thus, though an RFP for the full process was required at the start, what was ultimately agreed to was a process shaped largely by their needs that would evolve over time.

RESPONDING TO APPEALS FOR HELP

The processes discussed earlier describe situations where public or private leaders decide that they want help in developing plans or making a decision. Many other times, those with authority spend time and resources creating a plan or crafting a decision that they then announce. Those announcements are sometimes met with negative responses that range from confusion to outrage. At this point, either the leaders or those protesting may turn to a facilitator and ask for help. Responding to these reactive processes creates a different set of challenges for the Transformative facilitator. These include issues related to power, impartiality, access to information, and many others.

One of the characteristics of reactive processes is a significant difference in perception of power. A plan or decision has been announced by those in a position to do just that—plan and/or decide. Those who rise up in protest are well aware that they are disagreeing with those who have the authority to move forward and that their disagreement is being expressed at the eleventh hour. In addition, the leaders who made the plan or decision are almost always the ones who have the resources to hire

External Constraints versus Party Choice   115

and pay a facilitator. Thus, in these situations a Transformative facilitator faces ethical questions as well as many practical ones. Assuming people are willing to enter into dialogue, can the facilitator reassure all participants about their own impartiality regardless of the fact that one side is paying the bill? And what responsibility, if any, does the facilitator have related to the unequal power that often exists?

These dilemmas exist for all facilitators. Because Transformative facilitators are committed to transparency, they will raise these issues whether or not others bring them up. They will then leave decision making about what to do about the unequal power up to potential participants, including whether or not to participate. Sometimes the facilitator can help people think about ways the process can be structured or modified in the face of power differences. These and other issues are discussed openly, and it is up to the individuals themselves to decide what to do in response to the situation they face. An example from the public sector illustrates this point.

A research institute developed a plan to rebuild the incinerator that handled its waste, including regulated medical waste from their research labs. The existing incinerator was old and out of compliance, and the institute's planners assumed that the community would welcome a new, state-of-the-art facility. Instead the public announcement was met with fierce opposition from a group of neighbors who lived near the incinerator. When representatives from the institute began to explain the rationale for their decision, the meeting devolved into a shouting match. The residents were very concerned about air pollution, especially from the medical waste that was being burned. They were angry that they weren't consulted before this decision was made. They did not trust the institute and feared they were being lied to. The institute representatives were caught off guard. They thought they had done a thorough job in researching the best kind of incinerator to build and expected to be thanked for their hard work. They believed they were wrongly attacked and were unsure of what to do next.

This is a common starting place for reactive conflict situations. Those on both sides were suspicious, fearful, confused, and angry—weak and self-absorbed. And the community, the institute and its neighbors, was certainly paralyzed and polarized. This was just the latest in a long history of tension between the institution and local residents. At the initial meeting, everyone retreated to their corners and got ready for another big fight, putting their energy into making their best arguments against the other side. In this instance, why it made sense to build a new incinerator *or* why a new incinerator was a bad idea. This focus on winning a narrow argument meant no one was thinking calmly and clearly about the complexity of the situation.

A Transformative facilitator who faces a situation like this usually begins with either one-on-one meetings or in meetings with small groups of people who share a similar perspective. The facilitator listens as people talk about the situation and share their perspective, their view of the history, and whatever else they choose to talk about. It makes sense to begin by listening because Transformative Dialogue is grounded in the assumption that those involved in the situation have the best understanding of what the problem really is.

So the next day, when I got a call from the research institute asking for help, I suggested that I meet with them to gain a better understanding of their perspective on the situation. The representatives explained that while they stood behind their proposal, they valued their relationship with the community. They were frustrated by the community's mistrust and suspicion. Their institute provided many well-paying jobs and benefited the community in many ways. But they acknowledged that they had rarely if ever consulted with the community before making decisions. In addition, they admitted to me that they wanted to expand their research facilities, which would mean new buildings as well as more medical waste. They would need the town's permission for their expansion. If residents were already angry with them about the incinerator, they feared they would have a harder time getting the town to allow their planned expansion.

They asked me if I could help by facilitating communication between the institute and the community. I talked with them about my commitment to a co-created dialogue process and asked for their input on the focus of the dialogue, who might be involved, and what it might look like. They explained that they were willing to put just about everything related to the incinerator on the table except for nonaction. The existing incinerator needed to be replaced with something that allowed them to handle the existing waste and had the capacity to manage their planned expansion. In terms of who should be involved, they suggested that scientists from their institute should join the planners who had made the initial presentations. Their goal was to find a mutually acceptable solution in six to eight months. They were less clear about a format and wanted to hear what community members suggested. They also agreed to cover the costs involved, within reason, and suggested that I develop a proposal after the initial negotiations. Before I met with community representatives I checked in about sharing what they had told me. They said I was free to share much of what we had talked about other than their future expansion plans.

Only a subset of community members who had been at the initial meeting were available to meet with me about next steps. Things got off to a rocky start. People let me know how angry they were with the institute's history of making decisions unpopular with the community. They felt that they should have been consulted at the start of the process rather than informed about a decision after the fact. They didn't understand what waste was burned and why and wondered if there were alternatives to incineration. Their anger was not alleviated when I explained that the institute had agreed to rethink their decision and were open to a facilitated dialogue process that I would lead. Instead they were suspicious, questioning both the institute's willingness to negotiate in good faith when they had the power to do what they wanted and my ability to be impartial if the institute was paying the bills. I reflected what they said to let them know that I had heard them and to allow them to make any clarifications. Then, rather than being defensive, I spoke directly to their questions about my impartiality. I explained that I was committed to a process where participants would make decisions about both process and content. My goal was to be transparent. I would explain the reason behind any suggestions I offered and ensure that others were free to ask questions or make different suggestions. I then asked them to think about the "how" and the "who" of a dialogue and consider what, if anything, could address any remaining concerns. After talking privately, they agreed

External Constraints versus Party Choice 117

to consider dialogue if the institute agreed to a process that included representatives from the neighborhood, the local municipalities, and local environmental groups. They also wanted at least one senior institute official at the dialogue sessions. As we wrapped up the conversation, I checked in with them about how much of what they had told me could be shared with the institute.

These two initial meetings reflect several important points about the value of Transformative Dialogue. As each "side" talked about the conflict, their understanding of the situation evolved. It was no longer just about whether or not to rebuild the incinerator. Instead it was, most broadly, about the relationship between the institute and the community. In addition, once those I spoke with realized that they would be deciding together how to structure the process and who to involve, their suspicions eased. They also listened carefully to what I said about impartiality and were reassured by my actions, asking explicitly what I could and could not "carry" to the other side. Hearing all this, both sides decided that they were willing to give dialogue a chance.

It took several more separate meetings and two joint meetings for this dialogue process to take shape. They ended up deciding on a formal structure, designating a specific number of people from the research institute (including the vice president), the immediate neighborhood, and the larger community as "official" participants who would be decision makers. These people agreed to meet regularly, though anyone who was interested was welcome to attend and offer input or comments. They decided to try for consensus, but if that wasn't possible, they agreed to abide by any decisions supported by 60 percent of participants. Perhaps most importantly for the community, the number of institute participants was balanced by an equal number not directly affiliated with the institute.

THE ADAPTABILITY OF TRANSFORMATIVE DIALOGUE

Transformative Dialogue is an adaptable process that can be used in a wide range of situations including those that involve structured planning and decision making. The external boundaries and limits of such processes may at first seem to preclude the idea of co-creation. Nonetheless one-on-one meetings can help clients and leaders consider ways of opening up narrowly defined processes as they come to understand the value of co-creation and maximizing participation. Similarly, intragroup conversations can help even very angry individuals realize that a Transformative Dialogue that invites them into decision making about process as well as content may help them negotiate with more powerful legislative or institutional leaders so that their voices can be heard and their ideas incorporated into agreements and solutions.

Transformative processes not only help people get the clarity they need, even in the face of constraints. They also promote connections among participants who interact with each other as they grapple with challenging situations. These connections can foster new relationships that have positive benefits far beyond the particular situation being addressed by a dialogue.

11

Transforming Conversations

A Journey through Community Dialogue in Somalia

Vesna Matović

This chapter tells the story of the Community Dialogue Initiative, a Transformative Dialogue process that I led in Mogadishu, Somalia, from 2014 to 2017, while working for International Alert. This co-created process involved our project team meeting with numerous members of the community to develop a plan for dialogue based on their own analysis of their situation and needs and then recruiting local facilitators and forming dialogue groups that included women, youth, elders, IDP camp wardens, religious leaders, service providers, and local authorities.

This process unfolded in a context that included three major challenges that I explore in detail in this chapter. The first was security. Somalia is a challenging place to work on a dialogue process, especially one organized around the principles and premises of Transformative Dialogue. The context I was working in was similar to many postconflict countries, but Somalia has had particular challenges in establishing a viable state. Thus, the security situation is often dire with choices frequently dictated by the need to maintain safety.

The second major challenge was a result of the expectations I encountered from Somalis who were used to the more directive approaches standard in most peacebuilding initiatives. In postconflict areas around the world, international and local NGOs are engaged in peacebuilding activities that often include dialogue of some form. But the focus of the larger initiatives and the dialogues within them are often top-down initiatives where outsiders bring in a predetermined process rather than follow a community-driven one. Detailed, solution-focused plans are drawn up by the NGO and followed by those implementing the initiatives. Community members often receive stipends or other material incentives for participating and often attend activities to receive these incentives rather than to focus on improving their communities. These standard practices are in many ways the exact opposite of a Transformative approach.

The third major challenge was culture. Historically Somali society is both traditional and patriarchal. Its governance system is largely structured around the clan, which controls much of social, economic, and political life. Within the constructs of the clan, decision making is generally preserved exclusively for men, and they are the ones chosen as leaders and legitimate clan spokespersons. Women are often excluded from clan-based decision making and have been excluded from appointments at senior level positions in government. Cultural social norms promote sexual and gender-based violence (SGBV), such as early forced marriage or female genital mutilation, practices being challenged by the larger project that sponsored our initiative. Navigating these cultural forms was made more challenging by my own identity as a European woman. In this chapter I describe how I applied the principles and skills of Transformative Dialogue while facing these challenges.

WHAT WE DID

The dialogue project began in 2014, when International Alert, the NGO I worked for, was asked to offer dialogue in two districts of Mogadishu. The dialogues were part of a larger project conducted by CISP, the International Committee for the Development of People, along with International Alert. The wider project focused on social norms around SGBV. Dialogue was chosen as part of the project so that communities could freely raise issues of concern and explore and address these issues together. Given these goals, I chose to use a Transformative approach, which best met these goals and would allow different actors from communities to participate in decision making. A Transformative approach also maximized the opportunity to build capacity so that dialogue could be used not only for existing issues around the project themes but also for dealing with other tensions within or affecting the community.

We began planning the Community Dialogue Initiative's scope in 2014. The first thing we did was put together a Dialogue Working Group (DWG), consisting of Somali and Kenyan staff from the two NGOs. Members of the DWG went through an extensive capacity-building process. This included training on conflict and gender sensitivity, SGBV, context analysis, principles, practices and skills of Transformative facilitation, monitoring and evaluation, and a training for trainers. From that point forward, the DWG played a key role in developing the dialogue process, liaising with local authorities, interacting with the communities, and training community facilitators.

After devoting more than a year to preparation, DWG members went to the two districts in Mogadishu that had been selected for the project. The dialogue process began as they met one on one with different community members to get their perspective on the situation, consider logistics, recruit and train facilitators, and do more planning, informed by information from each community. It was only then, two years later, that we started to have dialogue sessions. The members of the DWG were insiders, people who had experience working with these communities, so gaining entry was not a problem.

Dialogues were facilitated by teams of facilitators from the community. There were twelve dialogue facilitators (six women and six men) who worked in pairs, each facilitating one community dialogue. DWG members supported and supervised the community facilitators, offering coaching and additional trainings as needed. DWG members were also responsible for monitoring and evaluating the dialogue process. Each group held eight dialogue sessions with consistent community participation from August to November 2016. An additional four sessions were added in early 2017. These groups included women, youth, elders, IDP camp wardens, religious leaders, service providers, and local authorities.

Everything we did was informed by our commitment to Transformative principles. Our goal was to provide a safe space for communities to come together and talk about issues of concern, and we knew that only the community itself could figure out what was safe. Using Transformative Dialogue, a bottom-up approach, allowed community members themselves to determine what to talk about. Rather than focus on finding solutions to predetermined problems, we wanted to support community members in improving their relationships to each other and in increasing mutual understanding. This would allow communities to address their issues in constructive and creative ways. Our hope was that by moving the dialogue away from the goal of solving specific problems, we would enable communities to talk openly about any issue or problem they had, to increase their understanding of those issues, and to include more perspectives in considering how those issues were affecting different groups in the community and how they might respond.

SECURITY CHALLENGES

Security was a serious concern in Mogadishu, shared by all who were involved in the project. Though the situation was improved by the withdrawal of al-Shabaab in 2011, the city was still faced with regular attacks (including improvised explosive devices and targeted assassinations). At the community level, there were many security concerns, which means that people were often afraid to talk about the issues affecting them. Furthermore, the protracted conflict resulted in a complex picture for internally displaced persons (IDPs). IDPs live in both camps and within host communities in urban areas. In Mogadishu, they form a significant proportion of the population. At that time, there were around thirty thousand IDPs in Mogadishu, with the largest groups coming from Lower Shabelle, Bay, and Middle Shabelle, three adjacent Somali regions near the capital Mogadishu.[1] There were considerable tensions between host and IDP communities.

The need for safety impacted the project's design. We did all that we could to ensure safe access for community members. Obtaining permits from local authorities became an integral part of project logistics. Unfortunately, security concerns were sometimes exploited to exercise control, such as denying access to community members based on perceived security risks. In response to security information, project activities needed to be adapted or canceled or locations changed, requiring all of us to remain agile, responsive, and adaptable to the prevailing security context.

These challenges and decisions about how to address them proved to be a real test for the Transformative approach. We did our best to ensure that every decision was made through a consultative process, involving the dialogue participants, facilitators, and members of the DWG. Listening to concerns and respecting local knowledge became a hallmark of our collaborative decision making.

How we chose venues for a dialogue provides an example of how security issues overlapped with control by local authorities. Security played a crucial role in venue choice. The dynamics with local authorities varied across districts. In one district, where a positive working relationship existed, collaboration was easy and fruitful. In contrast, in another district, local authorities insisted on holding dialogue sessions in district headquarters offices. Participants were concerned about this association with the government, explaining that this perceived connection could jeopardize their safety, particularly in the context of threats from groups like al-Shabaab. Consequently, several individuals withdrew from the dialogue group. Recognizing the increasing challenges and people's reluctance to participate in the dialogue if it were held in district headquarters, the group collectively decided that the venue needed to be both safe *and* neutral, not closely tied to or owned by local authorities. When we explained to local authorities that the decision to change venues was made by the dialogue group members themselves, they agreed to the change.

While the Community Dialogue Initiative was able to turn much of the decision making over to community members, we understood the security system as a limitation that had to be factored in. Safety was ultimately the responsibility of each person involved. We could not guarantee safety, but we could be open and transparent with people about this external constraint, making sure that each person took this into account when they decided whether and how to participate in the process. And in keeping with Transformative principles, we respected the different calculations that each individual made as they weighed how much to participate and how much to say.

CHALLENGES CREATED BY THE WORLD OF INTERNATIONAL AID

Changing the Rules of the Game

There is a large presence of international aid agencies in Mogadishu providing services and humanitarian aid, managing development projects, and working on peacebuilding, indirectly if not as their main priority. The current way in which aid and development are delivered creates a set of "rules of the game," to which communities adapt and respond. It can look like a well-practiced game—communities learn how to behave, what to expect from aid agencies, how to "participate," and how to answer the questions when asked. This is in most ways the exact opposite of a Transformative approach.

Establishing an initiative based on an approach so different from the existing ways of working was a big challenge, requiring considerable learning for the DWG from the beginning, as well as a lot of "unlearning." One of the biggest challenges was to put into practice a Transformative approach to dialogue, allowing communities to own the process and to make their own decisions.

In other projects being implemented in the same districts, communities had very clear instructions on what they needed to change and how. They were offered schedules and curricula to follow by development actors. The expectation was that the information and knowledge would come from outside with communities on the receiving end. The same expectations were held by project staff, who were used to being on the "delivery side," where they were given manuals, instructions, and clear tasks. They were then expected to follow the prescribed process in their work with communities.

In contrast, the goal of our project team was to work with community members to develop a process, without "knowing in advance" what issues the communities wanted to talk about. The DWG followed the community rather than a strict plan. This change was not always easy. The project staff were used to working from externally developed manuals that allowed them to begin a dialogue knowing what would be talked about and how they would answer any questions that were asked. I explained to them that we were not going to have any predeveloped manuals because the community members in the dialogue were going to decide what to talk about. When they heard that, I saw fear in their eyes. How would they know what to do? How could they answer questions? They explained that they wanted lessons that they could teach. I asked them to think back on their previous work and consider if these prepared lessons had succeeded in changing attitudes and behaviors. They acknowledged that community members came most often because of the material incentives and tended to disregard a lot of the content. I also asked them if they thought Somalis needed to be told by foreigners, outsiders from NGOs, how their culture and behavior should change. They agreed that they certainly didn't need this. As they thought about this further, they realized they wanted to be treated with trust and respect. But this core lesson of Transformative practice, supporting the agency of dialogue participants and allowing them to be decision makers, was a hard lesson to learn. We reinforced it continually in all our work with these team members. In this way the planning of the dialogue—or co-creation—was itself dialogical.

Incentives for Participation

One distinct challenge arose from community members questioning the benefits of their participation in dialogue without getting any tangible material incentives in return. This expectation reflected a culture of dependency that had developed over the years: international organizations usually offered material goods, most often money, in exchange for community participation in the projects they organized.

Instead we provided only light refreshment for community members, as a symbolic appreciation of their participation but also to show understanding of cultural norms relating to hosting meetings. We also were able to reimburse participants for travel expenses. When they realized there would be no material incentives, many community members expressed their disappointment and said they didn't want to participate in the dialogue.

We addressed this concern by talking about how this dialogue was going to be different than others. We talked with potential participants about our belief in the community's ability to decide topics and collaboratively address issues—one of the core Transformative premises. We asked them how much had changed after their participation in earlier projects, and they acknowledged that the answer was not very much. We encouraged them to give this a try, explaining that they could decide whether or not to continue based on what they experienced. Despite their initial skepticism, the approach proved successful, demonstrating community interest and a willingness to engage in dialogue even in the face of unconventional incentives.

Participant Selection

In our endeavor to initiate and co-create Transformative Dialogue, we encountered significant challenges, particularly in the realm of participant selection and decision making. Early on, we identified a series of assumptions that required careful examination and, at times, challenge. The challenges were internal as well as external. Many of these assumptions were initially made by members of the DWG, who presented them as integral aspects of the community's cultural norms that we needed to respect and adhere to.

One such assumption was that local authorities and community leaders would be responsible for selecting dialogue participants and facilitators. This contrasted with the Transformative principle of a community-driven approach. We wanted members to volunteer for the dialogue and propose others they wished to engage with. Through a series of meetings and conversations with diverse community segments— including service providers, community leaders, IDPs, women, youth, security personnel, and religious leaders—we observed a high level of interest across all groups. We had enough interest from community members to form six dialogue groups.

Expecting Fast Solutions

Another expectation of both NGOs and community members was quick solutions for their problems and issues. This expectation was shared among DWG members and facilitators, and so it became a norm. Their expectation was that community members would share their different issues in each dialogue session, decide which one to focus on during the session, and then generate options and possible solutions. The expectation was that they should be able to solve at least one problem in each dialogue session. In fact, solutions created in this fashion rarely withstood the test of time. The fact that these fast solutions didn't last helped us move participants to a more Transformative approach. We emphasized the importance of supporting interactions that strengthened the group—their relationships, trust, freedom to express themselves and to explore issues together, to respect each other, to appreciate other opinions, etc.

This took time, in some cases almost half of the overall process. But it made a significant difference in how participants interacted. Eventually sessions started to look more like "dialogue" sessions and less like problem-solving workshops. At that point, instead of finding solutions for predefined problems, groups started to develop joint initiatives and plans for addressing the issues *they* had prioritized. They also started to bring their "insights" and "learning" into their family life and other forums. One participant explained how "I have started sharing all things discussed—first with my family, then relatives, then some of the villagers; they like what we are doing and asked if they can join us." Another person explained how their community wanted to organize dialogue on a variety of issues they cared about, including "how to build peace in the community, how to care about street boys, migration and similar issues."

Groups started to appreciate the opportunity to explore issues together and emphasized many times how their interactions were now different because they had developed trust. They also emphasized the importance of new friends and networks. Some members could speak openly for the first time. One participant said that "the biggest change I observed was about participation. In the beginning, only a few talked, and after a few weeks everybody contributed and felt free to discuss and suggest." When their opinion was appreciated, it became the moment of recognition. That gave strength to dialogue members. Several commented on how the dialogue had given them confidence. One woman said, "Now, I see myself talking in front of people, sharing my opinion, raising topics of interest, and I was happy to see myself as a brave woman, who can share what she learned in a crowd of people in the community." Another said, "I am now less afraid to speak in front of elders, leaders, and authorities." Interestingly, when insisting that communities not follow a predetermined process of problem solving but figure out topics and issues themselves, it led to strengthened relationships and more confidence to participate and even communicate the resulting discussions to their communities and their leaders. It also led to *real* problem solving.

Monitoring the Dialogue and Defining Success

Most dialogue initiatives monitored success by counting the number of topics covered or the number of problems solved. But, consistent with Transformative principles, the Community Dialogue Initiative understood success as members' increased agency, their willingness to consider the perspectives of others, their active participation in decision making, and positive changes in the quality of interactions among them. The quotes in the previous paragraphs are examples of indicators of such increased agency and new relationships. But documenting this kind of change requires focus and can be challenging.

Those tasked with monitoring the dialogue process had a difficult job. Although a monitoring and evaluation group was established and trained together with other members of the DWG, different staff were sent to monitor the sessions because they were based close to the community in question, and this meant the security risk for others was reduced. But this also meant that the actual monitors didn't have any training to enable them to understand the dialogue project or how to monitor progress.

Indicators of success were also developed Transformatively, with the participants of the dialogue. It took some time and a lot of effort to come to a shared understanding about what is a "measure" of a successful dialogue process. From that point, the focus was more on the interactions within the dialogue groups, the atmosphere, the expression of opinion, the general dynamics (including power dynamics), the quality of the discussion, the depth of exploration of the topic, and the participation of all members. What we noticed is that at that point people were opening up topics that were quite hard to discuss and that were uncomfortable for some members. They were more emotional and stronger reactions started to appear. One participant said, "I gained a lot from the dialogue process; it was my first time to participate in discussions where I can benefit from the participants' ideas. It opened my mind to the world. I used to feel shy to speak and fear standing in front of people, but after the third week of dialogue, I changed and became brave and shared my opinion." Another noted how, "another benefit is that not all participants were aware of different issues in their communities, so they learned a lot, and understood more. It also became normal to talk about difficult issues, things that were taboo before, such as rape."

CULTURAL CHALLENGES

Clan Dynamics

Another significant factor related to power, control, and engagement was navigating the intricate dynamics of clan structures in the dialogue process. Our team knew this would be challenging because our initial context analysis underscored the importance of the clan structure and its power dynamics. We needed to understand various clan dynamics within a district, including the influence of majority and minority clans on social, economic, and political life. This understanding played a pivotal role in how we recruited facilitators and engaged participants.

Local authorities exerted pressure to recruit dialogue facilitators exclusively from their own majority clans and to exclude minority clan members. The majority clan in a given district often expressed concerns about losing decision-making power in a dialogue process where decisions were made by everyone. They hinted at their ability to obstruct the dialogue project if they were not reassured. In the southern areas of Mogadishu, the heightened insecurity faced by minority clans posed challenges for their participation in the dialogue, exacerbating their already marginalized position. In addition, the DWG was concerned about the genuine risk that the project might inadvertently support and strengthen these and other existing power structures.

Navigating these clan dynamics became an integral aspect of the broader challenge of managing power dynamics, control issues, and relationships with local authorities. Team members did not openly challenge existing power structures. Rather, they engaged local authorities and clan leaders in much back and forth, asking questions, considering responses, and suggesting options. They found again and again that this strategy of engagement was the way to promote change. Proactive measures like this, along with their nuanced understanding of the local culture, helped them ensure that the dialogue process was inclusive, representative, and not reinforcing existing inequalities within the communities.

Working with Local Authorities

Though local authorities were not part of the dialogue process, a successful process depended on at least their implicit support. They proved to be a challenging group, indispensable yet occasionally prone to overinvolvement. We needed them for their support, and as part of the community themselves they were important stakeholders. They were generally supportive of the dialogue, offering to provide the venue, giving advice, and sharing security information. But their overinvolvement created problems. We worked hard to establish a relationship that allowed them to be supportive but not controlling. In some cases, we came close to realizing that ideal. Sometimes we were less successful.

One example of this was our attempt to procure refreshments. The project staff followed an agreed-upon procurement policy for all the elements of the project. However, a problem occurred with the contract to provide the refreshments for the dialogue sessions. A group of women had provided the refreshments for community meetings that were part of a different project happening in the same district. They expected that they would receive the contract again. When this did not happen, the women complained to the local authority who responded by denying participants access to the dialogue sessions. The dialogue sessions were put on hold while the project staff negotiated with the authorities and explained that our project had a procurement policy that the women had not followed. Luckily for us, the local authority advised the women's group to comply with procurement procedures next time so that their application could be considered. The local authority then allowed the dialogue sessions to continue.

This challenge was not only about the procurement process but also about the need for the local authority to maintain control within their districts. It was not always easy to navigate these issues. Sometimes we felt like giving up. But the communities we were working with were motivated to continue with the dialogue, so we decided to live with some challenges, overcome others, and try to minimize their negative impacts.

Gender

Our DWG was well aware that the aim of the wider project was to contribute to improving the response to and prevention of SGBV against women and girls through a multifaceted approach that included capacity building, support to service provisions, awareness activities, research, and advocacy. We understood that Transformative Dialogue's emphasis on supporting participants' agency could assist with these goals, especially awareness and capacity building.

The design of the dialogue project was partly informed by the findings of research that documented linkages between the conflict in Somalia and social norms related to SGBV. That research showed that SGBV in Somalia was deeply rooted in unequal gender relations, discriminatory and harmful gender social norms, as well as social exclusion. Almost all study participants indicated that SGBV is equally "normalized" by host and IDP communities (majority and minority groups). Host and nonhost households have adopted certain behavioral and social norms toward SGBV, with minority groups remaining silent in order to avoid social exclusion. This normalization of SGBV is also related to a complete lack of or limited communication and dialogue among Somali communities at the household, societal, and national level, not only on SGBV and harmful social norms but also on peace, reconciliation, and antiviolence after the civil war.

Because of these findings, we designed our dialogue initiative to offer a different and very important opportunity to start opening up communication. We worked hard to understand the interaction between conflict and gender and the implications of that interaction for the intervention.

One of the ways this played out was the perceived reluctance of women and youth to participate in the same group as community leaders, elders, and religious figures. The assumption was made by many, including members of the DWG, that women and youth would not have the freedom to express themselves in mixed groups. Rather than accept this, we decided to ask potential participants to make their own decisions. When we talked with individual women and young people, we asked them about the kinds of groups they would be willing to join. We offered the option of mixed dialogue, as well as separate women's and men's groups. This approach produced four mixed groups, one women's group, and one men's group, guided by the choices expressed by participants. The experience underscored the importance of questioning assumptions and biases and letting people make their own decisions, which is consistent with Transformative principles. It also meant that these dialogue groups did not reinforce existing power structures and decision-making dynamics.

Age was another factor that played a great role culturally. Young people (across all other identities) were less confident and were not encouraged to express their opinion. Like the women, when we invited young people to participate, they agreed. Then, during the dialogue, we supported all who wanted to speak. The youth gained confidence as they realized that they could use the dialogue space to contribute to discussions and influence decisions. To quote one of the community members, "It was like planting a seed; young women who started to speak out, will change their family and those close to them."

CONCLUSION

The Community Dialogue Initiative was marked by complexities and triumphs. We navigated our way through security challenges; changed the way we, as an NGO, interacted with the local communities; and worked with the complexity of Somali culture. We followed rather than led, attending to ethnopolitical conflicts, power dynamics, gender intricacies, and external limitations. In doing all this, we witnessed the transformative potential of genuine community conversations.

This venture was not without its hurdles, but in each challenge, we found seeds of growth. As I share these insights from this experience, I hope to inspire a deeper understanding of the inherent power of Transformative Dialogue, even in the most challenging contexts. In the Somali community engagement, we discovered the strength that emerges from collaborative decision making, the resilience of individuals embracing change, and the profound impact of sincere dialogue in fostering connections. Our journey reflects not just the challenges overcome but also the collective spirit of change and understanding that dialogue can bring to communities in conflict.

Amid the challenges, all of us involved with this dialogue project found moments of profound personal growth and transformative learning emerged. All of us were involved in a continuous process of unlearning preconceived notions and accepting the power of cultural exchange. Embracing a collaborative decision-making model became the cornerstone of our approach. Recognizing the inherent wisdom within the community and actively involving local voices in shaping the dialogue process was not merely a strategic choice but a heartfelt commitment to fostering empowerment and ownership among the participants. Each collaborative decision became a testament to the transformative potential of shared leadership and co-creation. Speaking personally, I realized that my own worldview expanded as I engaged with the richness of Somali culture, delved into the nuances of their societal structures, and witnessed the resilience of communities in the face of conflict. These reflections encapsulate the intricate dance of personal insights and transformative experiences encountered while bridging the cultural gap in the pursuit of dialogue and peace in Somalia.

I understand this chapter not as a conclusion but as a call to others to continue developing the potential of Transformative Dialogue. In the varied threads of these conversations, there lies a continuous invitation for dialogue to be a catalyst for positive change, breaking barriers, and fostering resilience within communities facing the complexities of ethnopolitical conflicts.

NOTE

1. http://www.jips.org/system/cms/attachments/1120/original_Mogadishu_Profiling_Report_2016.pdf.

12

Navigating Dialogue in Complex Conflict Systems

The Transformative Dialogue Experiences of Interpeace Kenya

Abiosseh Davis and jared l. ordway
With Lopode Paris, Murshid Dubahir, Kenedy Rotich,
Job Mwetich, and Hassan Ismail

This chapter explores the experiences of five Kenyan facilitators working with the NGO Interpeace in areas of Kenya affected by chronic conflict and intermittent violence. Both of us have watched these facilitators make choices that align with the premises and principles of Transformative Dialogue. Because of this experience, when we were invited to co-author this chapter, we decided that the best way to proceed was to invite those we've worked with together to have a conversation about their work. So we asked Interpeace Kenya's country representative Hassan Ismail and team members Lopode Paris, Murshid Dubahir, Kenedy Rotich, and Job Mwetich to reflect on their own experiences.

We share here excerpts from our conversation that highlight the many ways that the work of our Kenyan colleagues aligns with Transformative practice. The conversation touches on themes of identity, insider and outsider roles, the value of intragroup dialogue, gender and patriarchy, cultural appropriateness of interventions, and the capacity of local communities to deal with conflict constructively on their own terms. Our conversation also notes challenges to working Transformatively when donors and local or national authorities have expectations of speedy results and concrete outcomes. Finally, our colleagues point to the dilemmas that are raised between wanting to halt violence, which creates an imperative to work directively, and wanting to respect participants' agency, which requires time.

BACKGROUND

Since 2021, we have been working through the independent, international peace-building organization Interpeace to support practitioner teams conducting mediation and dialogue in the violence-affected arid and semi-arid regions of Kenya's Northeast and North Rift Valley, as well as Marsabit County. Interpeace has been active in Kenya since 2014, when it entered into partnership with Kenya's National Cohesion and Integration Commission (NCIC), a government agency mandated to foster lasting peace and cohesion between Kenya's various ethnic communities. This formalized partnership began in 2015 with a pilot program in Kenya's Mandera County on the border of Somalia and Ethiopia.

The work in Mandera was largely successful in stopping cyclical communal violence while establishing self-directed local peacebuilding initiatives such as Ceasefire Monitoring Committees (CMCs) that are now widely able to manage intermittent clashes (Interpeace 2023). This success led NCIC to recommend the adoption of the Mandera County model for locally owned and locally driven peacebuilding in *all* forty-seven counties of Kenya. Today, Interpeace works extensively with the Kenyan organization Network for Peace, Cohesion, and Heritage Trust (NEPCOH) who together have carried out similar activities in regions across northern Kenya.

The people of Mandera County along the Kenya-Somalia border are pastoralists who commonly keep sheep, camels, cows, and goats and historically move from place to place with their livestock on a seasonal basis. The two predominant clans in this area are the Garre and Degodia, both of which are principally Muslim, with Somali cultural traditions informing customary laws and practices. Interclan disputes between the Degodia and Garre communities of Mandera County have happened for generations and grew particularly intense in 2010 through 2015, when violent conflict claimed countless lives and led to livestock raiding and property destruction. During that time, many farmers found themselves uprooted from their ancestral lands, their fruit trees cut down and irrigation farms destroyed. Major tensions continue. Interpeace Northeast team's success in supporting a self-sustaining ceasefire agreement between the communities since 2019 is noteworthy.

In the North Rift Valley, the Pokot and Turkana are among the seminomadic agropastoralist communities spread across five counties. Violent conflict between the Pokot and Turkana communities have been documented for over a century, with clashes that have resulted in tragic losses of lives, displacement, and the destruction of property. Deep-seated perceptions of historical injustices and rivalry have helped to perpetuate new cycles and patterns of violence.

WORKING IN THIS CONTEXT

Understanding how conflict occurs in nomadic communities or why nonviolence remains elusive is not always straightforward. Based on the premise that peace must be built from within societies, Interpeace Kenya has centered practices of listening to conflict parties and the issues they want to bring into focus as the main means for supporting and sustaining peace. This work entails the use of dialogue to support changes in interaction and relationships both within and between groups in order to strengthen the capacity of various actors to prevent and manage conflict. In addition to facilitating dialogue, the program's teams help to draft, archive, and implement the various communities' peace accords, support communities in creating collaborative frameworks related to community peace, and more.

A key part of the practitioner teams' approach to these conflicts has been the use of *participatory* analytical activities that engage communities in examining conflict dynamics. These methods embody Transformative principles, convening people from a single community as an "intragroup" exercise, and have functioned effectively as a starting point for further "intergroup" meetings. These spaces have fostered important exchanges and nuanced understandings well beyond conventional conflict analysis. This, in turn, enables the co-design of dialogue processes.

Building on the customary community practices of circle gatherings, these opportunities for reflection have invited communities to examine their experiences and concerns in relation to conflict as well as their visions for peace. Through that, communities' own observations of cyclical and episodic nontransformation of violent conflict highlight various impediments to peace while also unpacking these issues through gendered and generational lenses.

Through this work we have seen that the core premises and principles of Transformative Dialogue align closely with the teams' own adaptive and pragmatic approach to process design and dialogue facilitation in these complex contexts. The processes co-created by the teams and the participants have led to direct and resounding reductions in intercommunal violence while temporarily interrupting and limiting the ways in which elite political actors have instrumentalized conflict or fomented violence for their personal economic and political gains.

THE CONVERSATION

Putting Parties at the Center

The first part of our conversation is about the importance of prioritizing party decision making and self-determination. This emphasis on self-determination has emerged from experience and the many failed peacemaking attempts since Kenya's independence in 1963. Experience has shown that if the process is rushed or does not respect self-determination, there will be no local ownership of any resulting agreement, which will then be largely ignored. This respect for party choice is coupled with respect for the usual ways villages or communities consult with each other. In this way, respect for party choice supports more culturally appropriate activities, including where dialogues are held.

This part of the conversation also highlights several tensions and dilemmas that exist for practitioners. First, decision making by local communities is in tension with the imperative of bringing violence to a halt, which has in the past been accomplished when mediators or public officials, believing that an immediate settlement will achieve the goal, pressure parties to sign an agreement that is not genuinely their own. Second, in an area with scarce resources and great distances, committing to more time for party decision making means more risk and more costs. In the vast geographic expanse of North Rift counties, some villages take hours to reach over rough terrain with minimal or no roads. Many villages are only available via heavy four-wheel drive vehicles or on foot. Teams can be caught in gunfire or risk criminal attacks. In the meantime, state security forces may move to enforce a securitized peace. Returning home without a fixed agreement also means ongoing uncertainty and greater risk of violence.

Abi: In the complex environment where we work, does the Transformative Model make sense?

Lopode: We really believe that we don't necessarily bring [expertise] to people. One thing [we know] is that the community has the power. We are not directing anything or imposing anything. They know everything. They know the problems. They have the possible solutions. We are just there to [support them] when we see the strain a little, but not imposing what we want.

Murshid: The whole thing is about coming with the perception that you don't know [or assume] anything and that the communities have the solution at hand, and you are there to help put that into perspective.

And [as trusted insiders] we might be in some way the "initiators" of that process but we give [those decisions] back to the communities to help them sustain that process . . . there's an automatic impact from the process where people move away from conference-based, boardroom-based peacebuilding toward more community-oriented mechanisms, you know, people can sit under trees using their own mechanisms, host each other, *become* the process themselves. What this means is there is a shift from the more incentive-oriented peacebuilding so people can just discuss anywhere, in their own farms near their own livestock areas.

Hassan: It is a challenge to identify [root causes]—where do we start? [There is a lot of superficial blaming] and issues change over time. Because of the long history, it becomes easy [for parties] to frame the problems superficially. As much as we affirm, we also challenge [community members] to acknowledge and deal with complexity and patterns. [By doing so] it becomes easier for them to [open] and give answers to how to address [the situation], so they move away from a superficial understanding and deepen their approach.

jared: The way you understand how pastoralist communities work really matters . . . when you go out and spend time sitting with communities, process co-creation is front and center. Enabling parties to draw upon the practices they do regularly not only fosters a co-created process, but perhaps more importantly, materializes community ownership.

Murshid: Yeah. Helping people understand or building their thinking capacity to really be part of the process itself takes time. What stood out throughout the process in Mandera was how our interaction with communities created some level of the communities' own understanding about process. That's the main role we played, helping them understand that *they* really have the power to make decisions on their own, and that everyone has some role or level of involvement for the entire process to be successful. And people understood [then that] if this process fails, then this is *my* role that has led to the [outcome]. [We work toward] making things simple and moving away from a centralized [mediator-centric] position toward more consensus building and community led [process].

jared: Lopode, you inferred earlier that the decision making is the responsibility of the parties you work with. Do you have an example of this?

Lopode: We [were to facilitate] a meeting between Pokots and Turkana around October [2023]. We went thinking at this meeting they'll sign a [ceasefire] accord and open the area [which had closed after widespread violence]. But when we met with them, [the Pokot] community had outstanding security concerns [and could not come to agreement]. They said: "let us go deliberate further [involving more of our villages in consultation]. Then we will have a meeting in January where, maybe we can sign an accord, maybe not." Since they said, "let us go deliberate further," we as facilitators realized that even if we had asked them to sign an accord [that day], no one would have really supported it.

In Lopode's last example, she signals the facilitation team decided to follow the parties, despite their hopes for a signed agreement that day. That meant exercising patience given their request for more time and respecting the customary practices of consultation that are relevant for any agreement to become truly acceptable to the wider community and therefore durable. It is important to remember that "agreement" here refers to ceasefires. Ceasefire agreements are typical in the North Rift and often don't result in anything concrete. Though conflict interveners often see agreements as an endpoint, here they are often merely a starting point. Ceasefires are a way that intercommunity dialogue about important issues can get started. They often include a framework of important points that require further dialogue within and across communities if they are to be implemented. As their conversation reveals, there are often important relational changes that happen along the way; people resume interactions that had stopped as a result of violence.

Teams also know that these framework agreements, like many, provide a platform for further dialogue work between conflict parties. They often highlight the need to involve and invite other relevant institutions and organizations to engage as well. One reason for involving other stakeholders, often at the parties' requests, is because key conflict dynamics are inextricably linked to local economic and development-related challenges that cannot be addressed by one actor or institution alone. Participants may call for inputs from county-level governance institutions and/or humanitarian or development organizations. In this sense, teams know that supporting transformative outcomes means supporting dialogue work beyond the ceasefire. An early ceasefire agreement between two communities is a start, not an end point.

There are also challenges to the process because of the pressure from international donors to get to an agreement and deliver on project goals. There are a lot of restrictions with funding from donors, but there is no doubt that participatory methods produce better outcomes, whether in terms of relational changes and conflict transformation or concrete agreements when they are signed. There are also powerful actors who have an interest in the conflict continuing, and this is a big challenge. These complications are discussed in the following segment.

ON AGREEMENTS

Abi: We don't all stop when there is an agreement, a settlement, or a peace accord. In the international community, the idea of agreement means one big agreement, whereas in our experience, both in Northeastern and North Rift, there have been a series of sequential agreements. Could you talk about how several agreements help move along a process, or fit within a larger process that brings about change, rather than one big agreement being the pinnacle outcome?

Lopode: When we first came in, we learned that there have been big agreements like the Koloa Agreement, which was signed by Members of Parliament, governors, big people, but no one followed through. It was just like a show for the media, then people went home. Nothing happened [afterward]. For me, the signing [of a ceasefire agreement] is just the beginning. It's not the end. If we leave [parties] after signing, everything will crumble in a month or two months. But now that's where we start. For instance, if [parties] say they want the markets to be open or roads [to be opened]. These are things they can do themselves, or we can [support them to] do. That's when I will start planning to bring the other communities together for [additional] meetings. [Meantime], they start to interact and start using the roads together.

We follow [up on] the tangible outcomes [parties] can achieve, not necessarily big achievements which we cannot see [happening] in the foreseeable future. A year from now we can't [achieve total] disarmament. [But we know] communities can "silence the guns" themselves. These miniscule details add up. So if they silence the guns [in practice], even if the community has the guns but doesn't use them, the area will be calm.

If parties are signing and they just go home [the agreement won't be followed]. Sometimes the outcome they want [requires] something other organizations can [help them to accomplish]. If they want a school to be open, then we engage the Ministry of Education, we can go engage at the school themselves, see what the setting is, why the school closed down, asking, "this was a peace dividend, it brings communities together, how can we help?"

jared: Lopode and Kenedy, you also stressed your choice to support the Pokots' request for time to consult widely across their villages. What happened as a result of that decision?

Lopode: If we look at the number of [violent] incidences such as before we had that meeting, the roads were impassable. But now you check your incident reports, and you see one [incident every] two weeks and so forth. So you realize [the parties] are working in the background, yes.

Kenedy: After these meetings and agreements, you find that in communities, businesses will start to pick up and people will start to move to the [town] center. Or you find that they'll be visiting their friends again. And communities are very happy when you convene them because you find that they [have known] each other in the past. Another thing is that everyone participates in these meetings. Old or young, everyone loves peace. It's because of fear that you find a gap [in people's interactions]. But once they come together and they start speaking, they are longing for the good old days when they used to have peace.

However, during some recent intercommunity dialogue with leaders from [two warring] communities, we found that despite us engaging the leaders, members of the local government from both sides, the [process] had some setbacks because a key political gatekeeper was not into it. He [wasn't convinced] that leaders [should] meet. And now we are still waiting for the next meeting.

jared: So on the one hand, supporting party self-determination in terms of enabling customary practices can bear fruit. On the other hand, your convening is the gesture that gives people permission to move beyond fear. Yet you also acknowledge that there is more needed than fostering intergroup trust and supporting self-determination. The example of a powerful political or economic actor exercising control over how parties engage is not uncommon. Those individuals influence processes significantly, even while they themselves may not participate in the intercommunity dialogues you facilitate. How do you make sense of that?

Kenedy: It demoralizes your spirit because you find that most of the [community] leaders are willing to speak about [conflict] to end it. But people with serious power have [personal] interests. They have a certain number of cattle and want to forcefully graze on other people's land. They support [financially and in other ways] the theft of animal[s], which [intermediary] criminal actors then sell on the market at a lower cost.

jared: This is a good illustration of how powerful actors can influence the decision making of communities in conflict and a localized peace process itself. As you have said, their influence can instrumentalize conflict as well as hinder peace efforts. But you also noted that community dialogue has empowered communities to resist and counter-balance powerful efforts to impede peace (Interpeace 2023).

Abi: This notion of centering community dialogue rather than working on high-level agreements also seems to be a departure from the business-as-usual model of peacemaking and peacebuilding in Kenya. As I understand it, the typical approach used by national and international actors alike is a bit of a helicopter approach, where mediators (and in many cases community leaders/representatives) are flown

138   *Abiosseh Davis and jared l. ordway*

in, hosted in upscale hotels, reaching for agreements that are often not genuine, and typically disconnected from the communities who neither know, own, or even agree with their contents. These agreements tend not to hold and, in some cases, even become part of bigger problems. I imagine that in the beginning, adopting this Interpeace approach of centering efforts within and among *those most affected* by the conflict was not an easy transition, particularly for team members who were used to the status quo approach. [In this case] to have patience to say, "okay, we don't work *only* for an agreement, we work for letting the parties decide." Have you felt challenged in this? What are the difficulties?

Lopode: [Before I came to the team] I worked in county government, so the governor was [the one presiding over] signing [ceasefire] agreements. We had some [agreements] that extended across borders of Turkana County, Ethiopia, and Uganda. But you see that the signing [is promoted by] a small group of political leaders or [external NGO] professionals, not by the *communities* [doing the direct fighting]. The communities themselves don't even know what these "agreements" are. They're not framing *their* agreements in [a signed accord]. They themselves don't come out straight and say, "we are agreeing to stop; we are going to stop using the gun, immediately." But [government] [would have] to go back to the office and now frame [their discussion] as an agreement [in their own words]. Sometimes you won't get the words you want, the words you expect. [In our work, we] go with what the community themselves say. But for the "professionals" they literally write down their points in the agreement format, "we, the Turkana community, agree to . . . from Day X henceforth, we will do this, and this, and this."[1]

jared: That is a practice consistent with seeing agreements as a terminus for process. The insistence on a signed agreement, or the conflation of agreements with a lasting outcome seems to miss an important point. From what you said earlier, your approach to co-creation starts by listening for what the communities need. This illustrates how agreements are just a beginning for longer dialogue work to begin.

Lopode: Yeah. So that's why sometimes you [understand] that parties have agreed [on certain issues], but you can't make them sign anything. If they've agreed there won't be any attacks on the highway, then that will be stopped for some time. But at the same time [what] they're [really] saying [is], "we have to go and discuss this further," even if they have already agreed [to stop shooting each other]. So you don't stop at the signing, even if they've agreed, yes. They have to then go back to their communities and discuss what's next.

ON INTRAGROUP WORK

jared: That illustrates your orientation to co-creation. It is in part the reason why you have also supported plenty of *intra*community dialogue activities too. Why does the *intra*group work matter as part of intergroup dialogue, or even prior to leader-level mediation?

Navigating Dialogue in Complex Conflict Systems 139

Job: Intergroup dialogue is [typically] the result of several *intra*community talks. [Key] issues [of concern] come out very clearly from the community. The [intragroup space] is a critical [first] phase for raising questions. [Someone might say,] "what if we meet with the Pokot later; what if we see our [stolen] goats in their homestead, what do we do?" It gives them an opportunity to reflect and say, "let's try to mitigate [violent revenge cycles]." Those are some of the things that [wind up] in the agreements that they have signed, so even if they encounter such temptations, they work to forgive. In Suguta Valley, one of the CMC members [recalled] once he was doing outreach and when he was arriving, he said: "I saw my stolen animals taking water [there on somebody else's property]." But because we had [previously] agreed to move forward and commit to the existing peace [he said to himself], "let him use the animals in peace." Such kinds of public remarks by an elder give the rest of the community pause. It challenges their ways of thinking in this environment.

Hassan: If you want to cut the trail of historical violence that has happened for a long time, you need [an equally] historical step. Starting here, let's stop [violence], let's refocus. When [parties] look around and reflect, they see the environment is a toxic one. Everybody sees that, in fact, everybody has been criminally liable—fathers, brothers, uncles, cousins. Somebody has always stolen from another family.

jared: This drives home the value of listening and intragroup dialogue as a means to support shifts that address cyclical revenge. You don't impose that on parties. Once again you are working in ways that respect a community's customary practices. Intragroup work structures the space for a single community to reflectively engage with one other. That's consistent with the core principles of Transformative Dialogue.

Murshid: A cornerstone achievement has been putting the conflict participants at the steering wheel. When our work started in 2015 in Mandera [County], there was a situation of armed conflict. People wanted us to go mediate in the "professional way," the *conventional* way of doing things. We came [instead] with [consultative methods], a very long and serious process [informed by participatory action], but it has really transformed people, transformed conflict actors to become peace agents.

A very good example is Rhamu town, where there had previously been very serious postelection violence. In 2017, everybody was fearing that the same thing might occur again. We held several discussions with elders and authorities, and even had some peace pacts, but we saw that none of those things were really holding water. [Prior to that], we [had been] doing the same things all the other [mediators] were doing, the "usual thing" that the government will always do. But out of those discussions something came out. [We heard people say,] "back in 2013 something happened between two villages that were saved from the effect of conflict. They agreed and did something," and that is how the idea of the Inter-Village Dialogue Spaces came about. So [our team mobilized] to support those spaces, and 2017 was the most peaceful election in Rhamu. As facilitators, all we needed to do was to see that an opportunity had availed itself, and then you invest in that opportunity.

jared: That must have been a proud moment, given Kenya's experiences with electoral violence. But it required the use of dialogue practices that happened outside

140   *Abiosseh Davis and jared l. ordway*

a traditional boardroom, with you all listening and willing to support intervillage practices, with parties and their ideas "at the wheel."

ON GENDER AND WOMEN'S MEANINGFUL PARTICIPATION

We asked Lopode to comment on what role she plays in the team as a woman and about the challenges of supporting the opportunity for women to be part of these processes. Her reply highlights the barriers that the patriarchal cultural practices create for the full and active participation of women in official peace meetings. However, she also shows how thinking creatively about what dialogue is and where it takes place makes space for women to contribute. Women can speak openly on the margins of Barazas,[2] in the markets and in other informal settings, when purposefully engaged. What they say in these spaces can then be brought into the mainstream of the community conversation without violating principles of self-determination. Members of the Interpeace team have opted not to forcefully adjust power imbalances in these early stages but instead open dialogue in creative spaces and through women-only groups.

The combined power of careful *observation* and *attending* as core practices of a transformative facilitator are reflected strongly in Lopode's points. The example showcases the power of process co-design to enable broader community ownership about issues that are relevant to all, particularly on issues that men (in their unique gendered roles and perspectives) either dismissed or overlooked. By adapting to opportunities that come up she is following participants and supporting them in realizing these opportunities.

Lopode: Because the communities we are working with are highly patriarchal, we don't do so many meetings for women. If you [as facilitators] are imposing this structure, it's because we need to meet the target number of women in our meetings for donor requirements, that is imposing [on how the community works]. You'll speak with women and there will be no decision [from them] at all. Sometimes they won't even speak completely, and you have to push and ask directed questions, so the answers will be sometimes *yes* or *no*, or no response at all.

I do facilitation when we have women or when we have a meeting bringing men and women together. Yes, women will come to the Barazas, sit at the edges, but won't speak. In the whole Baraza, you have like ten women and one hundred men. So you have to take it a step further, just go have a normal conversation and engage two or three women who are sitting close to you to find out: *what are they facing, as women?* Or you go and buy sugar here and there, ask them how their kids are, and so forth. Then you get to realize what is pressing and see what you can do as an organization. It doesn't have to be broadcasted in the whole Baraza. You have to push yourself to engage these women. You see some of them are really frustrated.

Navigating Dialogue in Complex Conflict Systems   141

Abi: But at some point, these power imbalances may become important to confront more directly, right? Any reflections on dealing with these kind of power imbalances within and/or between the communities?

Lopode: The *intra* part helps a lot with this [power imbalance]. So if you are in a meeting and you discover that [only] one or two women have spoken, and they have so much to say but you feel like it's not really coming out well, you see broader parts [of their concerns] will also be missing. You can go a step further and organize *intra women-only* meetings where now you get all these ideas to come up. If you [later] convene the rest of the community, either you [as a facilitator] or the women can bring up the ideas, the key points you picked up from the women-only groups where you see [issues] coming out clearly, whereas not so many [men] were [previously] speaking about them. And [only then] you'll discover that they will *all* own [those issues].

An example is where the [Turkana] women themselves are saying, "Pokot women are suffering." When you bring it to the general community, you realize now the whole community owns this idea where they feel like Pokot are suffering, where they [recognize they] have to travel miles and can't access hospitals, or veterinary doctors who can't access areas when there's conflict.

So now they bring up these issues. The whole group was [ignoring this] because it was just women who spoke about it, [while] the men were [instead] speaking about cattle raids only; you miss out on this aspect where it's actually a key point that will bring these communities together because they share the challenge and share what they see: the other community is actually losing out or facing troubles. [These comments] actually show compassion. They actually start [further] conversation. If [we as facilitators then] go to Pokots and tell them, "Turkana women are feeling that you Pokot (women) are suffering so much," they're like, "oh, these guys are actually feeling for us, they have compassion for women, they have compassion for our children," and that drives the conversation further.

jared: What you describe there, Lopode, with the Turkana women acknowledging the suffering of Pokot women is what a Transformative practitioner would see as an important shift toward recognition. Nondirective facilitation and co-design starts at the *intra*group level; and it is as much about listening for what's *not* being said, or being said by certain members of the community, while being dismissed by others. The process thus supports more inclusive listening. Your facilitation role helps to enable a much broader, more inclusive, richer discussion around diverse needs and concerns.

Lopode: Yeah. Sometimes it's not really planned. You just adapt in the moment, adapt to the meetings. Sometimes you [engage/facilitate] an extra day because you [organize] a women-only meeting or a youth-only meeting to get these points to come out more clearly, so they can actually be owned [by the larger community]. A group of women in a community [name] these challenges and even sometimes come up with solutions. So mostly it's adapting, not what we went out there intending to do, but what we saw coming up as an opportunity.

142 *Abiosseh Davis and jared l. ordway*

ON IDENTITY

Identity plays a role in this work in several ways. There are tribal identities like Pokot and Turkana as well as clan identities like Garre and Degodia. And there are gender identities. But there are also identities as insiders and outsiders. Hassan's comments show that in addition to a facilitator's identity, trust in a facilitator is also determined by their integrity, which is a function of their history with the community. Other identities also matter, such as professional identities. These intersectional identities give license to ask hard questions and contest destructive patterns, provoking reflection without supplanting parties' decisions. Indeed, identity has become a conscious cornerstone of the Interpeace team's approach to Transformative Dialogue and facilitation roles.

The discussion here also shows the potential benefit of "insiders" and "outsiders" working together. The collaboration within teams across geographies and identities, such as the "outsider" role Hassan plays in the North Rift, has also proven effective for trust building with stakeholders at critical moments. This is yet another example of how the teams have combined the insight and wisdom of "insiders" with an orientation to principled co-design, making their work so effective.

Abi: How do your identities as facilitators play into the work you are doing?

Hassan: Identity always plays an important role, factoring into challenges around legitimacy. I have enjoyed across the board community trust in my engagement, even though I am a [majority clan] Garre, because of two things: (1) When people see a Garre facilitator and Garre leadership on board, they see [promise in it] because Garre are the biggest community in Mandera and hold most political power. And the other thing is (2) your role in the community and what you've done in the past. For example, [our colleague] Mahat who is team lead for Mandera, he comes from Wajir, but he's been a teacher in Mandera for so many years, and he comes from a minority group from another community. But since he's worked in Mandera for many years, when he appears and engages [conflict parties] there is already mutual respect. The issue is not just your identity but also your history, your capacity to influence changes positively, and your voice of condemnation for violence.

I could condemn both the Degodia and Garre in the same meeting for the permissibility of crime. I could criticize them. But if you use your one identity card or tribe [association] alone, it won't reinforce your mediative capacity [to support parties]. For example, I was also a teacher, and Kenya representative coordinator for humanitarian affairs, so [people] knew me for my role. People [now] say, "don't look at him just as his tribe." Identity is important, but it must be coupled with other traits and past experiences to really be relevant. If your history is not known, it will be difficult to [be effective in] the mediator role.

Abi: In complex environments, are there other identity-related challenges?

Hassan: When [one community is] humiliating the other, and you come with the message of peace, it's difficult for them to understand you. The way your identity supports you or not with the other communities, it can also go bad with your own group. They have also been killed and lost animals. So when you tell them, "Let's go talk peace," they say: "we are being killed," they look at you like a traitor, as a spy, [or] they want to influence you negatively by saying, "we want to defeat them and teach them a lesson." But [what matters is] your consistency of balance [to send the message] that it's not just about the conflict, it's about the future, and remind them: You are all neighbors. You may come from a *stronger or weaker* group, but in all these years, *no community has ever defeated the other one. That's the reality.*

Job: Particularly when your community is the powerful one—in my case, [people are] always [accusing] [my group, the Pokot, screaming,] "Pokot this, Pokot that!" When [I as a Pokot] stand to talk about peace, others will always question: "what are you telling us, because the example is just not there!" But if you show your stand about peace and share what the advantages [are], slowly, they will see the reasoning in what you are doing. For example, [in an area where we work] some Pokot politicians were [using speech to incite violence] and the [non-Pokot] communities were calling to ask me about my stand or opinion. I confirmed to them that peace is a superordinate goal. This opinion was going against the politicians whose words hold value. We use that opportunity to pose that type of challenging question. One of our strengths is that [our team] has representation from each community. If communities are not opening up simply because [I as] a Pokot [am] sitting there, we sometimes excuse ourselves and then the [team member] from that community takes the co-facilitation lead, trying to use the opportunity to vent and share the observations.

Abi: Can you say something about the significance of an "outside mediator" versus an "insider mediator," like yourselves?

Hassan: The mix is the best, if you are able to get an inside and outside mediator. [For outsiders] it takes time and learning, which [can] slow down the process. When outsiders work together [with insiders] or if an [outsider] mediator has had a similar experience, if they can relate to the inside mediation process, and have their principles clear, then it can be collaborative and supportive.

When there is an insider mediator, the real issues and cause of conflict will be [better] articulated, not some cosmetic cause—people will be genuine about impediments to peace and what they are fighting over. The insider knows what's happening in the environment and appreciates what is being discussed, [whether it] is true or slightly not true. They have the [linguistic] capacity to authenticate, to know who the gatekeepers and spoilers are, who is being sincere or not, and who to avoid or not. So that is very influential. But when the conflict has stayed for long, when it's interstate or protracted, when it's reached a point where insider mediators work is difficult, you will find better convening power by externals, due to [their multipartiality], who can provide more support to the team.

When I'm in the North Rift, I'm viewed as an *external*, so whenever there is suspicion [by communities that one or another of our team members] will undermine things, my presence provides external trust in the sense that I [don't have a local stake in the game], but I share similar history of experiencing violence, as well as how we got out of the challenges. That gives some elements of trust. The mix is good: an insider mediator [knows how to build] consensus quickly, while the external takes time to understand the context [but affords trust]. If you didn't have the experience of lifestyle like pastoralists, if you come from the cities and cannot appreciate the pasture and water fights, you cannot be effective. Though externals who bring a similar history [from elsewhere] can still add to that experience.

Even as an insider, absolute trust by the parties will be questioned, and that can be complemented by the external mediators who people will see as somebody who can be fairer, with no bias. All of us have human biases. Just because you as an insider [may] have been involved in other processes, you could be *over*exposed by other processes. You may assume you understand and take things for granted. You might be influenced by the environment and [easily] make too many assumptions. For example, if you are a Borana or Gabra mediating in Marsabit, it's easy to fit into the [dominant] narrative and undermine [if you] start forgetting the long history of violence. You [might not] be able to understand the inner core that can slip underneath you, the trauma, etc. You may have even the right set of mediation skills, but if there is a long history of violence, it may not be very easy as an insider to facilitate a process. In an intractable conflict, an external mediator could be better.

CLOSING REMARKS

We hope that the conversations and perspectives shared in this chapter will inspire other practitioners to see the benefits of the Transformative approach, especially at this time when others are seeing the value of making conflict intervention work itself dialogical and adaptive (see, for example, Lehti 2018 and Muto, de Coning, and Saraiva 2022). The promising outcomes associated with the efforts of Interpeace's teams in Kenya can inspire opportunities for conversation among practitioners, donors, and stakeholders about the benefits of Transformative work. We also hope this chapter encourages further exchange among practitioners across diverse socio-cultural and/or political orders about the adaptation and application of Transformative Dialogue beyond North America and Europe.

We are grateful for the insights that team members Lopode, Murshid, Kenedy, Job, and Interpeace Kenya's country representative Hassan Ismail have been willing to share about their past and ongoing efforts. Their stories and reflections illustrate coherence between Transformative Dialogue's core premises and their own work, fostering a basis on which to further explore and critically unpack those tenets and their applications in non-Western complex, conflict-affected contexts.

NOTES

1. Teams often refer to "the professionals" as external mediators or attorneys working in service of either the county government or peace NGOs that have historically been involved in organizing ceasefire processes.

2. *Baraza* is "a Kiswahili word meaning a public meeting(s) that is used as a platform for creating awareness, responding to issues affecting a given community."

13

Asymmetries among Allies

How Working Transformatively Can Contribute to Dialogue in Wartime Ukraine

Josh Nadeau

At the moment of writing this article, the full-scale Russian invasion of Ukraine has lasted for over two years and has caused massive destruction to life, livelihood, and civic infrastructure. It has spawned a global crisis, involved major powers, and is the largest land war in Europe since the Second World War. It has proved deeply complex and has had a major impact on both Ukraine and on the world. As of now, it is not clear how or when it will end.

As the most extensive war in Europe since World War II, there has been widespread destruction. There are estimates that civilian and military casualties on both sides have surpassed 150,000 and may be significantly higher (OHCHR 2024; Armstrong 2024; Mediazona 2024; UA Losses n.d.). There has been a massive destruction of infrastructure and in some cases entire cities. Displacement is now commonplace with between 3.7 to nearly five million citizens living as internally displaced persons (IDPs) throughout the country, and other European countries hosting approximately six million refugees as of early 2024 (People in Need 2024). The war is a cause of major psychological stress for citizens across the beleaguered nation, especially for soldiers who are currently or were formerly on the frontlines of fighting or civilians who have fled from or still live close to combat zones. Soldiers returning from active duty have been impacted by brutal violence and are at risk of reproducing violence at home. Government ministers, policy makers, and other officials are faced with complex decisions, often with more needs that must be met than resources to meet them.

That has not stopped many discussions among different parties about what an eventual peace could and should look like and what roles various actors may have in building that peace. One of the many groups asking precisely these questions is the Ukrainian Community of Dialogue Practitioners (UCoDP), a group consisting of mediators and dialogue

145

facilitators with long experience with conflict work in Ukraine. This network worked closely with researchers at the National University of Kyiv-Mohyla Academy's Mediation and Dialogue Research Center (MDRC), as well as with various international partners.

Between 2014 and early 2022 dialogues were convened to address issues like tensions between IDPs and the communities hosting them, the reintegration of returning veterans, disputes between government figures on key topics like transitional justice or how to reintegrate occupied territories, as well as creating space for discussion and exchange between Ukrainian and Russian citizens or between residents of government-controlled or non-government-controlled areas, the latter referring to territories occupied by Russia from 2014 until early 2022.

In addition to the many grassroots-level dialogues that were organized, often with international funding (Kyselova and Moseiko 2021), dialogues were also coordinated by international nongovernmental organizations (NGOs) like the Martti Ahtisaari Peace Foundation (CMI), the Centre for Humanitarian Dialogue (HD), or by international organizations such as the Organization for Security and Co-operation in Europe (OSCE). Many of the local practitioners facilitating or mediating these processes originally came from backgrounds other than peacebuilding, such as law, family mediation, activism, and others (Kyselova 2017). However, the realities of the conflict, as well as international attention and funding, prompted them to focus on the impact of the war.

In this chapter I will first discuss how the full-scale invasion has impacted the work of Ukrainian dialogue practitioners and raised questions about what dialogue is as well as what its role could or should be in wartime. Second, I will explore how the war has also revealed tensions between the way Ukrainian practitioners view the possibilities and limitations of dialogue in the current situation and the way certain international peacebuilding practitioners do, leading to a conflict between peace practitioners who, in many ways, are allies. This tension raises important questions about the relationship between peace and dialogue and the meaning of local ownership. Finally, I reflect on how Transformative Dialogue can address these challenges in ways that respect the experience of Ukrainian practitioners and center their agency while also pointing to the role that international interveners could play in supporting dialogue work. This chapter is based on the experience I have had working with Ukrainian dialogue practitioners prior to and following the Russian invasion in 2022, as well as with members of the broader international community of dialogue practice. It is important to note that I am writing from the position of a practitioner who condemns the Russian invasion of Ukraine and am writing about dynamics concerning Ukrainians and international practitioners who likewise find the invasion to be illegitimate.

THE UKRAINIAN COMMUNITY OF DIALOGUE PRACTITIONERS

The war has confronted Ukrainian dialogue practitioners with a number of challenges (Kryshtal, Kotiuk, and Kyselova 2023). Many have had to take care of their own safety in the early days of the invasion, evacuating from their homes and moving to other cities in Ukraine or even to other countries in Europe. Many put dialogue work on hold in order to help with humanitarian efforts, which especially in the short term involved evacuation and the provision of aid, both to IDPs and to heavily hit towns and regions. They have also worked on projects aimed at addressing their co-citizens' psychological needs.

For example, a number of UCoDP members served as mediators in "mobile teams," where they collaborated with psychologists in small groups that were deployed primarily to large cities with sizable IDP populations (Eihelson et al. 2023). There they could respond with substantial freedom and agility to emerging tensions around issues like regional stereotypes, the use of the Russian language, or other issues emerging between local residents, IDPs, NGOs, and local authorities.

But the war also prompted reflection—they had worked for eight years to address conflict, but war nevertheless erupted. This led to the emergence of major existential questions: What can dialogue do in the face of ongoing, armed clashes? Can practitioners support nonviolent approaches like dialogue alongside armed resistance? How can one justify allocating severely limited psychological or temporal resources to organizing dialogue during an acute humanitarian crisis? Tensions also arose regarding how to respond to international expectations of what Ukrainians should do, as well as to what the field of peacebuilding might suggest as solutions.

In response to this, the UCoDP initiated a reflective session to discuss whether they could reach consensus concerning the role dialogue could play at that particular moment. Their discussions resulted in a statement released in May 2022 called "7 Points on the War and Dialogue from Ukrainian Mediators and Dialogue Facilitators," released through the MDRC (7 Points 2022).

The 7 Points Statement raised a number of important issues regarding dialogue and war. The statement affirms the community's support for armed resistance while declaring that nonviolent mechanisms like dialogue are nevertheless crucial for building and maintaining lasting peace. However, and perhaps more significantly, the community also claimed that many types of dialogue were themselves inappropriate during the hot phase of the war.

While high-level negotiation and dialogue were seen as key for progress on technical issues like coordinating prisoner exchanges or grain export from Ukraine's Black Sea ports, UCoDP members warned that convening cross-contact line dialogue, that is, dialogue between Ukrainians on different sides of the contact line, or between Ukrainians and Russians, even Russians with pro-Ukrainian sentiments, was premature and potentially harmful for several reasons. First, because of the psychological asymmetries present, especially in the early days of the full-scale invasion: Ukrainians were thought to be more likely to perceive Russians as a threat than Russians were Ukrainians, placing them under additional stress and making dialogue more difficult for them than for the other side. "The expectation that, in this state," the statement reads, "people can actively listen and understand others, which are necessary components of dialogue, are unrealistic" (7 Points 2022).

Second, dialogue in a conflict setting is often thought to involve what is known as *transfer*—the process by which the insights and breakthroughs generated in a dialogue are hoped to impact the broader conflict context (Fisher 2020). This may take place through reports delivered to official negotiation teams, content generated for distribution through traditional or new media outlets, or by involving important policy makers in the dialogue itself (Çuhadar and Paffenholz 2020). UCoDP members claimed that fundamental political differences in Ukraine and Russia, with the former possessing a democratic and the latter an authoritarian governance system, meant that while Ukrainian citizens are able in theory to impact policy, even influential Russian dialogue participants were framed as having little influence over their government or army. A related but noteworthy asymmetry involves the fact that Russia lacks the sort of well-organized community of experienced dialogue facilitators that Ukraine enjoys, which may further inhibit the application of dialogue as a tool in that nation.

Instead Ukrainian practitioners highlighted more immediate ways to apply dialogue in the country, in forms that they viewed as less problematic. This included much of the work they had been engaged in since 2014: assisting with tensions arising from internal and external displacement; improving social cohesion among different social sectors; building relationships between residents, humanitarian actors, and local government; and consolidating bridges between government and civil society.

Of note here is the fact that the 7 Points Statement was produced in the early phase of the full-scale invasion and responded to the realities of that particular time. In a number of conversations I have had with practitioners who contributed to the statement, it was clear that further changes would come over time through additional reflection. Rather than being a statement against all possibility of cross-contact dialogue ever, it is important to note that members of the UCoDP released the statement in response to foreign pressure that pushed for immediate person-to-person dialogue across the contact line—it was meant as a way to inform the international community about realities as experienced on the ground as well as to prevent potential harm stemming from well-intentioned but potentially underinformed desires to work toward peace.

One aspect that the statement emphasized explicitly was the principle of *local ownership*, a concept broadly discussed in the peacebuilding field that refers to the push to center the agency of local actors in peace processes, rather than external actors and experts (Donais 2009). The idea of local ownership has been gaining traction in the international peacebuilding community over the past decade (Richmond 2012). In many conversations that I had, local ownership was often described as making sure that nothing of great import and with great implications for Ukrainians should be planned without the involvement of Ukrainians themselves.

In the current context, this could include consulting with Ukrainians on potential dialogue processes and hiring local facilitators when possible. At the same time, the UCoDP drew attention to the kinds of dialogue that were indeed seen as immediately necessary and appropriate to the moment. This included dialogue among host communities and IDPs (inside Ukraine) or refugees (outside of Ukraine), between civil society and the government, or to improve social cohesion among citizens, humanitarian actors, or administrative regions.

While these concerns were not developed at length in the 7 Points, a number of Ukrainian colleagues I have spoken to claim that many peacebuilding norms accepted as standard practice today were developed in response to intrastate conflicts that emerged in the period following the end of the Cold War. They claimed that strategies stemming from this experience fail to take into account the interstate, great power nature of the Russian invasion. In other words, the invasion was initiated by a government that is less amenable to the kind of influence these dialogues hope to produce, meaning that progress would likely be found primarily on the Ukrainian side. Thus, presenting dialogue as a means of addressing the war without taking into account this asymmetry could potentially amount to a false promise, which, in addition to other harms, may damage the reputation of dialogue as a tool among Ukrainians.

Important here is the notion of a theory of change, which is a theory of how an intervention (that is, dialogue) is supposed to lead to a hoped-for change in a given society (Shapiro 2006). Some dialogues are designed with particular theories of change in mind, for example, including influential participants in the dialogue who have the ear of policy makers in relevant countries (Fisher 2020). In a number of conversations I have had with Ukrainian practitioner colleagues, they argued that dialogue that doesn't have a theory of change is ineffectual at best and irresponsible at worst.

CONFLICT AMONG PRACTITIONERS

The text of the 7 Points Statement was an invitation on the part of UCoDP members to international practitioners who condemned the Russian invasion, framed as a way to offer a more informed allyship with Ukrainian practitioners. The 7 Points themselves were widely shared among conflict resolution professionals, many of whom used their positions and platforms to amplify the voices of the signatories (Berghof Foundation 2022; ICIP 2022; PCI 2022; Tolsdorff 2023).

That said, not everyone agreed with what the UCoDP proposed, even among international peacebuilders who supported the liberal world order and condemned the Russian invasion as immoral. Within the circles that I move in, criticism of the statement was focused on issues such as supporting armed resistance to the Russian army, the idea that certain kinds of dialogue were inappropriate, and the degree to which Ukrainian experience should be uniquely centered in discussions of how to reach peace.

The international critics of armed resistance in Ukraine that I have had contact with were motivated by a number of factors ranging from pacifist sentiment (the country would suffer less loss of life by resisting under occupation than from the ongoing war) to fears of escalation (the suffering of Ukrainians left under occupation, while tragic, would be nothing compared to the horrors of a potential nuclear confrontation between NATO and Russia). Many such critics assembled at the International Summit for Peace in Ukraine held in Vienna in June 2023. While the organizers in Vienna would change their language in their eventual statement, initial discourse around the summit highlighted NATO alongside Russia as a key root of the conflict and blamed Western weapons delivery to Ukraine as part of the reason why the war had not ended. Some even called for the halting of arms deliveries as a way to incentivize Ukraine's return to the negotiating table, which was hoped to hasten an immediate ceasefire.

This line of reasoning was concerning to many Ukrainians, including members of the UCoDP, as the supply of arms was seen as one of the only ways to resist further Russian destruction of cities as well as making possible the liberation of occupied areas, as had occurred in parts of Kharkiv, Kherson, and Donetsk regions in late 2022. Many Ukrainian practitioners worked to counter this line of thought by releasing additional statements like the Ukraine Peace Appeal, which advocated for what practitioners called a "more informed solidarity" (Ukraine Peace Appeal 2023). The appeal drew attention to a central dilemma: ending arms support without a symmetrical response from Russia could amount to Ukrainian capitulation and total Russian occupation of the country, likely resulting in suffering and mass migration from Ukraine into neighboring countries already under strain. Those left under occupation, often the elderly, the low income, and others unable or afraid to relocate, would suffer oppression and potentially even execution should pro-Ukrainian views be discovered.

Some international practitioners were also resistant to the claim that some forms of dialogue were not appropriate at that time. I have had conversations with a number of international colleagues who were deeply surprised when they read the 7 Points Statement, as they felt that there is always space for dialogue, or that when space seems not to exist, it is the task of the facilitator and the peacebuilder to create it, not to warn against dialogue. In certain conversations, I even heard concerns that, at best, Ukrainian facilitators may have been traumatized into us-them thinking instead of looking to transcend it, and, at worst, that UCoDP members were acting "territorially," not allowing for other professionals, ones with decades of experience, to do their work. In effect, these critics saw statements like the 7 Points as creating artificial and unnecessary barriers to forms of dialogue that were seen by these practitioners as necessary and timely.

A number of my Ukrainian colleagues have also argued for a shift away from classic peacebuilding approaches, which emphasize compromise and meeting the interests and needs of both sides (Miall 2023; Paffenholz et al. 2023). Such approaches may produce proposals advocating for changes to Ukraine's official borders, a commitment on the part of the country not to seek NATO accession, and other compromises in the interest of negative peace. These were perceived as an admission that Russian desires are more important than Ukraine's rights. Instead some UCoDP members propose a model where aggressors and victims are clearly defined and support is given to victims, in this case Ukraine. They framed this as a more "just" vision of peace (Right to Protection 2023).

Ukrainian practitioners and some international peacebuilders have also differed in their approaches to local ownership. Many Ukrainian practitioners, as well as other members of Ukrainian civil society, declare the primary conflict as between Ukraine and Russia and argue that framing Ukraine as a privileged victim in the conflict, and reacting accordingly, is key to challenging structural patterns that create asymmetries like the one that Ukraine is experiencing now with regard to Russia (Sustainable Peace Manifesto n.d.). Certain international practitioners have instead identified two to three loci of conflict, with Ukraine-Russia being only one. The others include (1) a "cold war" between Russia and NATO and (2) conflicts inside Ukraine itself, especially but not limited to those between Ukrainians who support Kyiv or Moscow (Miall 2023; Paffenholz et al. 2023). Private conversations I've had with international colleagues also highlight the stakes of the war as an argument against total local ownership: the dangers of escalation are high, and the potential for a nuclear war means that Ukrainians' needs are not the only ones that need to be taken into account.

In contrast, conversations among Ukrainian colleagues recognize these dangers but nevertheless warn against the potential of these arguments to erase the harsh realities of present Ukrainian suffering, or that they may be used to "sacrifice" Ukrainian well-being on an altar of nonescalation, as it were.

Following the release of the Ukrainian Peace Appeal in the wake of the Vienna conference, members of the UCoDP organized their own conference in Kyiv where they promoted "Ukrainian approaches to a just and lasting peace" that highlighted these dilemmas and attempted to center Ukrainian voices and agency in the debate. In this and other forums, Ukrainian practitioners warned their allies and other outside observers that not all types of peace are equal: a ceasefire that does not address the root causes of the conflict would in effect "freeze" the conflict, leaving Ukrainians to suffer under occupation in exchange for a deescalation that could ultimately prove temporary. Furthermore, some suggested that proposals to hand over some or all of the occupied territories to Russia as a condition for peace could embolden Russia to come back in a future invasion to take more land (Right to Protection 2023).

Such interprofessional conflicts between peacebuilders, and dialogue facilitators in particular, have the potential to take up time and resources and divide response to what is, in effect, a hot war. Time spent on addressing such conflicts is time not spent on preparing joint action, conceptualizing innovative visions of peace, and laying the groundwork for eventual dialogue on the ground. With the high stakes involved in the war, these divisions amount to, in my opinion, a tragedy. Peacebuilders are, as it were, fighting with each other rather than fighting for peace.

TRANSFORMATIVE DIALOGUE

Transformative Dialogue is characterized by a number of traits that are relevant to this discussion. Rather than being driven by a goal of peace, Transformative practitioners are driven by a belief in Transformative premises that posit that people have the motivation and the capacity to connect meaningfully with others and to make self-determined choices even in situations of adversity. The goal of a Transformative organizer or facilitator of dialogue is therefore to support, but never supplant, people's agency as they figure out what is best for them in a given situation. A Transformative practitioner would always start from the position that people themselves know their situation best, and because they have to live with the consequences of their decisions, they should be the ones making them. Thus, it is not up to the facilitator to decide whether or not dialogue is appropriate; it is up to the potential participants.

Because of this focus on the agency of people in conflict, Transformative practitioners do not make assumptions about what kind of dialogue is most appropriate. Intergroup dialogue is not favored over intragroup dialogue. Instead people themselves work with a facilitator or organizer to find out who needs to talk to whom, about what, and how. Rather than try to make space for dialogue in a way that ignores the context of the situation, Transformative practice follows the participants and, in that way, co-creates a process that meets the needs on the ground in ways defined by people themselves.

A major focus here is on learning to "live with no," even if practitioners hoped to reach a "yes" (Cleven, Bush, and Saul 2018). This entails a lack of pressure to reach a "yes" or to engage in dialogue that feels designed to push parties toward that option. While this may seem to slow proceedings, this is only the case if the goal is peace. If, instead, the goal is to support people as they make decisions for themselves in difficult circumstances, then it is exactly what is needed in the given situation. It is certainly clear that agreements reached as a result of pressure are likely to be less sustainable over time. In addition, when that pressure is absent, it may make the thought of dialogue more palatable for actors who would not otherwise participate in the process, thereby making it potentially more inclusive.

That said, the focus of this chapter is not only the Russian invasion of Ukraine but also the dispute between conflict resolution practitioners with different ideas of what peace should look like and how to build it. As with the war, this conflict is asymmetrical—one party, namely the Ukrainian dialogue practitioners, is uniquely affected in a way that their international counterparts are not. Furthermore, the conflict between professional dialogue communities, while minor in comparison to the ongoing war, may nevertheless have an impact on the capacity of the Ukrainian practitioners to respond effectively to the consequences of the invasion. That said, Transformative principles can point to ways forward through this dispute.

First, the Transformative approach would center the experience of those particularly affected by the conflict, in this case the Ukrainian practitioners. Importantly, this does not mean that the concerns of certain international practitioners are less legitimate. Indeed, concerns about possible escalation and world war are deeply legitimate. Instead this would be an invitation to view the experience of the Ukrainian practitioners, along with their arguments that not all types of dialogue with various Russian parties are appropriate, not as a barrier to "real" dialogue that needs to be removed in order for the work to begin but as the very starting point of the work itself. For international practitioners who disagree with the sentiments expressed in statements like the 7 Points or the Peace Appeal, this can mean engaging in dialogue with their Ukrainian counterparts, not as outside experts or facilitators but as participants themselves. In other words, "centering" the Ukrainian experience may express itself first in acknowledging and taking into account the unique situation of Ukrainian facilitators as conflict-affected practitioners rather than amounting to immediate agreement with the content of the statements.

Second, the Transformative approach also lends support to the Ukrainian request to focus not only on cross-contact line dialogues with Russian representatives but on other types as well This includes dialogue within Ukrainian society whether between government–civil society, IDPs–host communities–local government, or among distinct societal groups. Dialogue may also assist with conversations between Ukrainians remaining in the country and those living outside its borders, as well as between Ukrainians and international allies. For international practitioners who see dialogue as an immediate tool that should be used to address major issues like the Russian offensive, growing militarism, or the risk of nuclear escalation, the forms of dialogue promoted by the UCoDP may be framed as a first step toward addressing these necessary concerns. One type of dialogue that is especially possible right now is dialogue between these international practitioners and their Ukrainian counterparts where they bring these legitimate questions to the table. Instead of framing Ukrainian practitioners as an obstacle to dialogues on those themes—or bypassing them completely, which historically has contributed to resentment or resistance on their side—international practitioners may engage with them directly.

Third, I deeply believe that one of the most important traits of any dialogue process must involve not looking at Ukrainian conflict affectedness with condescension or as a "disbalance" that needs to be "healed" before talking about perceivably more serious issues like militarism or escalation. Instead Ukrainian experience, in this context, is a teacher for all groups involved. And international practitioners have the opportunity to journey with their Ukrainian colleagues through this process.

Finally, a key element in the Transformative approach is highlighting agency and choice as a way to address feelings of powerlessness, asymmetry, or vulnerability. I had a moving conversation with a Ukrainian colleague where she described herself as having two "hats," one of which is her practitioner "hat" with which she recognizes the complexities of the conflict from multiple sides, and one of which is her Ukrainian "hat" with which she experiences the conflict from the inside. Processing this paradox is a unique element of the journey Ukrainian practitioners are taking right now, and the Transformative approach may help international practitioners who disagree with the Ukrainian statements to create space for processing this Ukrainian experience in ways they find acceptable while also leaving the door open for exchange, insight, and progress on particular issues. By highlighting agency and choice and conversations that bring more clarity about the situation, Transformative work also supports and strengthens local capacities that are important at every stage of the process from war to peace.

There is potentially much more room for movement than international practitioners may have suspected after first reading the 7 Points, which was itself a strongly worded statement released near the beginning of the full-scale invasion. I have participated in conversations and dialogues with Ukrainian colleagues, their allies, and their advisors in which we have discussed the nature of what Russian-Ukrainian dialogues could be in the future. Finding themselves in a space of agency, strength, and resourcedness may indeed enable my Ukrainian colleagues to face other dialogue tasks from a position of increased capacities. International practitioners can help enable this process, presenting fewer barriers to its development by acknowledging the legitimate concerns in a Transformative manner and letting them form the ground floor of the discussion instead of framing them as issues to be overcome in order to begin dialogue work. Statements like the 7 Points or the Peace Appeal do not demark the boundaries or an end point after which dialogue cannot take place. Rather, from a Transformative perspective, they may indicate a conflict-sensitive, locally informed place to start.

CONCLUSION

Applying the approaches embodied in Transformative Dialogue could provide a useful way for dialogue practitioners to move forward as they approach disputes and differences within their communities against the backdrop of a full-scale war. The method's focus on agency and choice, its acceptance of people where they are, its openness to the importance of intragroup conversation, and its acknowledgment that small steps matter whether or not "big" peace deals result can itself form the basis for difficult conversations between practitioners who disagree on what peace should look like and how to build it.

14

Monitoring and Evaluating Relational Outcomes in Transformative Dialogue Processes

Erik Cleven

WHY THIS CHAPTER?

It may seem strange to include a chapter on monitoring and evaluation in a book that is focused on how to co-create a dialogue process. If this seems strange, it may be because evaluation, the systematic effort to understand changes that result from our work or what difference that work made, is often thought of as something that is done at the end of a process, when the work is finished. Because monitoring and evaluation involves time and resources it often becomes little more than a box-ticking activity, in spite of the good intentions of those involved. In fact, evaluation is most effective when it is planned from the outset of a program or project, and it can be an important learning activity and an important part of the dialogue process itself. In the context of Transformative Dialogue, which is a co-created process, monitoring and evaluation is also co-created. It is the participants in the process who are best able to identify the significance of changes that have occurred within a given context and to define which changes really matter.

The chapters in this volume tell the stories of Transformative Dialogues that were carried out in a number of different contexts: in a postwar context with deep divisions between clans in Somalia; dealing with a racist incident in a workplace in the Netherlands; the way that Dayton, Ohio, dealt with the relationship between the police and the community after the death of a young Black man; relationships between different professional groups in a large healthcare organization in the United Kingdom and the Netherlands; and difficult conversations about race in southern Maryland. In all of these situations, communication was difficult and often characterized by mistrust, suspicion, stress and trauma, feelings of animosity, and a sense that people were not being heard. The goal of these dialogues was to alleviate these problems, but it's important to note that all of these problems are fundamentally relational.

Monitoring and evaluating any process is difficult, but it is even more difficult when what one is evaluating is linked to the type of relational change supported by the Transformative approach as in the previous examples. Relational change can be hard to "see" and is certainly more difficult to observe than concrete material changes, like building a school or installing wells. Monitoring and evaluation is also made challenging because different actors have different interests in evaluating program activities. Donors want to know their money was not wasted. Board members of an organization promoting dialogue want to document that the work is doing what it aims to do. Project managers want to know that what they are doing is making a difference, and they want to convince donors of this. Reflective practitioners want to learn from their activities and improve their work. Community members and participants also want to see clearly the positive changes that have taken place. At the same time, the kind of relational changes that dialogue work aims to promote can take time to develop. They don't necessarily happen after just one meeting.

Transformative processes aim to change the quality of conflict interaction from negative to positive and to ensure that participants are making the decisions about the process, content, participation, and outcomes of dialogue. How would one know whether such changes have occurred and how would one document that for participants, donors, or local authorities? For what overall end or purpose? What does it look like to do monitoring and evaluation Transformatively? Given the variety of contexts in which Transformative Dialogue occurs, how will we know what meaningful change looks like in a given context? To answer these questions, I will first introduce the idea of evaluation and what it is. Following this I will describe how Transformative practitioners can help individuals and groups document changes that result from dialogue and why monitoring and evaluation of Transformative processes must also be co-created. Finally, I will discuss why evaluation is important for Transformative practitioners. Because this book presents Transformative Dialogue in many contexts, I will use examples from a variety of situations.

WHAT IS MONITORING AND EVALUATION?

Evaluation is about assessing the value and meaning of something. It is often used to assess outcomes of a program or activity, to find out how it is operating, to assess its efficiency, or to understand why a program or activity accomplishes or fails to accomplish its intended outcomes. Evaluation can also be used to assess individual activities, like whether or not a training is successful. Evaluation is often carried out at periodic intervals or at the end of program or project activities. The questionnaire commonly filled out after a seminar is an example of this. But evaluation can also be integrated into an entire program, starting at the beginning, not the end. This *integrated evaluation* approach means that the process of evaluation is built into the

Monitoring and Evaluating Relational Outcomes in Transformative Dialogue Processes 157

program design from the very beginning. For reasons described in this chapter, this integrated evaluation is most appropriate for use with Transformative Dialogue.

Often evaluation focuses on two levels: internal and external validity. If an activity has internal validity it means that it was carried out well. If you say, "It was a good seminar," you are assessing internal validity. External validity is concerned with whether or not it was the right activity. In other words, even if the activity was done well or was a good activity, it may not have been the right activity to do in the given situation or to accomplish a desired end. If a dialogue process succeeds in improving relationships in a divided community, it was probably the right activity to carry out.

Monitoring is the systematic effort to track the achievement of program outcomes, often *during* but also at times following the completion of a process or project where significant complexity is involved. This sentence is full of jargon. So before talking about how to evaluate the relational outcomes that are a key goal of a Transformative Dialogue, let's define some terms and introduce the idea of the impact chain and the difference between activities, outputs, and outcomes. The impact chain can be expressed as follows:

Input → Activities → Outputs → Outcomes → Impact

Let's look at each term here individually:

- *Inputs* are the money, resources, skills, and time put into the work.
- These inputs make it possible to carry out *activities*. An activity could be a meeting, a dialogue session, a mediation, or a training.
- The *outputs* are the products of the activities in terms of things we can count: the number of trainings or the number of participants attending these sessions, the number of brochures printed and distributed, the number of hits at an internet site, etc. But these numbers do not tell us whether these activities, even if they involved a lot of people, were done well and actually made any difference to them or, if so, what kind of difference they made.
- The *outcomes* are the benefits or changes experienced by the participants in the activities. This could include
  - new knowledge or competence (for example, the skills to mediate as a result of a training),
  - new relationships and connections,
  - changed relationships or interactions (for example, conflict interaction could change from negative to positive),
  - changed attitudes or views, or
  - changed behaviors.
  One could say that outcomes are the answer to the questions, "why did our activities matter?" or "what difference did our activities make?"
- *Impact* is achieved if the participants in a program affect members of the community who were not directly involved in the program. For example, participants in an educational seminar put what they have learned to use in

158 *Erik Cleven*

the community and do things that positively affect or involve others. In other words, impact relates to participants' interactions with the wider community who did not participate in activities directly. We achieve impact to the extent that our participants are able to interact differently with others who did not participate directly in the program.

Because Transformative Dialogue is a co-created process where participants make the decisions about process, participation, content, and outcomes, monitoring and evaluation of Transformative processes also involves co-creation. In Transformative Dialogue one outcome that we work toward is always the same: that participants are able to interact in more positive and constructive ways, even when there is continued disagreement or conflict. This can be seen in empowerment and recognition shifts that occur as people interact with one another. Other outcomes may include changed relationships or patterns of interaction between different members of a community. These outcomes also may involve changed interaction across group divisions, but they may equally involve changed interaction between members of one group. But as we will see shortly, how we know whether these changes have been achieved is context specific, and it is up to participants to define which changes are really significant and how we would recognize them.

Evaluating both the internal and external validity of activities is something only participants can do. Was a particular activity the right activity to do? Community members need to answer that question, not external interveners. But as with other aspects of Transformative Dialogue, interveners give community members and participants the support they need to answer these questions.

OBSERVING RELATIONAL CHANGE

It is easy to count the number of participants at a meeting or the number of hits at a new website, but how do we observe outcomes, especially the relational outcomes that Transformative Dialogue seeks to promote? Remember, the goal of Transformative practice is to promote pro-social interaction, which means to support the individual empowerment and recognition shifts that allow people to interact with others from a place of clarity and responsiveness, whether or not they agree. We don't always think of relationships as something we can see, so we need a way to observe how relationships might shift or change both during and after a dialogue and whether or not there are ripple effects seen elsewhere in relevant spaces in the wider community. What would allow us to "see" empowerment and recognition shifts, changes in people's attitudes, and new ways that people are interacting?

We do this with *indicators*. Indicators are things we observe that tell us something about the people or organizations we are working with. Relational indicators can be things people say or the ways they interact. For example, in Lida van den Broek's chapter in this book she noted how participants arriving at a dialogue meeting did not shake hands. After the meeting they did shake hands before departing.

Monitoring and Evaluating Relational Outcomes in Transformative Dialogue Processes 159

Relational indicators might also be policy changes or the way policies are carried out, for example, with regard to service provision. For example, Anja Bekink and Angie Gaspar in their chapter describe how dialogue meetings in a healthcare setting led to a change in how shifts at a hospital were staffed. Outcomes and impacts manifest themselves in visible indicators, things we can actually see. For example, as people experience empowerment shifts, they become clearer and more decisive and they feel more confident and stronger. In Dayton, Ohio, Thomas Wahlrab describes how one participant felt they now were free to talk and had a voice, even though disagreement persisted. As people experience recognition shifts, people are less defensive and more responsive to others and are able to take the perspective of others and acknowledge why people have acted as they have. We can actually see this as people get calmer and acknowledge others in conversation.

Changed attitudes about members of another group may result in people who never interacted previously meeting for coffee in a local coffee shop. It might be hard to observe changed attitudes, but you can observe people having coffee together. This would indicate a changed relationship. Here are some categories of indicators to help you think about how you might "see," that is, monitor and evaluate, relational change.

Things People Say

Stories—What stories do people tell about themselves or about their conflict? How do they talk about themselves or members of other groups? Are others portrayed as adversaries? Are stereotypes expressed?

Statements—What kind of statements do people make to you? What kind of statements do people make in seminars or to the press? What do these statements tell us about how people view others or how they view the possibility of change?

Social media posts—What are people saying online?

Ways People Interact

Connections—Who is connected to whom? Do members of different groups in the community have connections with each other, to people in different communities or countries? Do they have connections to decision makers? Are people connected on social media?

Networks—Are there informal networks that are important to life in the community? How are they structured? How are they changing over time?

Conversations—What conversations take place (or don't) in the community or organization? Who talks to whom? What conversations do you see or hear when you visit the community? Do conversations happen only when initiated by a facilitator or are people themselves taking the initiative to interact with each other? Who comments on whose social media posts? What is the nature and tone of those comments?

Meetings—Who meets with whom? Who organizes or calls meetings?

160   *Erik Cleven*

Social events—What kind of social events happen in the community? Do members of different groups attend each other's social events such as weddings, high school graduations, funerals, etc.? Where do people socialize and who do they socialize with?

Transactions—Where do people shop? Which service providers do they use? Think about doctors, schools, parks, and recreational activities.

Divisions—Where are the lines of division in the organization or community? There may be groups in the community defined by ethnicity, race, religion, clan, sexual orientation, politics, or class. Which identity is most salient and creates separation? Are there *intra*group divisions? If you are working in an organization, divisions might be professional or disciplinary ones.

Cooperation—What kind of cooperation takes place, if any, across lines of division? Are there examples of cooperation that used to take place but no longer do? Have new forms of cooperation developed?

Competence, Institutions, and Policy

Knowledge and skills—What knowledge, skills, or competencies do people have? What skills do they lack?

Organizational structure—What characterizes the structure of organizations you are working with? How diverse are the organizations? Are there organizations that are diverse with regard to race, ethnicity, or religion or not? This could relate to religious organizations, sports clubs, voluntary associations, NGOs, and so on.

Institutions—What characterizes the institutions in the community, that is, schools, religious organizations (for example, churches, synagogues, or mosques), or the municipality?

Services—What characterizes the services offered by organizations or institutions? Who receives these services and who does not?

People can reveal a lot about their attitudes and opinions in the stories they tell and statements they make. If we ask people to tell us about a conflict or ask someone who they are, the answer will usually be in the form of a story. Transformative Dialogue involves many opportunities to hear people express these opinions either in one-on-one conversations or in meetings or seminars with others.

By paying attention to these categories of indicators we can learn something about relationships in the community, but the significance of each has to be understood in context, through the conversations we have with participants or community members. Thus, not only is the process of Transformative Dialogue co-created, the evaluation of its effectiveness also requires the participation of those involved.

LEVELS OF CHANGE

In addition to the categories of indicators described earlier, Transformative Dialogue practitioners look at outcomes and impacts across four levels of change, each of

Monitoring and Evaluating Relational Outcomes in Transformative Dialogue Processes 161

which can tell us something about how people relate to one another in an organization or a community: personal, interpersonal, changes in types or levels of civic engagement, and institutional change. Let's look at each of these in turn and some examples of what might indicate that change has occurred.

Personal—The personal level refers to attitudes and opinions that individuals hold. This can include what someone thinks of others or how much they trust others. It might also refer to how someone feels about their place in an organization or in the community, or how they feel about the possibilities for change. The personal level also refers to skills. Skills might be specific, like learning to mediate, or they might be more general, like becoming a better listener.

Examples of indicators of personal outcomes:

- You are talking to a community member after a dialogue meeting about community-police relations and they say, *"I understood the officer differently than I have before. It was really helpful to hear his perspective."*
- A participant expresses the following toward the close of a community conversation on race: *"I was impressed by the deep and genuine sentiment expressed by those present here today to be part of something that can improve our community."*
- You have a one-on-one conversation with a community member to consider next steps in a dialogue process and they say, *"After Friday's session, I'm more optimistic for success than I've been for a long time."*
- A participant speaks to you after a dialogue session in a country that has experienced violent conflict and says, *"I came here ready to defend my position against these guys [from the other side], but now I realize that their experience was not that different from mine and I understand how they feel."*

Interpersonal—The interpersonal level refers to relationships, interactions, and social ties with others in the organization or the community.

Examples of indicators of interpersonal outcomes:

- A community member calls you after a community dialogue meeting to say, *"I wanted to tell you that as a result of the meeting yesterday, particularly the discussion groups, I have dates for further conversations with two people I had not met with before."*
- You are working in a community with strong ethnic divisions and segregated schooling. On a Friday night you are in town and you see high school students from different ethnic groups going to a disco together, something you have never seen before.
- You are working in a rural community in a country where there have been high levels of election violence. Outside a school, you chat with some elementary school students. They wave to a child of a different ethnic group and say, *"Hey, there's our friend!"*
- You find the following comment on an evaluation form after a dialogue meeting: *"On the way out of the forum, I had better conversations."*

162   *Erik Cleven*

- In an ethnically divided community, one café in town became a point where people from different ethnic groups could meet and talk.
- You are working on a dialogue initiative in a large healthcare organization and members of two different professional groups agree to establish channels for regular communication and dialogue.

Civic engagement—Increased involvement in community activities, creating new community initiatives.

Examples of indicators of civic engagement:

- You meet a community member on the street who tells you, *"I reached out to an elected official that I met at the community forum."*
- After a dialogue meeting several participants join together to start a police-community committee to address community policing issues.
- In a rural community in a postconflict setting, parents from different ethnic groups at a school you are working with formed an association to help each other with the harvest.

Organizational and institutional change—Depending on the type of work you are doing, this could refer to changes in an organization, for example, the way the administration is organized, which positions exist, how decisions are made, how board members are recruited, etc. It can also refer to laying groundwork for policy and procedural changes within institutions or local communities.

Examples of indicators of organizational or institutional change:

- After a community forum attended by the chief of police and representatives of a group representing people with disabilities, the city's event application form is modified to include a requirement to submit an accessibility plan to any event application.
- In a postwar country an NGO is working on returning refugees to the communities they fled from during the war. After a dialogue meeting where refugees and local authorities were present, the municipality begins to offer the same service provisions to returning refugees as the rest of the population.
- In the same country at an ethnically divided school, a joint classroom for children of any ethnic group is established with computers for the children to learn computer skills.

HOW TO MONITOR AND EVALUATE RELATIONAL OUTCOMES

Monitoring and evaluating relational outcomes involves a process of creating a baseline, thinking about relevant indicators, and recording and documenting those indicators. If we claim that interactions in a community have changed, we need to be

Monitoring and Evaluating Relational Outcomes in Transformative Dialogue Processes 163

able to say what they were initially. The previous examples of indicators are all examples of changes that were observed. But the baseline documents what things were like before the changes occurred. Baseline indicators might include things like "members of different ethnic groups frequent different cafés" or "high school students socialize only with members of their own ethnic group." The previous examples would then indicate positive change. For a Transformative practitioner baseline indicators are identified in conversation with members of the community or organization the practitioner is working with. This can be done in one-on-one conversations and/or in meetings with small groups of people. We could say that creating the baseline involves answering the following question:

- What characterizes the attitudes, motivations, and relationships of people in the community, organization, or institutions you are working in at the start of the program or project?
- What do you see that indicates [are the visible indicators of] these attitudes, motivations, and relationships?

Once you have defined a baseline, you need to think about what might constitute positive change. As you do this, it's critical to be sensitive to context and realistic about the progress you expect. Ideas about positive change can come from asking participants questions about change:

- If interactions improve in the community and/or the institution you are working with, what will you expect to see or hear? What would you see or hear in the long term? What would you see or hear in the course of the next year?
- If you are working in an organization or an institution, and if positive changes were made in organizational structure, what would you expect to see?
- If the organization or institution you are working with provides services to the community, and if positive changes were made in the services offered, what would you expect to see?

Again, you will be looking for these changes by considering the categories listed earlier: things people say, ways that people interact, policies, and the way these policies are enacted. It is people in the organization or community you are working with that will know which changes would constitute meaningful change in that particular context. An outside intervener cannot assess what kind of changes would be truly meaningful. In the previous examples, high school students going to a disco might seem completely insignificant in one context, but in another context it might be a sign of significant changes in community relations.

With a baseline defined and a tentative idea of what positive change may look like, you now need to continually monitor indicators of relational change. This means monitoring changes in informal, daily interactions (through stories, conversations, etc.) as well as through the more formal interactions within organizations and institutions and as services are provided.

It is critical that you take time to record and document these changes. How can the changes described earlier be recorded or documented? The most important way this can happen is by project workers and facilitators taking careful notes of their personal observations at the end of each meeting, conversation, or project visit. This may sound easy, but it requires commitment and discipline to actually carry out. When project activities are at a peak it is easy to think that the activities are far more important than the monitoring and evaluation. It is easy to think that you will remember things you hear about people's relations and interactions, but if they are not written down they will be of far less quality than if you record them each day.

One way to document change is to use a field notebook (or laptop if you wish and have one) to make these notes each day. Other methods might include field report forms, either online or on paper, with the previous categories listed to help you be systematic. Periodic meetings or phone calls with team members can also help recognize and capture important observations. It is important to develop tools that help people provide feedback in ways that are natural to them. This may or may not involve the use of writing or digital tools. If you are working in a cultural context where literacy is low or people are more comfortable with oral than written communication, then that should be reflected in the methods developed. Here too co-creation is important to ensure that the tools developed will be culturally appropriate and ones that will actually be used.

As you monitor and document changes, pay attention to those things that were not included as you imagined what change would look like. Ask community members to think about questions like these:

- What unexpected factors or external influences have come up during the program or project period?
- How did this influence relations in the community? Examples might include episodes of violence, elections, or the activities of other NGOs.

At the end of a program we also document the state of interactions and policies. This will make it possible to report on changes as the program proceeded but also how much was achieved during the whole program.

THINKING ABOUT INDICATORS

At any point during your program, after participating in a conversation or attending a meeting, it may be helpful for you and for team members to think about the following questions:

- What did you see or hear that indicated new trust or openness on the part of those present?
- What comments did you hear that indicated changes in attitude?

Monitoring and Evaluating Relational Outcomes in Transformative Dialogue Processes 165

- What comments were made that indicated a person or group is feeling better about their place in the community?
- Did you hear about or observe any new connections between individuals or groups?
- What did you see or hear that indicated new or increased involvement in the community?
- What new ideas surfaced about ways to involve others not present?
- What suggestions were made for changes in policy and/or procedures?

It can also be important to remember that there may be outcomes that can be observed but are not necessarily articulated by those involved.

At the end of a program period, if you have monitored and documented the changes your Transformative Dialogue has contributed to, you are ready to report on the following:

- The actual resources used
- The activities that actually were carried out
- The outputs of those activities (how many people participated in activities or were served by the program)
- The changes you have seen taking place and why the activities you carried out made a difference
- Possible influences of external or unexpected factors
- The extent to which your objectives have been achieved

Remember that you may want to think about both internal and external validity. In other words, were activities done well and were they the right activities? If not, what could have been done differently and why?

WHAT MONITORING AND EVALUATING ACCOMPLISHES

As you can see from the previous discussion, the idea is not that you *never* report on activities but that you do not *only* report on activities. The most important level becomes reporting on the outcomes achieved, that is, why this mattered to the people and communities involved. Monitoring and evaluation is often thought of as a distraction from the real work of conflict transformation and dialogue. It can seem like a bureaucratic burden that involves report writing and filling out forms. But if monitoring and evaluation is done Transformatively it is an important part of dialogue work for several reasons.

First, monitoring and evaluation can help participants and all community members reflect on and become conscious of changes that have occurred in an organization or community, even if conflict is still present. Transformative Dialogue makes it possible for people to experience conflict and disagreement as more constructive and positive if they are able to hear one another and to recognize one another's humanity. Being able to see the ways that this happens can be important to the people living in the community and an important part of the process of getting clear.

Second, engaging in monitoring and evaluation can help donors and local decision makers understand the importance of your work. Donors often want to see concrete results from program funding. Telling them that fifty people participated in dialogue meetings and talked is not nearly as convincing as showing concretely how attitudes and relationships changed in the community. Transformative Dialogue work can have profound effects on people who participate in dialogue, but it can be hard to show what those effects are. Monitoring and evaluation is an effective way to educate donors about how relational change works and how it benefits individuals and communities, and how these benefits can occur even if reconciliation or agreement is not achieved.

Finally, seeing clearly how activities positively impact people can help interveners remain motivated to do the work of facilitating and organizing dialogue because they can see how their work is making a difference.

Bibliography

7 Points on the War and Dialogue. 2022. https://md.ukma.edu.ua/wp-content/uploads/2022/05/Public_Statement_War_and_Dialogue_Ukraine_ENG.pdf.

Armstrong, B. K. 2024, February 25. Ukraine War: Zelensky Says 31,000 Troops Killed since Russia's Full-Scale Invasion. *BBC*. https://www.bbc.com/news/world-europe-68397525.

Autesserre, Severine. 2021. *The Frontlines of Peace: An Insider's Guide to Changing the World*. New York: Oxford University Press.

Beck, Aaron T. 2000. *Prisoners of Hate: The Cognitive Basis of Anger, Hostility, and Violence*. New York: Harper Perennial.

Berghof Foundation. 2022. "Peace for Ukrainians Means Their Own Resilience to Withstand Aggression." https://berghof-foundation.org/news/peace-for-ukrainians-means-their-own-resilience-to-withstand-aggression.

Blackmon, Traci, John Dorhauer, Da Vita D. McCallister, John Paddock, and Stephen G. Ray Jr. n.d. *White Privilege: Let's Talk—A Resource for Transformational Dialogue*. United Church of Christ. http://privilege.uccpages.org/.

Bush, Robert A. Baruch, and Joseph P. Folger. 1994. *The Promise of Mediation*. San Francisco: Jossey-Bass.

Bush, Robert A. Baruch, and Joseph P. Folger. 2005. *The Promise of Mediation: The Transformative Approach to Conflict*. San Francisco: Jossey-Bass.

Bush, Robert A. Baruch, and Joseph P. Folger. 2012. "Mediation and Social Justice: Risks and Opportunities." *Ohio State Journal on Dispute Resolution* 27 (1): 1–52.

Bush, Robert A. Baruch, and Sally Ganong Pope. 2002. "Changing the Quality of Conflict Interaction: The Principles and Practice of Transformative Mediation." *Pepperdine Dispute Resolution Law Journal* 3: 67–96.

Cleven, Erik. 2011. *Who Needs to Talk to Whom, About What, and How? Transformative Dialogue in Settings of Ethnopolitical Conflict*. Westport, CT: Institute for the Study of Conflict Transformation.

Cleven, Erik, Robert A. Baruch Bush, and Judith A. Saul. 2018. "Living with No: Political Polarization and Transformative Dialogue." *Journal of Dispute Resolution* (1): 53–63.

Cleven, Erik, and Judith A. Saul. 2021. "Realizing the Promise of Dialogue: Transformative Dialogue in Divided Communities." *Conflict Resolution Quarterly* 38 (3): 111–25.

Çuhadar, Esra, and Thania Paffenholz. 2020. "Transfer 2.0: Applying the Concept of Transfer from Track-Two Workshops to Inclusive Peace Negotiations." *International Studies Review* 22: 651–70.

Donais, Timothy. 2009. "Empowerment or Imposition? Dilemmas of Local Ownership in Post-Conflict Peacebuilding Processes." *Peace & Change: A Journal of Peace Research* 34 (1): 3–26. https://doi.org/10.1111/j.1468-0130.2009.00531.x.

DuVernay, Ava, and Jason Moran. *13th.* USA, 2016.

Eihelson, Iryna, Inna Tereshchenko, Olga Kukharuk, and Natalia Bezkhlibna. 2023. *How to Work with Conflicts in Communities in the Times of War: A Guide to the Concept of Mobile Groups.* Kyiv: National Platform for Resilience and Social Cohesion. https://national-platform.org/how-to-work-with-conflicts-in-communities-in-the-times-of-war-2/.

Fisher, Ronald. 2020. "Transfer Effects from Problem-Solving Workshops to Negotiations: A Process and Outcome Model." *Negotiation Journal* 36 (4): 441–70.

Folger, Joseph P. 2010. "A Transformative Orientation to Team Development Work." In *Transformative Mediation: A Sourcebook. Resources for Conflict Intervention Practitioners and Programs*, edited by Joseph P. Folger, Robert A. Baruch Bush, and Dorothy J. Della Noce. Association for Conflict Resolution and Institute for the Study of Conflict Transformation.

Folger, Joseph P. 2020. "Conflict Analysis and Conflict Intervention: Do Theoretical Understandings of Conflict Shape Conflict Intervention Approaches?" In *Comparative Dispute Resolution*, edited by Maria Federica Moscati, Michael J. E. Palmer, and Marian Roberts, 74–86. Research Handbooks in Comparative Law. Cheltenham, UK: Edward Elgar Publishing.

ICIP. 2022. "Opinions about the War in Ukraine with the Prospect of Peace." https://www.icip.cat/en/opinions-about-the-war-in-ukraine-with-the-prospect-of-peace/.

Interpeace. 2023. "The Mediation Experiences of NCIC and Interpeace in Mandera County and the North Rift Region." https://www.interpeace.org/resource/the-mediation-experiences-of-ncic-and-interpeace-in-mandera-county-and-the-north-rift-region/?utm_source=rss&utm_medium=rss&utm_campaign=the-mediation-experiences-of-ncic-and-interpeace-in-mandera-county-and-the-north-rift-region.

Kryshtal, Andrii, Olga Kotiuk, and Tetiana Kyselova. 2023. *Civil Society Organisations in the Field of Mediation and Dialogue in Ukraine: Changes, Challenges and Trends after 24 February 2022.* Kyiv: Danish Refugee Council. https://pro.drc.ngo/media/zlpa2v51/organisations-in-the-field-of-mediation-and-dialogue-eng.pdf.

Kyselova, Tatiana. 2017. "Professional Peacemakers in Ukraine: Mediators and Dialogue Facilitators Before and After 2014." *Kyiv-Mohyla Law and Politics Journal.* http://dx.doi.org/10.2139/ssrn.3106731.

Kyselova, Tetiana, and Andrii Moseiko. 2021. *Mapping of Dialogue and Peacebuilding Organizations and Initiatives in Ukraine.* CivilM+. https://md.ukma.edu.ua/wp-content/uploads/2021/07/Mapping-of-Peacebuilding-and-Dialogue-Actors-2021-ENG.pdf.

Lang, Michael D. 2019. *The Guide to Reflective Practice in Conflict Resolution.* Lanham, MD: Rowman and Littlefield.

Lang, Michael D., and Alison Taylor. 2000. *The Making of a Mediator.* San Francisco: Jossey-Bass.

Bibliography

Lehti, Marko. 2018. *The Era of Private Peacemakers: A New Dialogic Approach to Mediation.* New York: Palgrave Macmillan Cham.

Maalouf, Amin. 2000. *In the Name of Identity: Violence and the Need to Belong.* New York: Arcade Publishing.

Maoz, Ifat. 2000. "Multiple Conflicts and Competing Agendas: A Framework for Conceptualizing Structured Encounters between Groups in Conflict—The Case of a Coexistence Project of Jews and Palestinians in Israel." *International Journal of Politics, Culture and Society* 17 (3): 563–74.

Mediazona. 2024. "Russian Casualties in Ukraine." https://en.zona.media/article/2022/05/11/casualties_eng.

Meeks, Catherine, ed. 2016. *Living into God's Dream: Dismantling Racism in America.* New York: Morehouse Publishing.

Miall, Hugh. 2023. *Can Conflict Resolution Principles Apply in Ukraine?* Policy Brief No. 153. Tokyo: Toda Peace Institute. https://toda.org/assets/files/resources/policy-briefs/t-pb-153_conflict-resolution-principles-in-ukraine_miall.pdf.

Muto, Ako, Cedric de Coning, and Rui Saraiva, eds. 2022. *Adaptive Mediation and Conflict Resolution Peace-Making in Colombia, Mozambique, the Philippines, and Syria.* New York: Palgrave Macmillan Cham.

OHCHR. 2024. *Two-Year Update. Protection of Civilians: Impact of Hostilities on Civilians since 24 February 2022.* United Nations Office of the High Commissioner for Human Rights. https://ukraine.un.org/en/261245-two-year-update-protection-civilians-impact-hostilities-civilians-24-february-2022.

Paffenholz, Thania, Alexander Bramble, Philip Poppelreuter, and Nick Ross. 2023. *Negotiating an End to the War in Ukraine: Ideas and Options to Prepare for and Design a Negotiation Process.* Geneva: Inclusive Peace, 2023. https://www.inclusivepeace.org/wp-content/uploads/2023/08/UKR-negotiations-preparations-report-2023.pdf.

PCI. 2022. "Public Statement on the War and Dialogue from Ukrainian Mediators." https://peacefulchange.org/news/public-statement-on-the-war-and-dialogue-from-ukrainian-mediators/.

People in Need. 2024. "Ukrainian Refugee Crisis: The Current Situation." https://www.peopleinneed.net/the-ukrainian-refugee-crisis-current-situation-9539gp.

Press, Sharon, and Ellen E. Deason. 2021. "Mediation: Embedded Assumptions of Whiteness? Jed D. Melnick Annual Symposium: Presumptive ADR and Court Systems of the Future." *Cardozo Journal of Conflict Resolution* 22 (3): 453–98.

Richmond, Oliver P. 2012. "Beyond Local Ownership in the Architecture of International Peacebuilding." *Ethnopolitics* 11 (4): 354–75. https://doi.org/10.1080/17449057.2012.697650.

Right to Protection. 2023. "Ukrainian Approaches to a Just and Lasting Peace: R2P Organized an International Conference in Kyiv." https://r2p.org.ua/en/page/ukrainian-approaches-to-a-just-and-lasting-peace-r2p-organized-an-international-conference-in-kyiv.

Shapiro, Ilana. 2006. *Extending the Framework of Inquiry: Theories of Change in Conflict Interventions.* Berghof Handbook Dialogue No. 5.

Sustainable Peace Manifesto: Never Again 2.0. N.d.. https://sustainablepeacemanifesto.org/.

Tolsdorff, Tim. 2023, July 31. "How Ukraine Overcomes the War and Its Consequences." Robert Bosch Stiftung. https://www.bosch-stiftung.de/en/storys/how-ukraine-overcomes-war-and-its-consequences.

UA Losses. n.d. https://ualosses.org/en/soldiers/.

Ukraine Peace Appeal: Towards a More Informed Solidarity. 2023. https://www.ukrainepeaceappeal2023.info/.

Index

activities, 157, 165
adaptability, of Transformative Dialogue, 117
Advocacy Program, Calvert Library sponsoring, 93
agency, of participants: practitioners respecting, 2–3, 152; privilege and, 19; Transformative approach highlighting, 153. *See also* self-determination
agreements, 136–38
"Another Voice" (statement), 73, 80, 82–83
antiracism policy, in public schools, 94
appeals for help, responding to, 114–17
Articulated Model of Practice, of Dayton Mediation Center, *27*
attending, observation and, 140

Baltimore Mediation team, of Phipps Senft, 94
Baraza (public meetings), 140, 144n2
BC-DRaP. *See* Big Conversation on Dismantling Racism and Privilege
beginning, of Transformative Dialogue, 86–87
bias: decisions not impacted by, 88; nondirective approaches avoiding, 10; police reform and, 104; trust and, 16

Big Conversation on Dismantling Racism and Privilege (BC-DRaP), 91
Big Conversations, 12, 89, 91, 93
Bij1 (political party), 63, 72n2
Black history, 93–94
Black Men in White Coats (program), 93
Blackmon, Traci, 90
breakthroughs, 89–90
Brown, Michael, 81
Bush, Baruch, 10, 26

Calvert County (Maryland), 85–86
Calvert Library, Advocacy Program sponsored by, 93
capacity, 2, 5, 13, 23
case workers, 42–43, 45, 48–49
Ceasefire Monitoring Committees (CMCs), 132
ceasefires, 12, 144n1; intercommunity dialogue beginning with, 135–36; Interpeace Kenya supporting, 132; Ukraine and, 150–51
Centre for Humanitarian Dialogue (HD), 146
change, levels of, 160–63
check-ins, 78

171

Index

children, safety of, 40
Children and Youth Services, 50
child welfare, 40, 42, 48–49
choice, Transformative approach highlighting, 153
circle gatherings, 133
civic engagement, 161, 162
clarity, 20–21; through co-creation, 20–21, 56; interactions increasing, 72; pro-social interaction with, 2; through reflection, 28
class dynamics, 126–27
clients: facilitators in relation to, 110–11; normalized/dominant *versus* nonnormalized/minority identities of, 49; process driven by, 110; safety lacked by, 47–48
CMCC. *See* Community Mediation Center of Calvert
CMCs. *See* Ceasefire Monitoring Committees
CMI. *See* Martti Ahtisaari Peace Foundation
coaches, 105–6
co-creation, 9, 36–37, 138; beginning of, 64–65; clarity through, 20–21, 56; of dialogue, 14, 31, 61; by participants, 109, 158; of process, 74
co-facilitation, 59–60
co-facilitators, 31–32, 35–36
collaborative decision-making model, 129
collective story building, 33
comfort, safety distinguished from, 47–48
communication, weakness and self-absorption impacting, 3
communication forms, 57–59
communities, polarizations in groups and, 25–26
community dialogue, agreements contrasted with, 137–38
Community Dialogue Initiative, 119, 122, 125, 129
community mediation, 9 hallmarks of, 26
Community Mediation Center of Calvert (CMCC), 86, 89, 139
community members, facilitators as, 88–89
Community Relations Service for, Department of Justice, 75
competence, institutions and policy and, 160

Concerned Black Women of Calvert, 89
confidentiality, 18
conflict, 1, 48; among practitioners, 149–51; asymmetry in, 152; disempowerment and, 49; gender and, 128; interprofessional, 151; in nomadic communities, 132–33; polarization and, 94; reactive, 115; self-absorption during, 45; transformative theory of, 3–5, 4; violent, 12; weakness during, 45
conflict intervention, 5, 25
conflict resolution practitioners, disputes between, 152–53
connections, 159
conversations, 133–36, 159; Big, 12, 89, 91, 93; challenging, 98–100; decisions about, 78; homogeneous, 7–8; intergroup, 66–67, 101–2; intragroup, 101–2; small group, 34, 76–77; social constructs and, 95; supporting, 92–93; transformative, 21–22. *See also* one-on-one conversations
cooperations, 160
COVID-19 pandemic, 51, 52, 60–61, 103
Crawford, John, 81
Crisis/Rapid Response Family Meeting Program, 39
crisis/rapid response family meetings (CRRFMs), 40–41
cross-contact dialogue, 148
CRRFMs. *See* crisis/rapid response family meetings
cultural challenges, 126–28
cultural humility, 49–50
cultural practices, patriarchal, 140
culture, in Somalia, 119
custody disputes, 40

Dayton (Ohio), 81, 82–83; HRC for, 73; police reform in, 12, 98–99; public safety in, 107; race in, 12
Dayton Mediation Center (DMC), 12, 26–27, 79–80, 97, 100, 107
Dayton Police Department, 97–98
Deason, Ellen E., 10
decisions, 1, 42; bias not impacted by, 88; capability to make, 74; about conversations, 78; about dialogue, 10,

Index

173

12; facilitators helping with, 2, 36; participants leading, 7, 15, 17, 29, 33, 43, 68; about process, 17, 26, 48, 59, 100; Transformative approach tested by, 122. *See also* agency
Degodia (clan), 132, 142
Department of Justice, Community Relations Service for, 75
dialogue, 1, 6–8, 22, 147–50, 154; benefits of, 17–18; co-creation of, 14, 31, 61; cross-contact, 148; decisions about, 10, 12; education about, 16–18; facilitators starting, 92–93; impact of, 129; intercommunity, 135–36; intergroup, 138; mediation contrasted with, 15; monitoring of, 125–26; peace and, 146; problem-solving workshops contrasted with, 125; start of, 100–102; transfer and, 148; during war, 147. *See also* conversations
Dialogue Working Group (DWG), 120–21, 123, 128
digital communication, 60
directive peacebuilding, 12, 119
disagreements, misunderstandings and, 67–69
divisions, 160
DMC. *See* Dayton Mediation Center
documentation, 13, 164
donors, 166; international, 136; managers and, 156; outcomes and, 13, 131
Dubahir, Murshid, 131, 134, 135, 139
DuVernay, Ava, 91
DWG. *See* Dialogue Working Group

education, about dialogue, 16–18
emotions, facilitators tackling, 102
English, Kylen, 73, 75–76, 79, 81–82
ethical relation, between interveners and the parties, 21
ethnic violence, 18
European Union, United Kingdom withdrawing from, 52
evaluation, 155; integrated, 156–57; of relational change, 156; of relational outcomes, 162–64; what is accomplished by, 165–66. *See also* indicators
external validity, 157, 158, 165

facilitation: co-, 59–60; family crisis meeting, 39; of large group meetings, 44–46; racial issues and, 87–89; trauma-informed, 46–48
facilitation team, parties followed by, 135
facilitators, 61, 98–99, 147–50, 154; clients in relation to, 110–11; co-, 31–32, 35–36; as community members, 88–89; decisions helped with by, 2, 36; dialogue started by, 92–93; emotions tackled by, 102; guiding and following by, 68–69; identity of, 18–19; listening by, 29–30; managers as, 53–54; marginalized groups not spoken for by, 10; noticing by, 70; outsiders as, 56; participants differing from, 105; as process guides, 100–101, 105; roles of, 6–7; self-determination supported by, 2; transparency prioritized by, 115; whiteness acknowledged by, 88. *See also* practitioners
Fairchild, Darryl, 74, 82
faith community, 11
Family Engagement Initiative (FEI), 40, 49
family meetings, 11, 39–44, 46
fast solutions, 124–25
FBI, 74
FeedbackRadar, 51
FEI. *See* Family Engagement Initiative
Ferguson (Missouri), 81
field notebook, 164
first contact, 27–31, 36
Floyd, George, 12, 97
Folger, Joe, 10, 26, 27
following, by facilitators, 68–69
Foster, Irv, 85

Garre (clan), 132, 142
gender, 128, 140–41
generalizations, avoidance of, 103
goals, values and, 110
grief, 94
grounded, staying, 49–50
ground rules, 44, 45, 102–3
group meetings, 75–80
groups: marginalized, 10; people in, 8–9; planning, 32–33; polarization in communities and, 25–26; trust impacting, 125

174 *Index*

guardians, 43
guiding, by facilitators, 68–69

HD. *See* Centre for Humanitarian
Dialogue
healthcare organizations, 11, 51, 52–53, 61
holding space, 28, 36
homogeneous conversations, 7–8
HRC. *See* Human Relations Council
human beings, social connections of, 4
human identity, core of, 5
human interaction, 4, 5
human nature, 6
Human Relations Council (HRC), for
Dayton, 73

identity, 5–6, 18–19, 49, 142–44
IDPs. *See* internally displaced persons
images, transcultural communication
deepened by, 57–58
impact, 3, 88, 125, 157; of dialogue, 129;
intention and, 70; short- and long-term,
81–82
indicators: developing meaningful relational,
13; of relational change, 158–59;
thinking about, 164–65
informal contact, trust built through, 56
inputs, 157
"insiders," "outsiders" contrasted with,
142–43
institutional change, 162
institutions, competence and policy and,
160
integrated evaluation, 156–57
intention, impact and, 70
interaction, pro-social. *See* pro-social
interaction
interactional shifts, policy outcomes and,
106–7
interactions, 71–72
intercommunity dialogue, ceasefires
beginning, 135–36
intergroup conversations, 66–67, 101–2
intergroup dialogue, intragroup work
within, 138
internally displaced persons (IDPs), 121,
145, 147
internal validity, 157, 158, 165

international aid, challenges created by the
world of, 122–26
International Alert (NGO), 119, 120
international donors, 136
international peacebuilders, Ukrainian
practitioners differing from, 151, 153
International Summit for Peace in Ukraine,
150
Interpeace Kenya (organization), 12, 131,
133, 144
interpersonal level, of change, 160–61
interpersonal relationships, working
environment mirroring, 58–59
interprofessional conflict, 151
interveners, 166; ethical relation between
the parties and, 21; neutrality of, 16;
one-on-one conversations by, 22–23
Inter-Village Dialogue Spaces, 139
intracommunity talks, 139
intragroup conversations, intergroup
conversations equated with, 101–2
intragroup meetings, 65–66
intragroup work, 138–40
Ismail, Hassan, 131, 134, 139, 142, 143–44

Jordan, Susan, 10
justice, Transformative Dialogue and, 9–11

Kantharos (film), 63
Kenya, 12, 18–19, 131–33, 138, 139
knowledge, skills and, 160
Koloa Agreement, 136
Ku Klux Klan, 63

Lang, Michael, 27
large group meetings, facilitation of, 44–46
legislative aides, 106
Lemons, Meredith, 10
life experiences, challenging, 92–93
listening, 139; by facilitators, 29–30; "hold
space" during, 28; Interpeace Kenya
centering, 133
listening sessions, 34–35, 101
Living into God's Dream (Meeks), 90
local authorities, 122, 126–27
local decision makers, 166
local government, 102
local ownership, during peacebuilding, 148

Index

175

MACRO. *See* Mediation and Conflict Resolution Office

managers, 60, 61; donors and, 156; as facilitators, 53–54; Transformative Dialogue supported by, 55

Mandera County (Kenya), 132, 139, 142

"Many Wounds to Heal" (conversation), 93

marginalized groups, facilitators not speaking for, 10

Marsabit County (Kenya), 132

Martti Ahtisaari Peace Foundation (CMI), 146

MDRC. *See* Mediation and Dialogue Research Center

MDTs. *See* multidisciplinary teams

mediation, dialogue contrasted with, 15

Mediation and Conflict Resolution Office (MACRO), 94

Mediation and Dialogue Research Center (MDRC), 146

mediation response unit (MRU), 107

Meeks, Catherine, 90

meetings, 159; family, 11, 39–44, 46; group, 75–80; intragroup, 65–66; large group, 44–46; small group, 7, 31; women-only, 141

Middleham and Saint Peters Episcopal Parish, 89

misunderstandings, disagreements and, 67–69

Mogadishu (Somalia), 119, 121

monitoring, 132, 155; of dialogue, 125–26; outcomes tracked through, 157; of relational outcomes, 162–64; what is accomplished by, 165–66. *See also* indicators

moral grounding, self-management and, 35–36

moral impulse, 4

motivation, 2, 9

MRU. *See* mediation response unit

multidisciplinary teams (MDTs), 52, 55, 57

multiparty conflicts, co-facilitators attending, 35–36

Mwetich, Job, 131, 143

NAACP. *See* National Association for the Advancement of Colored People

National Association for Community Mediation (NAFCM), 26

National Association for the Advancement of Colored People (NAACP), 77, 89

National Cohesion and Integration Commission (NCIC), 132

National Health Service Trust (NHS), 51

National University of Kyiv-Mohyla Academy, 146

NATO, 150

NCIC. *See* National Cohesion and Integration Commission

NEPCOH. *See* Network for Peace, Cohesion, and Heritage Trust

the Netherlands, racism in, 63

Network for Peace, Cohesion, and Heritage Trust (NEPCOH), 132

networks, 159

next steps, 31–34

NGOs. *See* nongovernmental organizations

NHS. *See* National Health Service Trust

nomadic communities, conflict in, 132–33

nondirective approaches, bias avoided through, 10

nongovernmental organizations (NGOs), 146

Northeast Rift Valley (Kenya), 132

Northern Ireland, 20

North Rift Valley (Kenya), 132, 143

not-for-profit organizations, 113

noticing, by facilitators, 70

observation, attending and, 140

one-on-one conversations, 7, 19, 20, 34, 42–44; family meetings explored through, 41; by interveners, 22–23; value for Transformative Dialogue of, 15

oppression, 9–10

organizational change, 162

organizational structure, 160

Organization for Security and Co-operation in Europe (OSCE), 146

outcomes, 13, 106–7, 131, 157, 165

outputs, 157

"outsiders," "insiders" contrasted with, 142–43

parenting class, 49–50

parents, 42–43

176 *Index*

Paris, Lopode, 131, 134–38, 140
participants: co-creation by, 109, 158; decisions led by, 7, 15, 17, 29, 33, 43, 68; facilitators differing from, 105; practitioners supporting, 10; reflection by, 80–81; selection of, 124. *See also* agency
participation, 123–24, 140–41
participatory analytical activities, 133
parties: centering of, 133–34; ethical relation between interveners and, 21; facilitation team following, 135
patience, 135
patient visiting scheme, during COVID-19 pandemic, 60–61
patriarchal cultural practices, 140
peace, 146, 152
peacebuilders, international, 151, 153
peacebuilding: classic approaches to, 150; directive, 12; local ownership during, 148; top-down initiatives and, 119
peacebuilding, directive, 12, 119
Pennsylvania, Office of Children and Families in the Courts for, 40
people in groups, 8–9
personal growth, 129
personal level, of change, 160
Phipps Senft, Louise, 94
planning groups, 32–33
Pokot communities, 132, 139, 141, 142
polarization, 25–26, 94
police reform, 103, 107; bias and, 104; in Dayton, 12, 98–99; Transformative Dialogue and, 97
policy, institutions and competence and, 160
policy outcomes, interactional shifts and, 106–7
postelection violence, in Rhamu, 139
power, in reactive processes, 114–15
power imbalances, 48–49
practice, 131; premises underpinning, 4–5; pro-social interaction promoted by, 158; purpose driving, 75
practitioners, 145–48; agency respected by, 2–3, 152; conflict among, 149–51; disputes between conflict resolution,

152–53; participants supported by, 10; self-determination respected by, 2–3
preparation, 90–92
Press, Sharon, 10
Prince George's County (Maryland), 85–86
privilege, 19, 87–88, 105
proactive process, 111–12
problem-solving workshops, dialogue contrasted with, 125
process, 56–57; agreements terminating, 138; clients driving, 110; co-creation of, 74; decisions about, 17, 26, 48, 59, 100; proactive, 111–12; reactive, 114–15; RFP predefining, 112–13; self-organizing, 77
process consultants, 105
process guides, facilitators as, 100–101, 105
"Progress and Challenges in Our Schools" (conversation), 93
The Promise of Mediation (Bush), 26
pro-social interaction, 110; with clarity, 2; increasing, 60–61; listening sessions increasing, 101; practice promoting, 158; with strength, 2
public safety, in Dayton, 107
public schools, antiracism policy in, 94
purpose, practice driven by, 75

quality of care, 55

race, 11–12, 95, 99, 104–5
racial issues, 85, 86–89
racism, 9, 68–69, 87, 91, 94; in the Netherlands, 63; weakness and self-absorption exemplifying, 12; in workplace, 11
reactive conflict, 115
reactive process, 111–12, 114–15
recognition, shifts toward, 69–71
reconciliation, truth before, 92–93
records, 164
referrals, 41–42
reflection, 32, 78; clarity through, 28; during co-creation, 34; by participants, 80–81
relational change: documentation of, 13; evaluation of, 156; indicators of, 158–59

relational outcomes, evaluation and monitoring of, 162–64
request for proposal (RFP), 111–13
research institute, community suspecting, 115–16
RFP. *See* request for proposal
Rhamu (Kenya), postelection violence in, 139
Rhoades, Vicki, 95
Robert's Rules of Order, 102
Rotich, Kenedy, 131, 137
Russia, 145–46, 150, 152

Sabelis, Ida, 63
safety, 40, 47–48, 119, 121–22
safety considerations, 44
safety plan, family crisis meeting focusing on, 46
St. Mary's County (Maryland), 86
SCLC. *See* Southern Christian Leadership Council
security, 119, 121–22
"Seeing the Face of God in Others" (workshop), 86
self-absorption, 58–59, 87–88; communication impacted by, 3; during conflict, 45; racism exemplifying weakness and, 12
self-determination, 75, 133–34, 137; capacity for, 5, 13, 23; facilitators supporting, 2; NAFCM focusing on, 26; practitioners respecting, 2–3
self-management, moral grounding and, 35–36
self-organizing process, 77
services, 160
"7 Points on the War and Dialogue from Ukrainian Mediators and Dialogue Facilitators" (statement), 147–50, 154
sexual and gender-based violence (SGBV), 120, 128
Simons, Sylvana, 63
skills, knowledge and, 160
Skype, 90
small group conversations, 34, 76–77
small group meetings, 7, 31
social connections, of human beings, 4
social constructs, conversations and, 95

social events, 160
social media posts, 159
social movements, 10
Somalia, 12, 119, 128
Southern Christian Leadership Council (SCLC), 77
Southern Maryland History Coalition, 94
statements, 159; editing of, 79; UCoDP releasing, 147–48; writing of, 78. *See also specific statements*
Stop-Start-Continue (exercise), 59
stories, 159
strength, pro-social interaction with, 2
success, defining, 125–26
Suguta Valley (Kenya), 139
summaries, 78–79, 93
Suriname, 63, 72n1
Susquehanna Valley Mediation (SVM), 39, 50
system stressors, 52

team spirit, 55
13th (film), 90–91
Thirteenth Amendment (United States), 90–91
top-down initiatives, peacebuilding and, 119
trainers, 106
transactions, 160
transcultural communication, images deepening, 57–58
transfer, dialogue and, 148
transformative conversations, 21–22
Transformative Dialogue. *See specific topics*
transformative theory, 1, 3–5, *4*
transparency, 32, 45, 48, 105, 108–10, 115
trauma-informed facilitation, 46–48
truancy, 41
trust, 79; bias and, 16; groups impacted by, 125; informal contact building, 56
truth, before reconciliation, 92–93
Turkana communities, 132, 141
Turkana County (Kenya), 138

UCoDP. *See* Ukrainian Community of Dialogue Practitioners
Ukraine, 13, 145–46, 152

178   *Index*

Ukrainian Community of Dialogue Practitioners (UCoDP), 145–51
Ukrainian Peace Appeal, 150, 151, 154
Ukrainian practitioners, international peacebuilders differing from, 151, 153
understanding, shifts toward, 69–71
United Kingdom, European Union withdrawn from by, 52
United States, 18, 90–91, 107. *See also* Dayton (Ohio)
"The Urgency of Awareness" (training), 49

validity, internal and external, 157, 158, 165
violence, postelection, 139
violent conflict, 12

Wahlrab, Thomas, 12, 85
Walker, Robert, 74, 82
war, 147, 154
ways people interact, 159–60

weakness, 58–59, 87–88; communication impacted by, 3; during conflict, 45; racism exemplifying self-absorption and, 12
Whaley, Nan, 97–98
whiteness, facilitators acknowledging, 88
white privilege, 87–88
White Privilege (Blackmon), 89–90
women, participation of, 140–41
women-only meetings, 141
working environment, interpersonal relationships mirrored by, 58–59
workplace, racism in, 11
workplace stressors, 52
World War II, 145
Wright State University, 26

young people, 128

Zoom, challenge of, 103–4

About the Editors and Contributors

Erik Cleven is a professor in the Department of Politics at Saint Anselm College, where he teaches courses in international relations and comparative politics. He is also a Fellow and former board member of the Institute for the Study of Conflict Transformation. With institute colleagues he has helped develop Transformative Dialogue. He has extensive experience with dialogue in postconflict settings in the Balkans and other places and has offered Transformative Dialogue training in Kenya, Jordan, the Netherlands, Norway, and the United States.

Judith A. Saul is a Fellow and former board member of the Institute for the Study of Conflict Transformation and, through the institute, a Certified Transformative Mediator. She founded and ran a community mediation center in Ithaca, New York, for over twenty-five years and has extensive experience mediating interpersonal disputes, planning and facilitating organizational and community dialogues, and training mediators. She developed Transformative Dialogue with Institute colleagues and has trained others in it nationally and internationally.

Anja Bekink is a Certified Transformative Mediator, trainer, dialogue facilitator, and coach. She is a board member of the Transformative Model Foundation and president of the Institute for the Study of Conflict Transformation's board. Besides mediating, Anja works as interim manager and project leader in healthcare, mainly in hospitals. In these roles she uses her knowledge and experience of Transformative Mediation, Dialogue, and conflict coaching with groups of healthcare professionals, impacting the quality of teamwork, which in turn impacts the job satisfaction of healthcare professionals and the quality of healthcare.

About the Editors and Contributors

Abiosseh Davis is the head of global design, monitoring, evaluation, and learning at Interpeace. She has over fifteen years of work experience in the fields of peacebuilding and governance, providing technical advice and management support for the design, implementation, monitoring, and evaluation of peacebuilding, democracy, and governance initiatives in Africa, Asia, the Middle East, and Latin America. She has led and continues to lead research on topics such as gender, mental health and psychosocial support, resilience, inside mediation, and governance.

Angie Gaspar has worked in the United Kingdom's health system for over thirty years. In the past twenty years she developed support services for the National Service Trust and its fourteen thousand staff members. These services include therapy, responses to traumatic incidents, communication training, stress management, and conflict resolution services. Angie is a former board member of the Institute for the Study of Conflict Transformation and is a Certified Transformative Mediator. She has a master's degree in mediation from Queen's University, Belfast.

Arch Grieve is an author and political science lecturer at two Ohio colleges. He is also a Certified Transformative Mediator through the Institute for the Study of Conflict Transformation and utilizes Transformative Mediation in his private practice, specializing in divorce mediation. Arch began his work in mediation as a volunteer at the Dayton Mediation Center, where he later worked full time overseeing a range of programs. He has also led facilitations and trainings in the Dayton, Ohio, area and in multiple countries.

Cherise D. Hairston is a Certified Transformative Mediator and fellow of the Institute for the Study of Conflict Transformation and a certified professional coach. She is a community mediation practitioner with more than twenty-five years of experience at the Dayton Mediation Center, where she has facilitated dialogue processes for community groups, churches, and organizations. Cherise currently teaches conflict coaching at the Jimmy and Rosalyn Carter School of Peace and Conflict Resolution at George Mason University. She is also a National Association for Community Mediation board of directors elder.

Susan Jordan is in her tenth year as executive director of Susquehanna Valley Mediation, a community mediation center in Selinsgrove, Pennsylvania. She has over twelve years of experience mediating interpersonal disputes and facilitating community dialogue. Using Transformative Dialogue processes, she has co-designed programs with partners from human services, the courts, and local government. She is a Certified Transformative Mediator, trainer, and board member of the Institute for the Study of Conflict Transformation.

Meredith Lemons grew up in central Pennsylvania before moving to Colorado to attend the University of Denver. After moving back to her hometown post-graduation, she became the crisis/rapid response family meeting coordinator at

About the Editors and Contributors

Susquehanna Valley Mediation. Through her work with families in the child welfare system, she developed a passion for mediation, helping families and children in crisis, and social justice. She is now pursuing a graduate degree in social work at the University of North Carolina at Wilmington.

Vesna Matović is an experienced peacebuilding and conflict transformation specialist with more than twenty years of experience as a consultant, facilitator, mediator, analyst, and trainer on conflict and peace issues. Vesna teaches peacebuilding, conflict transformation, and the psychology of conflict and peace at UK universities. She is a board member of the Institute for the Study of Conflict Transformation and contributes to the development of Transformative Dialogue theory and practice in ethnopolitical contexts. Her dialogue experience is extensive, including work in the Balkans, Europe, the Middle East, Africa, and Central Asia.

Josh Nadeau is a dialogue facilitator and research fellow at Ottawa Dialogue. He holds an MA in conflict studies and has been based in Eastern Europe for nearly a decade. He has conducted dialogue projects and facilitation training across the post-Soviet space and works with both Ukrainian and Russian peacebuilding communities. His work also focuses on societal issues in North America, using dialogue practices to address ideological conflicts and sociopolitical polarization. He speaks English and Russian.

jared l. ordway is a peace practitioner and educator specializing in the co-design and facilitation of multistakeholder dialogue and mediation processes, participatory action research methodologies, and systems analysis. He works alongside institutions, organizations, networks, and groups committed to fostering transformative outcomes in violence- and conflict-affected contexts. jared serves in roles such as a dialogue advisor for the Institute for the Study of Conflict Transformation and as a senior associate with Interpeace's advisory team. He holds a PhD in peace studies from the University of Bradford.

Vicki Rhoades and **Dusty Rhoades** were partners in life for nearly six decades and Transformative Mediators since 2001. Vicki earned a BA in fine arts at St. Mary's College of Maryland. Dusty graduated from the US Naval Academy and then served for twenty-six years as a Navy carrier pilot and test pilot. They have co-mediated cases involving family, community, District and Circuit Court, discrimination (Maryland Commission on Human Relations), and foster care (Children in Need of Assistance) situations. They used their mediation skills to join with other community members to host conversations on race and privilege. That effort became a primary focus for them over the past dozen years. They were invited to join the steering group for the Big Conversations on Race and Prejudice in southern Maryland to help the group plan these conversations to effect the most construction community interaction. Vicki co-wrote the first draft of this chapter with Dusty but sadly passed away on June 10, 2023.

About the Editors and Contributors

Lida M. van den Broek, PhD, is an organizational anthropologist and founder of Kantharos (1983), one of the first training and consulting firms in the Netherlands specializing in managing diversity and dealing with racism, bullying, and harassment in the workplace. She is one of the founding mothers of the Transformative Model in the Netherlands, a Certified Transformative Mediator, and a teacher. She has published on racism, the position of women, and interventions related to bullying and harassment in the workplace.

Tom Wahlrab is a board member and Fellow of the Institute for the Study of Conflict Transformation. He is the former director of the City of Dayton's Human Relations Council (HRC) and the Dayton Mediation Center. He facilitated a dialogue that led to Dayton's formal designation as a welcoming and immigrant-friendly city by *Welcoming America*. Tom served as the HRC board chair and facilitated dialogues on police reform. He is involved with the restoration and sustainable management of land in Ohio and supports organizations engaged in similar missions.